THE KOSHER SUTRAS

A YOGI'S GUIDE TO THE TORAH

Marcus J Freed

freedthinker books

www.marcusjfreed.com

Freedthinker Books

www.marcusjfreed.com

Original version printed in Great Britain by Altaimage Ltd. Second version printed in Great Britain and United States of America.

First edition, 2013

Second edition, 2019

Library of Congress Control Number: 2012956373

British Library Cataloguing in Publication Data: A catalogue record for this book is available from the British Library.

Print version: 31

ISBN: 978-1-0886-8329-3

Book & cover design: Joshua Rudolph

Yoga photography: Timothy Reise

Back cover headshot photograph: Timothy Fielding

Editorial Advisors: Audrey Jacobs, Eric Rosen

A NOTE ON LANGUAGE IN THE BOOK AND FONTS USED

We have followed UK English spellings and punctuation styles throughout the book. The Kosher Sutras is essentially written using three different languages; English, Hebrew and Sanskrit. The last two always appear in transliteration. To differentiate these with different fonts:

Hebrew transliteration mostly appears in Trilogy Sans

Sanskrit transliteration mostly appears in *italics.*

The Hebrew transliterations are generally written with the modern Sephardic pronunciation, e.g. Shabbat rather than Shabbes, Shabbos or Shobbos. To represent the guttural 'Chet' sound (as in Chanukah or L'Chayim), we have written either an underlined H, e.g. Hanukkah, or just left the 'Ch' in place.

The 'chet' sound is hard to accurately pronounce by the written word alone, without vocal instruction. You will know it is being said incorrectly when somebody articulates (or hutzpah) with a soft ch that isn't coming from the back of the throat (i.e. the 'ch' in cheese is not the 'ch' in chutzpah, but taking somebody's cheese without asking would be a chutzpah). If you really want to learn this distinction, I'd recommend viewing a video of Chaim Topol's Fiddler on the Roof recording of "To Life". Practice singing along with 'L'chayim' and you'll be well on the right path.

DISCLAIMER Please consult your health care provider and obtain full medical clearance before practicing yoga or any exercise programme. Practising under the direct supervision and careful guidance of a qualified instructor will reduce risk of injuries. The information in this book is strictly for reference only and not in any manner a substitute for medical advice or the direct teaching of a qualified yoga teacher. The author, illustrators, photographers and publishers assume no responsibility for injuries or losses that may result from following any of the advice contained herein. If, however, your life significantly improves as a result of reading, we will gladly join you to celebrate! Now, practice in safety and good health!

PRAISE FOR THE KOSHER SUTRAS

"An inspirational and insightful offering to help navigate our spiritual journey with integrity".

Max Strom *Teacher and author of the book, A Life Worth Breathing, and the DVD, Learn to Breathe; to heal yourself and your relationships.*

"As Marcus J Freed points out in the Kosher Sutras, 'the very essence of Hatha Yoga is using asana (physical postures) to stabilise our body and make our mind calm and focused.' The importance of the relationship with the body as a means of enhancing one's relationship with one's spiritual and religious path and tradition is what is expertly explored within these pages".

Freed's eloquently written and well-released practice manual unites the Western Jewish ritual, textual, and historical traditions with the philosophy and practice of Hatha Yoga. This book is a welcome guide for those looking for a means to express the deep longing of the heart for union with G-d and the divine while connecting with the vessel of the body in this human life. No matter your religious tradition or background, this work will deepen your practice".

Felicia Tomasko, RN *Editor-in-Chief, LA YOGA Magazine and Find Bliss Magazine*

"Marcus J Freed's sensitive and skillful renderings and applications of Hasidic texts has opened a new window through which their timeless lights may shine".

Rabbi Dr Dovid Ebner *Rosh Yeshiva, Yeshivat Eretz HaTzvi, author of The Library of Everything and Perhaps this Poem*

"The Kosher Sutras merges the knowledge of Yoga and Torah into beautiful harmony".

Rabbi Yonah Bookstein *Author of Prayers for Israel and founder of Jewlicious Festivals*

"The adaptation of Eastern ideas and practices to the Abrahamic traditions and the consequent rediscovery of Western mysticism, is one of the most important developments in modern religion. With this book, Marcus Freed has made an important contribution to this favorable trend. Like bagels, "The Kosher Sutras" offers value to Jews and non-Jews alike. Yogis of all faiths will find inspiration, insight and practical tools for spiritual growth in these pages".

Philip Goldberg *Author of American Veda: From Emerson and the Beatles to Yoga and Meditation, How Indian Spirituality Changed the West*

"Marcus J Freed is a master of his craft. Within these pages you'll find passages that give the gift of insight and practical ways to connect to a space of possibility and freedom that brings wonder back into daily life".

Elisha Goldstein,PhD *Author of The Now Effect and Co-author of A Mindfulness-Based Stress Reduction Workbook*

"The great 20th century scholar, mystic and poet, Rabbi Abraham Isaac Kook wrote: "We have forgotten the holiness of our bodies." To remedy this spiritual malady, Marcus J Freed offers us clear techniques for transforming the stories of the Bible into experiences designed to wake us up to the holiness of our not only our bodies, but our whole lives. Kosher Sutras is a generous outpouring of creative and intelligent scholarship that integrates classic Jewish and Yogic teachings and practices".

Diane Bloomfield *Author of Torah Yoga: Experiencing Jewish Wisdom Through Classic Postures*

"Marcus J Freed connects to Judaism from the inside out. By marrying the physical dimension of Yoga with classical Torah teachings, he has found a compelling way of conveying Jewish wisdom. He is a breath of spiritual fresh air at a time when this is most needed".

David Suissa *Jewish Journal of Greater Los Angeles*

"This takes the integration of yoga and Judaism to an entirely new level Marcus J Freed's Kosher Sutra is the first embodied Torah commentary. Blending text, his wonderful insights into its meanings, and yoga postures into a seamless multi dimensional exploration of Torah, Marcus allows you to enter into the world Torah is away study alone cannot do".

Rabbi Rami Shapiro *Author of Amazing Chesed: Living a Grace-filled Judaism*

"Marcus J Freed has produced what I consider to be one of the most important Jewish Yoga books of his generation. Seamlessly bridging the ancient practice of yoga with each parashah of Torah, Marcus takes us on a physical and spiritual journey through the stories of our people and brings them to life with modern insights, philosophies and deep connection to ourselves. This book leads the way for all of us who walk the physical and spiritual path of seeking greater meaning in our lives through Jewish study and practice".

Lisa Levine *Author of Yoga Shalom*

"The Kosher Sutras" beautifully weaves teachings of Torah and yoga. Marcus J Freed's entries are heartfelt, informative, and provide practitioners the tools and inspiration to practice mindfully. If you're interested in integrating Judaism into your yoga practice, this book belongs on your bookshelf".

Zack Lodmer *Om Shalom yoga*

"Marcus J Freed is a Jewish yogi and teacher par excellence. This book is an embodiment of both Marcus personally and of Jewish yoga generally. It is about the complementary blending of two ancient spiritual traditions for well-being and advancement on all levels of the body-mind-spirit continuum".

Steven J. Gold *Author of Yoga and Judaism*

"Marcus skillfully and seamlessly weaves together the texts of the Jewish people with yogic practice and philosophy, finding genuine connections between the two, while maintaining the authenticity of each tradition. His unique approach is inspirational. As a committed Jew and a yoga instructor, his teachings have been key to developing my personal practice as well as my teaching voice".

Rabbi Lisa Tzur *Positive Jewish Living*

Special Thanks

Estelle Eugene, founder of Yoga Mosaic and The Jewish Yoga Network, for your generous support of *The Kosher Sutras*.

DEDICATION

For Mum and Dad who first taught me to stretch my horizons.

CONTENTS

THE KOSHER SUTRAS

BIBLIYOGA POSES

ACKNOWLEDGMENTS

Thank you to the following people who have all made this book possible: Firstly, a huge thank you to Audrey Jacobs for cracking the whip and encouraging me to keep the weekly discipline of writing the Kosher Sutras. Thank you to Joshua Rudolph for ongoing design expertise, on paper and beyond; to Rabbi Yonah, Rachel Bookstein and Jewlicious Festivals for being such gracious hosts when I moved to Los Angeles to complete the book. Thanks to Gillian Freed (Mum!) and Steven J. Gold for proofreading help. Thank you to Dr Maya Shlanger for major support during the book's crowdfunding campaign and to the folks at Jewcer.

Thank you to my teachers, who encouraged me to infuse sacred teachings with my own understanding; Rabbi Dovid Ebner, Rabbi Chaim Brovender, Rabbi Shlomo Riskin, and Chief Rabbi Lord Jonathan Sacks. Thank you to my yoga teachers who have given me so much support over the years – to Edward Clark and Tripsichore Yoga Theatre for so much love, handstands, intellectual nourishment and yogic fun; to Elizabeth Connolly, Rachel Krentzman, Lisa Walford and Marla Apt. Thank you to the many ad-hoc editors; friends who have supported and given feedback and support to the Kosher Sutras over the years; Eric Rosen, Yair Walton, Rabbi Hillel Simon, Rabbi Gideon Sylvester, Rabbi Jason Demant, Rabbi Chaim Rappaport, Rabbi Hillel Simon, Rabbi Shlomo and Olivia Schwartz, Rabbi Mendel Gordon, Rabbi Hertz and the Kingsley Way Yeshiva Gedolah. To my lovely little sister Lauren, who I've sometimes forgotten to thank publicly over the years, THANK YOU LAUREN!

Thanks to; Dr. Raphael Zarum, Jaqueline Nicholls, Lord Robert Winston, Harriet Goldenberg, Natalie Marx, Toby Gillingham, Yasha Michaelson and Mimoda, Moshe Bellows, Binah Weiss,

Lisa Friedman-Katz, Jason Isaac, Metuka Daisy Lawrence-Cohn and Steve Lawrence. Thank you to my other important teachers, including Clive Lawton and Lisa Akesson. A huge thanks to my 'family' in the Limmud community, for everyone in Britain who came along to the early Bibliyoga workshops at Limmudfest in sunny Sussex and the winter sessions in Nottingham and Warwick, and to the thousands of folks who who've attended my classes at Limmud conferences internationally.

FUNDERS

This book was made possible through a combination of grants and crowdfunding support. Thank you to the National Coalition of Independent Scholars for their generous research grant. Thank you to Lynne Schusterman and ROI for their microgrant that helped with the completion of this book. Thank you to the folks at Jewcer, especially Amir Giveon and Shira Shimoni for their support and encouragement throughout the process. Thank you to all of the following people who have bought the book at pre-sale through the Jewcer website www.jewcer.com. You are officially part of the Bibliyoga family and it was your support at this critical stage that made the entire publication possible - thank you! Aaron Freeman, Aaron Itzkowitz, Aaron Philmus, Alisa Fineman, Amir Give'on, Amos Nadler, Amy Solomon, Andrea Hodos, Ashley and Ayalah Hirst, Avi and Dafi Shlanger, Barnaby Nemko, Barry & Gillian Freed, Baruch Tauber, Batsheva Frankel, Bobby Bray, Bonnie Heft, Carmel Grant, Chaya Schneider, Clive & Susie Walters, Dean Levitt, Debbie Luce, Deena Pearlman Weisberg, Eric & Estee Rosen, Estelle Eugene, Esther Pasternak, Gwen Wexler, Harry & Dorit Nelson, Rabbi Heather Altman, Helen Coren, Ittai Anthony, Jason Rosenbaum, Jeff Starin, Jeremy Stowe, Jodie Mendelson, Jonathan Colman, Josh & Eve Sacks, Lady Li, Lara Walklet, Rabbi Laura Novak-Winer, Lisa Levine, Lois Tepper, Marcus Burstein, Margery Diamond, Melissa Kurtz, Michelle Katz, Mira Niculescu, Moshe Sheinfeld, Pam Chanin, Rabbi Lydia Medwin, Rabbi Micah Greenstein, Rabbi Wendy Spears, Rabbi Yonah & Rachel Bookstein, Rachel Wasserman, Rik Vig, Rob & Kelly Messik, Roman Libov, Sam Talbot, Salvador Litvak & Nina Davidovitch, Sandra Safadirazieli, Shawn Donley, Shifra Hastings, Shira Leorah, Simon & Emma Kisner, Susan Seely, Suzy Railly, Victoria Albin, Zack Lodmer and Zvia Hempling.

THE KOSHER SUTRAS

PREFACE TO NEW EDITION

Life can change overnight. On November 3, 2017 I was walking across the road en route to a Shabbat dinner in Los Angeles, hit by a car, thrown onto the bonnet and flipped onto the ground. I immediately started suffering from a major brain haemorrhage and had less than two hours to live. Emergency brain surgery at Cedars Sinai hospital saved my life. Four days later I had another brain haemorrhage and a second brain surgery. I survived by the grace of God.

A teacher once said to me "your principles only count when you are put under pressure". This was the time to see if my principles would stand up to the test.

The moment I stood up after being hit by a car, my head was bleeding but I immediately deepened my breath. I internally relaxed so that there was no unnecessary physical tension within my body. This was the precise moment I had been training for my entire life, the exact time to apply my 18 years of yoga training. Any fear or tension may have exacerbated my injuries and sped up my decline, but I was going to do everything I could to stay alive.

The Kosher Sutras was the first book I published, with the intention of providing an embodied spiritual approach to the weekly Torah reading. These short episodic essays contain a verse from the Torah - the "Kosher Sutra" - along with a Rabbinic teaching, an idea from one of the classic yoga books, and a posture or yoga asana so that you can physicalise the teaching. The yoga asanas (physical poses) are somewhat interchangeable. The most important thing, in my opinion, is that you find *some* form of physical expression.

This entire project began for me in 2001 when I had just started a regular yoga practice whilst studying physical movement at the Webber Douglas acting conservatoire in London with my teacher Edward Clark, an accomplished Yogi. This practice shed light on the restlessness, or *shpilkes* I experienced every Shabbat morning when sitting in shul for three hours, barely moving. From that point on there was no option. I had to incorporate physicality into my prayer. I quickly discovered there were thousands of other people who felt the same!

This approach is not for everyone. There is a fairly easy way to level criticism at yoga from a more traditional Jewish perspective. Yoga may indeed be called a form of *Avodah Zarah*, idol worship, although I (obviously) disagree.

I preferred the historical-philosophical approach of yoga scholar Merce Eliade who argues that yoga originates in the *Samkhaya* tradition, a strictly secular track within the six schools of Indian philosophy. Yoga did not originate within Hinduism according to Eliade, is not originally based upon the pantheon of Hindu gods, but lies within the secular tradition.

On different occasions I have personally and respectfully engaged in this discussion with representatives of the Hindu community, both in an opinion article I had published in the Washington Post's "On Faith" section, and when I represented the

Jewish community at a World Yoga Conference in Portugal. At the conference I politely explained the Jewish problem with a practice that is rooted in Hindu polytheism. The loving swamis I met approached me after the talk and compassionately explained that every Hindu god is merely a representation of the one true God, and they are indeed monotheists.

This is a highly contentious issue from a more traditional Jewish approach, but I have had respected Orthodox rabbis supporting my teachings right from the very beginning. I also heard many people attack this fusion of Jewish practice and yoga, so ultimately you must decide for yourself what you want to do. My only request is that if you are deeply offended and hugely disagree with my teachings, please make as much noise about it as you possibly can so that the books gain some controversy. "There is no such thing as bad PR".

If we look more deeply into this Hindu grey area, the name *Brahman* sounds very close to Abraham, and *Shiva* is the same as the Hebrew word *Sheva*, or indeed the Hebrew word Shiva which means "seven" and is used in the phrase *Sheva Brachot*, these seven blessings recited at a Jewish marriage ceremony, and the seven days of mourning following a Jewish funeral.

Enough already.

This is not meant as an apologetic or defence of yoga. The most frequent question I have heard in the last two decades is "Is Yoga Kosher?". Six years from publishing the first edition of *The Kosher Sutras*, this is still the main question that arises. Since I qualified last year as an Orthodox rabbi (even though I have no plans to publicly use the title but did it as part of my own spiritual journey"), my official rabbinic answer to the question of "is yoga kosher?", is "decide for yourself".

Last November, after I was hit by a car and sedated for brain surgery, nobody knew how long I had to live or whether the brain injury would leave me permanently damaged. Fortunately it did not, but nine months on I am still recovering from the physical trauma. I see the entire experience as a blessing from Hashem. Yoga has been an incredible part of my healing experience, and the daily practice of therapeutic Iyengar yoga helped me manage and almost completely eliminate headaches within eight weeks of the two brain surgeries. This was one of the many miracles I experienced, since doctors had told me I might expect to have headaches for the rest of my life.

I hope you enjoy the Kosher Sutras. This is a deep labour of love, the first of a trilogy of books, and I share it from my heart to yours.

With love and blessings
Marcus J Freed
Los Angeles, September 2019/Elul 5779

INTRODUCTION TO THE NEW EDITION

HOW DO I USE THE BOOK?

There are four main ways of using this book.

1. Read the chapters on their own and enjoy the concepts and teaching.

2. Adopt this book as a guide and study the chapters on a weekly basis, practising the postures and/or meditations in tune with the weekly Torah reading cycle.

3. For yoga teachers, use this book as a teaching resource, with week-by-week themes to introduce into your classes.

4. Use the teachings to support your practice as a yoga student, reading one before going into class and applying it as a personal focus during the class (respectfully and peaceably integrating the Bibliyoga practice into the class teacher's own method).

A NOTE FOR YOGA AND MEDITATION TEACHERS

Any yoga teacher can use this book as a practical resource. You can even, if I dare to offer, apply these concepts to other physical meditation practices, such as tai chi, chi gung, kung fu, or sports like tennis. How? By bringing awareness to what you are doing. Classical Hatha yoga is based around physical postures that are essentially a gateway to a deeper meditation but the ultimate aim is that we experience a sense of yoga in everything we do—yoga being oneness/unity with God, and the idea that we are experiencing this sense of unity in all we are doing. "Before enlightenment, I schlepped and carried water; oy", said the Yiddish Zen Buddhist monk, "and after enlightenment, I schlepped and carried water". Yes, this is a slight bastardisation of the classic proverb, but you get the point.

INTRODUCTION TO THE ORIGINAL EDITION

This is much more than a book about yoga. *The Kosher Sutras* is about healing your life. It is written for anybody who would like to strengthen their body, calm their mind, dissolve anxiety, engage their spiritual side and live life with passion. These teachings are for you whether you've spent the last 40 years on yoga mats, or if you never intend to get close to pair of spandex pants.

My yogic journey began in 2001. It was 10.45am on Saturday morning and I was getting restless. I always got restless around this time. 90 minutes of sitting in synagogue was usually enough to give me shpilkes[1], and I needed to stretch, dance or bang my head against the nearest wall. At that point a Hebrew verse leapt out from the prayer book, saying "all my bones will say God, who is like You?"[2]. This was a clear call to action. There had never been much space for moving one's bones in shul except for the circle-shuffle-dance that took place during an occasional barmitzvah. At least the Sufi mystics had a whirling dervish, but the best we came up with was the bottle dance from Fiddler on the Roof.

The questions suddenly began flowing: What does it mean to connect to God with our bones? Where is the body in religious practice? How can spirituality purely be expressed through verbal prayer and seemingly endless festive meals? More importantly, if we were to incorporate our bodies into our spiritual

---

[1]   Yiddish for nervous energy, or, 'ants in your pants'.
[2]   Psalm 35:10, from the Sabbath morning service

life, what would it look like? We continually talk about *shalom* or peace, but how can we embody the idea? If we were to give religion more of a physical vocabulary, where would we begin?

My rabbis in yeshiva[3] taught that there's one thing better than a good answer; a great question. And so, the journey of a thousand miles began a single question – how can I find peace in my body and soul? The journey took me through many spiritual books including the Bible, Talmud, Midrash, Rabbinic commentaries, The Zohar and beyond.

On the following Shabbat morning I decided to physicalise the psalmists' words "All my bones will say: God who is like You?". There seemed to be just one way to do it: yoga. The problem was that I only knew a few basic sun salutations. Still, I got up early, rolled out a yoga mat, set an intention and began practising the basics. After a 20 minute yog-ish session it was time to go to shul for the Sabbath prayers. Three hours later, the answer seemed obvious; something is wrong with the way we are practising religion in the West. It is unrealistic to expect a full spiritual experience without moving our body. And so, Bibliyoga was born.

I tried a few practice sessions at a cutting-edge education conference called Limmudfest which was then taking place at a retreat centre in Sussex, England, and before long I was being invited to teach throughout Europe, Israel, the USA and Australia. A community of like-minded Jewish Yogis was headed by Estelle Eugene in England and she invited me to join forces. We

---

3   Rabbinical seminary. Except I didn't become a rabbi. Yet.

rebranded to become the Jewish Yoga Network, which continues to grow each week.

The journey continues to go deeper. This is planned as the first of a series of books. The aim of Bibliyoga is to help you feel physically energised, emotionally uplifted and spiritually invigorated. A key principle of Bibliyoga, as it has now evolved, is that this is non-dogmatic, non-religious, and open to spiritual seekers of all disciplines. All you are asked to do is to commit to your own healing. The tools of Bibliyoga include asana (yoga postures), meditation and teachings from the Jewish spiritual tradition (including Kabbalah), and the more you commit to the practice, the greater the healing.

This book is the result of 10 years of work and the reason you are holding a 210-page book is because everyone advised me not to publish my 1500 pages of essays all at once (!). King Solomon taught that "there is no end to the making of books" (Ecclesiastes 12:12), so if you enjoy this book, please tell your closest 5000 friends.

WHAT IS A KOSHER SUTRA?

In brief, the principle of a sutra is that it is a short, memorable piece of text. Just as a medical suture is a short strip that brings healing to the body by holding together two pieces of skin across the wound, a Kosher Sutra is a short, memorable text that will bring healing to the body and the soul. Each Kosher Sutra is accompanied by a spiritual focus: the Soul Solution, a physical yoga practice (usually an asana, vinyasa, or meditative focus), and the benefits of that practice.

This short-form has been used for time immemoriam across wisdom traditions, whether it was for the Yoga Sutras, the Mishna, or indeed the infamous Karma Sutra. Our Kosher Sutras are Biblical verses that I have selected for their healing potential, and this book really is intended as a yogic/spiritual commentary that will help us bring peace to our entire being.

Each essay takes a different idea that ties in with the annual cycle of Torah reading, presenting a universal lesson that applies to all of us regardless of our background. The rabbis taught "it is not talking about it, but taking action that counts"[4].

So, please, stand at the front of your yoga mat and let us begin.

Marcus J Freed

Los Angeles, April 2013/Iyar 5773

---

4   Ethics of the Fathers 1:17. The loose translation is my own.

BIBLIYOGA: PHILOSOPHY-IN-ACTION

THE THEORY & PRACTICE OF BIBLIYOGA

Yoga is a path to inner stillness and deep fulfilment. From the Sanskrit word meaning "union", the practice involves uniting body and soul, finding peacefulness in every moment and becoming spiritually energized. The Kosher Sutras are a series of ancient Biblical teachings experienced through yoga, designed to infuse our body and entire being with this powerful spiritual wisdom. This is a path that has led me to experience deeper meaning and connection through the experience of spirituality in my body. If these tools help you, even a little, we will have achieved something important.

SPIRITUALITY OR RELIGION?

There is a gap: Many of us are living in the Western World, trying our best to earn a living and get on with it, be happy, and enjoy our days. "If life can be meaningful", we think, "then so much the better". Perhaps you get your spiritual buzz from attending synagogue, church, or mosque, or by going shopping. Lots of people seek to get it from yoga classes, where spiritual ideas are explored though the body. Nonetheless I felt that something was missing.

From my earliest years, I had been involved with Jewish practice, attending an Orthodox synagogue and living a vaguely traditional lifestyle. This meant observing the major holidays, eating mostly kosher food (except when McDonald's beckoned), and getting a basic Jewish education, until the age of 13. When I decided to become more observant at 19 years old, it satisfied certain spiritual needs—but there was still an unresolved question as to how to integrate my body within the spiritual practice. Surely there had to be more than eating, wedding-dancing in circles, and *shockelling* (swaying while praying)?

Yoga is usually taught in connection to Eastern philosophies, which makes sense since most yogic philosophy was developed in Asia. But we live in the West. What about Western spiritual traditions? Judaism, Christianity, and Islam all have an integral connection with the Hebrew Bible. Our question is; how can we connect to these sacred writings through the body and thereby embody the spiritual teachings?

THE BEGINNINGS OF YOGA

When Patanjali wrote the *Yoga Sutras* (~200 CE), he wedded secular Samkhaya philosophy to a physical yoga practice and took yoga in a more spiritual direction. The teachings of The Kosher Sutras rewind to the point before *asana* (yoga postures) and *vinyasa* (the flowing movement we find in sun salutations) were intrinsically connected with this Hindu-influenced philosophy. We are taking the classic yoga postures and realigning them with the Western spiritual tradition, beginning the conversation between yoga and Hebrew theology. This discussion will be informed by such as the *Yoga Sutras*, *Bhagavad Gita*, and *Hatha Yoga Pradipika*, all grounded in Jewish wisdom. The continual aim is provide more gateways to physical and spiritual fulfilment.

The earliest evidence of yoga postures dates back to the Bronze Age, where the Mohinjo-Daro seals show people in asana-like positions. These pre-date Hinduism, Buddhism, and the later religions with which yoga has been associated. It was relatively recently that Patanjali associated yoga into Hindu philosophy (again, under 2,000 years ago), and we are now embarking on a journey to spiritual and physical liberation through the alignment of yoga with the wisdom of the rabbis.

THE JEW & THE LOTUS

My path to yoga happened by accident. I was a frustrated spiritual seeker, several years into being *Shomer Shabbat* (Sabbath-observant) but still stuck with the unresolved question of how to use our bodies within a spiritual framework. The great Asian religions spawned Martial arts and other forms of choreographed movement that related to a spiritual practice but there was no great advice in the Jewish tradition, at least as far as I'd been taught.

Teachers appear when the students are ready, and it was at Webber Douglas Academy of Dramatic Art in South Kensington, where we were taught yoga to help focus our minds in preparation for acting. One day my teacher Edward Clark demonstrated an asana that stunned me, as he took a deep inhale whilst folded forward, before powerfully exhaling and lifting his legs into the air, holding the most incredible handstand I'd ever seen. I promptly lobbied Edward for months until he let me join his private yoga classes at home and agreed to train me personally.

Everything changed one Shabbat morning when my 28 years of frustration with Jewish spiritual practice came to a sudden end. It was as if I had discovered a hidden manuscript in a locked vault, blown off the dust, and arrived in the Promised Land. I had been diligently practising my yoga sequence every morning until then, in a bid to improve my acting ability, and it was on Saturday mornings that I began to compare how I felt after 30 minutes of yoga with 120 minutes spent in the synagogue. One experience left me feeling me calm and centred, whilst the other left me distracted and itchy to move.

There had to be a way to experience my own spiritual tradition through yoga, and it was time to find it. But there was a challenge. My rabbis had taught me a very strict way of interpreting Hebrew texts, as they had been taught; although it was fine to come up with an off-the-wall and creative teaching method, it had to "fit" the tradition. This meant either that an interpretation be backed up in the words of a previous teacher, or the new idea had to conform to traditional interpretations in an uncontroversial manner.

Here was the secret I discovered that day: combining the wisdom of the yogis with Torah teaching offered a way to feel physically great, emotionally clear, and spiritually fulfilled. From then on, the Bibliyoga philosophy started revealing itself in leaps and bounds. This system is open to anyone, regardless of background, affiliation, or physical ability. Everybody deserves to enjoy their body and find personal fulfilment.

THE BATTLE FOR KOSHER YOGA

There is an ongoing discussion over whether yoga is "kosher" and a legitimate practice for Orthodox Jews. The concern comes from yoga's sometime association with idol-worshipping customs (Hebrew: *Avodah Zarah*). Other faith traditions have similar concerns, and there is even an Orthodox Christian website that warns against the dangers of demons being released in certain yoga postures! The basic facts are that yoga pre-dates all formal Eastern religion: the earliest yogic texts were written well before Buddhism and Hinduism were forged in their modern forms. Although various forms of yoga were integrated into these religions at a later stage, yoga practice transcends all doctrines because it really helps us tie in with universal themes of peace, truth, and the soul.

The notion of interdisciplinary study is nothing new to Judaism; even the great Maimonides himself stated he had thoroughly learned Greek philosopher and the wisdom of non-Jewish astrologers. The last chapter of his *Hilchot HaChodesh* (The Laws of Months) explains how he took this knowledge and integrated it into his practice.

So as far as the question of whether yoga is kosher, for the purposes of this book, the answer is "Yes! Now let's move on". Alternatively, read the book and then decide for yourself. It may be of note that I have received resounding support of this work from a number of prominent Orthodox rabbis in Israel, England, and the USA.

THE TWOFOLD PATH

Bibliyoga has a twofold approach to incorporating Biblical wisdom with Hatha yoga: the literal and the metaphorical. I will first address the literal. There are references to moving the body throughout Biblical, rabbinic, and Kabbalistic literature. The Book of Psalms, attributed to King David, has comments littered throughout with direct references to physical movement, culminating in the final psalm which teaches us to "Praise Him with movement/dancing" (Psalm 150:4), and the oft-quoted "Let all that breathes praise the Lord" (Psalm 150:6).

There has always been some kind of literal physical interpretation of these verses, such as in the way Hasidic Jews put a special emphasis on swaying during prayer, using a back-and-forth motion that literally uses "all of the bones" in praising God. With Bibliyoga, we can take this notion of physical prayer much further: a gentle rocking motion does not engage all of the bones in the same way that a full-on sun salute or comprehensive yoga practice will achieve.

THE WAY OF THE LION

Rabbi Yitzhak Luria (1534-1572) is seen as the father of modern Kabbalah. Known as the *Ari* ('Ari' is Hebrew for "lion"), he introduced the idea of *Yihudim*, or "unifications", which effectively are mantras that aim to unify us with God. These *Yihudim*—these unifications—are the essence of yoga. If we set one of these mystical unifications as our intention (e.g., to bring light into the world) and then do our physical yoga practice, we can move towards a spirituality that involves both the body and soul. In his introduction to the early kabbalistic work *Sefer Yetzirah*, the "Book of Creation," Rabbi Aryeh Kaplan boldly suggested that:

> *"Meditative Kabbalah deals with the use of divine names, letter permutations, and similar methods to reach higher states of consciousness, and, as such, comprises a kind of yoga"* [1].

With *The Kosher Sutras*, we are metaphorically standing on the shoulders of great people who have gone before. What is amazing, and even revolutionary to the extent that, if properly appreciated, it could shake the foundations of every church, mosque, and synagogue in town, is that this is basically what the Ari was saying back in the 1560s: to integrate the body and soul. He described a walking meditation that imagines parts of the body as Divine energies (*sefirot*):

> *"When you walk in the street, meditate that your two feet are the Sefirot Netzach and Hod... meditate in this manner with regard to every part of your body. Also contemplate that you are a vehicle for the Highest Holiness. This is the meaning of the verse, "In all your ways know Him..." [Proverbs 3:6]* [2].

There are two challenges to integrating physical and Divine energies in the Jewish tradition. First, until now, there has been no system for putting this into practice. Second, the parts of the body that most Jewish leaders have focused on for the last 100 years are the head and the stomach (for thinking

---

1   Aryeh Kaplan, in his introduction to *Sefer Yetzirah*, p. 10.
2   Rabbi Yitzhak Luria, the Ari, as quoted by Rabbi Aryeh Kaplan in *Meditation and Kabbalah*, p258)

and eating). Bibliyoga is about finding ways to authentically experience these spiritual teachings throughout the entire body.

Yogic writings frequently discuss ethical and metaphysical ideas in an integrated way; they introduce a concept and present it within the context of a physical system. In the Yoga Sutras, Patanjali explains the yamas, or ethical principles of self-control, namely: nonviolence (*ahimsa*), truthfulness (*satya*), nonstealing (*asetya*), retention of vital fluids, or behaviour that respects the Divine as omnipresent (*brahmacharya*), and freedom from greed, or nonpossessiveness (*aparigraha*).

The style of Hatha Yoga taught by Krishnamacharya during the early 19th century taught concepts from the *Yoga Sutras* through the use of asana and vinyasa. The primary principle of ahimsa informs a person's yoga practice such that they should not be violent towards their own body nor force themselves into postures to cause them pain. It is surprising how many yoga students injure themselves in the name of yoga, which is intended to be a peaceful practice. Nonviolence includes gently respecting ourselves.

In yoga, and particularly in Bibliyoga, we are also looking to eradicate any violent thoughts that arise and to deepen the sense of peace. The theory is that once we have fully mastered a principle within our bodies, or at least gone some way towards internalising and understanding it, we can then live that concept and incorporate it into our daily behaviour. Rather than preaching the virtues of nonviolence to others, we begin to truly live it within our being and lead by quiet example.

BEGINNING THE DAY AND SALUTING THE SUN

There are many good reasons for the lack of a physical form of meditation in the current rabbinic tradition though the Talmud explains that the "ancient ones used to meditate for an hour before [formal] prayer in order to build concentration on God" (Talmud, Brachot 32b).

Although such meditation may never have been a widespread practice, it makes huge sense to set aside specific meditation time on a daily basis, regardless of whether one prays regularly. The literal Hebrew translation of quotation in the previous paragraph is "the ancient ones used to *wait* for an hour"; but the implication is that this is a form of preparatory waiting, full of presence and mindfulness, rather than sitting at a bus stop and reading the newspaper.

What we are discovering in Bibliyoga is not just a holistic exercise system, because the word "exercise" usually implies something self-serving and an end in itself. Rather, it is a movement towards enlightened living based on integrating spiritual wisdom with physicality, gaining balance for the body, mind and soul.

One of the true joys of yoga for me is that, as I deepen my practice and experience a greater sense of calm and well being, I also maintain a healthy body weight, increase stamina, reduce blood pressure, and find myself better equipped to deal with the aches and pains of everyday life. But these physical benefits are almost by-products of balanced living; they could be made into a goal unto themselves, but the engagement of Bibliyoga means that these arise instead as a result of the spiritual pursuit.

YOGIC BREATHING/ PRANAYAMA

*"All in whose nostrils was the breath
of the spirit of life..."*

GENESIS 7:22

YOGA ASANA PRACTICE

THE KOSHER SUTRAS

INTRODUCTION TO ASANA

"These photographs are intended as a guide to the yoga postures mentioned in the book. At the time of shooting the photographs, I was recovering from injuries to my right shoulder and right hip. Thus, I demonstrated each yoga *asana* to the best of my ability.

We all have the tendency to criticise ourselves when performing this kind of physical action. When I look back at the photographs with the eye of a yoga teacher, I can see how the upper back could be more straight at times, how the hips could be more open…but yoga is about the pursuit of perfection rather than the attainment. We are human beings, constantly in a state of moving forwards and doing our very best in any one moment. In other words, do the best with what you've got!

These pages are intended as a reference guide. Please follow the instructions carefully to move your body towards your best approximation of each posture, and in all cases it is worth learning with your local yoga teacher who can provide in-person feedback.

TRIPSICHORE SUN SALUTES /SURYA NAMASKAR

The vinyasa sequence was choreographed by Edward Clark of Tripsichore Yoga.

1. Stand with your feet apart.
2. **Inhale:** Extend hands outwards, to the sides.
3. **Exhale:** Bring hands into prayer position.
4. **Inhale:** Lift hands to come into a high arch, extending hands and ensuring an outward rotation of the shoulders.
5. **Exhale** into a forward bend.
6. **Inhale:** Draw the right foot backwards to a lunge position.
7. **Exhale:** Press the left foot back, pushing hands into ground and bending both of your knees.
8. **Inhale:** Move smoothly forwards into Cobra, briefly passing through either Low Plank/Chaturanga without stopping.
   For a modified version, move through kneeling, if you think your arms or wrists aren't strong enough; although this sequence is not about strength in the way you might think, so explore what is possible for you in this pose.
9. **Exhale** into Downward-Facing Dog, ensuring that the thighs are engaged (think "smiling knees"), that legs are straight but not hyperextended, and that the neck is relaxed.
10. **Inhale:** Bring the right foot forwards, keeping the energy forwards.
11. **Exhale:** Bring the left foot forwards to join the right foot, torso folding over.
12. **Inhale:** Straighten up to move into a high arch, driving the straightening motion from the legs and keeping the torso in the same open position it was in during the forward bend.
13. **Exhale:** Hands come down at the sides and into prayer position.

.01

.02

.03

.04

.05

.06

.07

.08

.09

.10

.11

.12

.13

SUN SALUTE A (JOURNEYING ON THE MAT) / SURYA NAMASKAR A

The sun salutation is driven by the breath.

1. **Inhale:** Begin with your feet hip-distance apart, shoulders down. Palms touch above the head. Look at thumbs. Keep ribs in, not jutting forward.
2. **Exhale:** Lower the torso into a forward bend. Press hands down to either side of your feet, in forward bend, on the floor.
3. **Inhale:** Elongate your torso forwards.
4. **Exhale:** Jump or float legs backwards into Chattaranga (Low Plank).
5. **Inhale:** Stretch into Upward-Facing Dog.
6. **Exhale:** Press back and lift the pelvic girdle up into Downward Dog. Hold for five breaths.
7. **Inhale:** Do a fifth inhalation.
8. **Exhale:** Bend the legs on your fifth exhalation.
9. **Inhale:** Jump or float the legs forward until you are in a standing forward bend.
10. **Exhale:** Straighten the legs without locking the knees.
11. **Inhale:** Inhale hands upwards to standing position, above the head.
12. **Exhale:** Release your hands to rest by the sides.

.01

.02 .03 .04

.05

.06

.07

.08

.10   .11

.09

HORSE STANCE BREATHING (HORSE STANCE WITH OCEAN BREATH/UJAYI PRANAYAMA)

.01

1. Stand in Mountain Posture, and step your feet apart so that each of your heels is on the mat with your feet (toes) pointing on the opposite diagonals.
2. Bend your knees outwards and lower your pelvis.
3. Keep your tummy tucked in, and bring your hands into prayer position with your thumbs by your heart centre.
4. Move your tailbone towards the earth so that your lumber spine is lengthened. This is Cat Tilt, and releases pressure on the lower spine.

.02

HORSE STANCE BREATHING

The key with Horse Stance Breathing is to make the movement last as long as your breath, and this is about measuring clear, smooth breathing. One of the most common challenges is to make sure that you have a gentle exhale that gradually releases the breath, rather than holding onto it.

1. Stand in Horse Stance, then inhale your hands out towards the sides, palms facing upwards.

2. Exhale your palms back together, coming back to Prayer Position, with your thumbs resting on your solar plexus.

3. Breathe in and out through your nostrils, enabling the ssssh sound to happen, which occurs when you use the Ocean Breath/Ujjayi Pranayama.

STAFF POSE/DANDASANA

.01

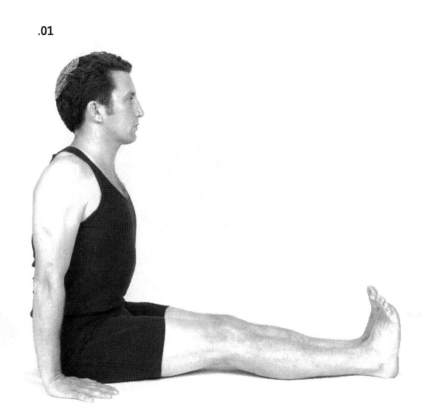

1. Sit with your legs straight in front of you, toes pointed outwards and thighs drawn in towards the bones.
2. Place your hands by the sides of your hips, with your fingers pointing forwards and your arms completely straight.
3. Keep your back straight.

ADVANCED Activate your abdominal muscles, keep the legs straight, and lift yourself upwards with both feet off the ground.

SEATED VARIATION Straighten both of your legs whilst sitting in a chair.

.02

SEATED FORWARD BEND/PASCHIMOTTANASANA

The pose shown is a modified version of Paschimottanasana, amended for people with tight hamstrings.

1. Sit in Staff Posture. Inhale, and lift your sternum upwards, without arching your back.

2. Exhale and lean forwards, taking hold of your ankles or hooking your forefingers around your big toes.

3. Aim to get your back as straight and open as possible. The idea is to maintain a clear alignment, rather than collapsing just so that you can "get the stretch". This is a really important point that bears repeating: the yoga postures are, first and foremost, about deepening the breath, rather than maximising the stretch at the expense of everything else.

4. Allow your elbows to bend outwards towards each side as you bring your head down towards your shins.

5. When you are comfortable in the position, take holds of the sides of your feet. Stay in the pose for several minutes.

VARIATION Loop a strap around the ends of your feet. Pull on the ends of the strap to draw yourself deeper into the pose. You can also place cushions or pillows on your thighs and rest your head on these for further remedial benefits.

ADVANCED Take hold of your right wrist with your left hand, in front of your feet.

INCLINED PLANE/PURVOTTANASANA

This pose is referred to as the Eastern Stretch because it stretches the front of your body, which is traditionally facing towards the east during a yoga practice.

1. Sit in Staff Pose. Straighten your arms behind you, palms resting on the ground facing forward. Inhale your hips up into the air, straightening your legs.
2. Aim to have your feet pressed flat into the ground. Drop your head backwards.
3. Engage the whole body, and breathe deeply.

VARIATION Come into Tabletop Pose, with your knees bent. Or just place your hands behind you in an approach to Staff Pose, arching your back slightly but not raising yourself into the full pose, to benefit from the mild backbend.

SEATED VARIATION Place your hands on either side of a chair, taking hold of the base of the back of the chair and pushing your elbows backwards. Raise your sternum and drop your head back.

COW-FACE POSE/GOMUKHASANA

1. Sit in Staff Pose with your feet straight out in front of you.
2. Bring your right leg over your left and bend both knees. Aim to have both feet pointing backwards, with your ankles in line with your hips (this is optional, and not shown in the photograph).
3. Inhaling, bend your right arm so that your palm is reaching over your back, and bend your left arm under, so that you are holding both hands together behind your back.
4. With every inhale, lift your head even further (by lengthening the spine, not tilting the head up), and maintain the energy.

BOAT/NAVASANA

1. Sit in Staff Posture, with your hands by your side, legs extended out in front of you, and back straight.
2. Press your legs together (inner thighs joined) and inhale, raising the legs to a 45° angle in front of you. Point your toes towards the sky and push out through your ankles.
3. On the same in-breath as for Step 2 above, raise your arms so that they are directly in front of you, palms facing one another on either side of your legs. Your arms should be parallel to the floor.
4. Remain in the pose for five breaths. Come down to sit cross-legged.
5. Place both hands on the ground and lift yourself off the ground in the cross-legged position.
6. Sit back on the ground and repeat Boat Pose.
7. Do this sequence five times.

MODIFICATION If you have problems with stability in the pose, keep your hands on the ground when you lift your legs. If you find yourself getting tired by one of the later repetitions, keep breathing and work harder! It's yoga, not sunbathing! (That is to say, there is something you'll discover by seeing through this challenge. Let yourself find it.)

ADVANCED MODIFICATION Stay up for longer. In between the boat poses, take yourself up to a full handstand.

ANOTHER OPTION While extended in Boat Pose, take hold of your big toes with the two first fingers of each respective hand.

SEATED VERSION This can be done in a chair quite easily and will work your abdominal muscles even more deeply. Take ahold of the sides of your chair, straighten your legs in front of you, and lift your buttocks off the chair. Make sure you keep breathing, relax the face, and focus all your energy on the posture at hand. Try to lift your sternum (imagine it floating upwards, but do not puff out the chest), and look forwards.

HERO POSE/VIRASANA

Young children often drop into this pose and plonk onto the floor quite happily. For adults, the pose can be fairly difficult when you start practising it, because over time, our bodies become tighter, and the hips and knees are prime areas for physical tension.

Fortunately, yoga makes you younger...

.01   .02

1.   Kneel on the floor with the tops of your feet flat on the ground beneath you.

2.   Move your feet to either sides of your hips, and place your buttocks on the ground in the middle.

3.   Raise your sternum, and place your hands on your knees, facing upwards.

.03

VARIATION Interlace your hands above your head, and take 10 breaths in this position.

MODIFICATION If you find Virasana too difficult on your knees, place a pillow, cushion, or block beneath your buttocks.

ADVANCED Take hold of your knees, bring your chin into the top of the sternum, and lift your chest. Keep your arms straight as you continue pulling up on your knees.

THUNDERBOLT POSE/VAJRASANA

This is a useful meditation pose that one may find easier than the various cross-legged positions.

1. Kneel on the ground with your shins next to one another.
2. Sit on your heels.
3. Straighten your back, draw your shoulder blades downwards, and place your hands facing down on either knee.
4. Look forwards.

VARIATION Place a pillow beneath your buttocks so that your knees don't have to bend as much.

BOUND-ANGLE POSE/BADDHA KONASANA

1. Sit comfortably on the floor. Bring your feet together so that the soles of your feet are touching one another.

2. Take hold of either side of each foot with your respective hand and draw your heels towards your groin.

3. Open your feet to either side so that just the outside edges of your feet (i.e., the side on the floor) are touching.

4. Lift your sternum upwards so that your chest is open and look directly ahead of you.

MODIFICATION If your hips are tight, sit on a block, and if your knees are in pain, place bolsters or cushions beneath your knees on either side.

PIGEON POSTURE/EKA PADA RAJAKAPOTASANA

1. Begin on all fours. Bend your right knee, to bring your right ankle so that it is behind your left wrist, side of your shin resting on the ground. Then push your right knee against your right wrist.
2. Straighten your left leg behind you and slowly bring your right hip towards the ground.
3. With one hand on either side of you, raise your sternum.
4. Repeat on the opposite side.

VARIATION Place a cushion below your bent knee to soften the posture and reduce the stretch.

ADVANCED Bend the left knee and take hold of your left foot with your left hand. Raise your right arm in the air and reach backwards, towards your left foot.

SPLITS (PREPARATION)/HANUMANASANA

Here, we focus on preparation for the splits rather than the full posture. There are enormous benefits in "just" this preparation.

1. Begin by resting on your knees.
2. Step your left foot forward and straighten your leg.
3. Ensure that your hips are evenly facing forwards.
4. Inhale, and then as you exhale, extend your torso over your straight left leg. You'll feel a stretch on the underside of your left leg, as you stretch the hamstring, thighs, and glutes.
5. If you find are comfortable in this pose thus far, sit your buttocks on your right foot and fold forwards. This is called Mahamudra, or "The Great Seal."

Practice this whole sequence on both sides. If you are comfortable, experiment with moving into full splits. Otherwise, simply repeat Steps 1–4.

MOUNTAIN POSE/TADASANA

Once you are established in Mountain pose/Tadasana, engage all of your muscles so that you feel a quality of strength and alertness, and meditate on the fact that all of your limbs are serving one greater purpose. This is Echad/Yoga. Feel the strength, the inner sense of community and the oneness.

1. Stand with your feet next to each other.
2. Straighten your back.
3. Engage your thighs
4. Root your heels into the floor. Notice how this opens out through the front of your body.
5. Gently lift your heartspace, and breathe deeply.
6. Adduct your legs (squeeze them together!).

EXTENDED MOUNTAIN POSE/TADASANA

1. Take Mountain Pose. Ground through your feet, and extend your hands out to the sides and up into the air.

2. Draw your shoulder blades together so that they are in alignment, and point the palms towards one another.

3. Ground through your feet, point your knees forwards, and roll your inner thighs towards one another.

4. Reach for the sky with your fingertips.

CHAIR POSE/UTKATASANA

The posture is Chair Pose or Fierce Pose (Utkatasana). It can be done anywhere.

1.   Stand up with your feet together.
2.   Bend your knees as if you were beginning to sit in a chair.
3.   Lift your hands upwards, and press your hands together.
4.   Press your buttocks backwards, and lift your chest so there is a slight curve in your lower back
5.   Gaze at your hands.
6.   Hold the pose for 5, 10, or 25 breaths.

7.   Begin to count your freedoms: freedom of speech, work, thought, love, and more. Try meditating on how your soul is ultimately free, eternal, and bigger than you can possibly imagine.

8.   Finally, focus on your breath, listening to the sound. Allow yourself to sweat, and push through the posture.

VARIATION Add a twist, placing your right elbow on your left knee, pushing your hands together in "prayer" pose, and twisting your spine to free your lower back from residual tension. Repeat in counterpose on the opposite side.

TRIANGLE POSE/TRIKONASANA

1. Jump your feet so that they are approximately one metre apart (or an equivalent length for your height) to land in a very wide stance.
2. Turn your right foot outward so that your toes point to the front of your mat. Turn your left foot until toes are angled to about 15°. Your right heel should be in line with the instep of your left foot.
3. Inhale your hands upwards, elongate your spine, and lean to the right side with your right hand extended, palm facing down.
4. Bend from the waist, placing your right hand on your thigh, shin, ankle, or foot. If it is available to you, aim to take hold of your right big toe with your right forefinger and thumb.
5. Raise your left hand into the air, palm facing forward.
6. Rotate your left hip upwards and outwards.
7. Look upwards.

8. Tuck your tummy in and lengthen your back.
9. Engage the muscles in your legs.
10. Raise the arches on both of your feet.
11. Be careful not to collapse your ribs or back. Your shoulders should be completely open and in a flat line. If in doubt, do a modified variation of the pose.

MODIFICATION Place a block to the outside of your right foot and rest your palm on that.

ADVANCED Place your right hand on the ground to the outside of your right foot.

SIDE-ANGLE POSE/UTTHITA PARSVAKONASANA

1. Begin in Mountain Pose. Inhale, and jump your feet one metre (about three feet) apart with your right foot pointing forwards (to the front of the mat) and your left foot parallel to the back of the mat. (The idea is to have the legs in a wide but stable stance, so adjust the distance according to your height.)

2. Exhaling, place your right hand on the floor to the outside of your right foot, while bending your right knee.

3. Inhale your left arm to reach over your left ear, engaging your body and energising the posture.

4. Look upwards, and ensure there is a direct line from your left foot through to the fingertips of your left hand.

5. Raise the arches on both of your feet.

6. Bring your upper arm over your head so that your armpit is drawn towards your ear.

MODIFICATIONS Rest your right forearm across your right thigh and bring both hands into prayer position, looking upwards.

Or put your right hand on a block behind your right foot.

ADVANCED Bind your right hand beneath your right thigh, taking hold of your right wrist behind your back with the left hand.

REVOLVED SIDE ANGLE/PARIVRTTA PARSVAKONASANA

.01

.02

.03

1. Begin in Mountain Pose. Inhale and jump your feet about one metre apart (or to a very wide stance; depending on your height), with your right foot pointing forwards and the outside of your left foot parallel to the back of the mat.

2. Exhaling, bring your left arm across your body, twisting the torso and placing your left hand on the floor to the right (outside) of your right foot.

3. Inhale your right arm to reach up and over, so that it is over your right ear, engaging your body and energising the posture.

4. Look upwards, and ensure there is a direct line of energy from your left foot through to the fingertips of your right hand.

5. Raise the arches on both of your feet.

MODIFICATION Rest your left forearm across your right thigh, and put both hands in prayer position, turning head to look upwards. Or place your left hand on a block to the right of your right foot.

ADVANCED Bind your left hand beneath your right thigh, taking hold of your right wrist (the torso twisted to the right).

WARRIOR I/VIRABHADRASANA I

1. Begin in Downward-Facing dog. Place your left foot so that it is parallel to the back of the mat or turned in to a near 15° angle.
2. Step your right foot towards the front of your mat, facing forward, and bend the knee, ensuring that your right knee is directly above your right ankle.
3. Raise both hands above your head, pushing your palms together.
4. Rotate your left hip so that it is facing forwards.

MODIFICATION The back heel can be raised off the floor, which makes the pose much easier.

WARRIOR II/VIRABHADRASANA II

With a focus on maintaining our inner power

1. Stand with your left heel at the back of your mat, toes at a 15° angle, pointing inwards.

2. Step your right foot to the front of the mat, toes pointing forward, positioning your right knee above your right ankle at a 90° angle.

3. Your back leg should be straight, with your hips opening towards the side.

4. Engage both legs, drawing up on your left quadriceps. Extend your arms, spreading your hands perpendicular to the floor, keeping shoulders down.

5. Hold for 15 breaths on each side—or until your muscles are shaking; that's when your real power kicks in.

PYRAMID POSE/ PARSVOTTANASANA

.01 .02

1. Stand in Mountain Pose. Inhale your hands out to the side. Exhale them together behind your back, clasp the hands together, push your elbows inwards and raise your arms towards the sky, keeping palms clasped.

2. Inhale and step your right foot forwards one-half metre (about 1-1/2 feet).

3. Rotate your left foot outward so that toes points to the left at a 45° angle.

4. Draw up the muscles on your legs, and exhale with your chest towards your right thigh.

5. Raise the arches on both of your feet.

.03

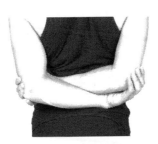

.04   .05

Aim to reach your chin on your shin and, gently but assertively, deepen the posture with every exhale. But do not overextend yourself. Hold "chin on the shin" as an aim, and let the body extend itself.

FORWARD STRADDLE BEND/PRASARITA PADOTTANASANA

.01 (FRONT VIEW)

1. Begin in Mountain pose and jump your feet one metre apart.

2. Make sure that your feet are facing forwards, place your hands on your hips and inhale your chest upwards.

3. Exhale folding forwards and put your hands on the ground in front of you. For the full version of the posture your hands will be on the same line as your feet.

4. Inhale and lengthen your torso with your head facing down.

5. Exhale and bring your head to the ground, whilst maintaining a straight back. Your forearms and elbows should be at right angles to the ground

.02

FORWARD STRADDLE-BEND WITH INTERLACED FINGERS/PRASARITA PADOTTANSANA C

This Bibliyoga posture will have initial cardiovascular benefits if you're not used to the pose, as the blood gets moving and the interlaced hands behind your back create more space around your heart. On top of that, your head is upside-down which also gets the heart working harder.

As you do the pose, try meditating on your heart, listening to your heartbeat and breathing deeply through your nose. Stay in the pose for as long as you are able and really focus on this sense of retuning to your heart. When you have completed the pose and continue on with your day, try to stay aware of the life possibilities that you are presented with— to see what you are motivated to do, where you are inspired to create something, whom you are driven to help. We all have some calling or other, but it takes a literal and metaphorical listening-to-our-heart to get back in tune with it.

1. Stand with one foot at either end of your yoga mat, in parallel position. Keep your legs straight; that is, your legs should now be making a triangle with the floor, with your pelvis at the top. Spread your toes, engage your thigh muscles, and ground yourself in the posture.

2. Interlace your fingers behind your back, arms straight, and lift your heart upwards on an inhale.

3. As you exhale, fold forwards, bringing your head towards the ground. Keep breathing, keep engaging your legs, and stay with the pose. Advanced practitioners will be able to get their hands all the way over on the ground in front of them, but for the rest of us "tighties," we'll do the best we can.

FORWARD BEND/UTTANASANA

.01

.02

1. Stand in Mountain Pose. Place your hands on your hips.
2. Fold forward from the hips, on an exhale, taking hold of either your shins or your big toes with the respective hand.
3. Keep your quadriceps engaged, but allow for a slight bend if the knees if you have any soreness in your back.
4. Use each inhalation to extend your spine. The ideal position is to have a straight spine. It is much better to be holding onto your shins with an extended back than to be holding onto your feet with a collapsed or rounded spine. As always, the emphasis is on alignment and clear breath.

VARIATION Seated Forward Bend. Aim for the same action whilst seated, reaching forwards and feeling the stretch on the back of your legs.

Try for straight legs, using a strap if necessary.

STANDING LEG RAISE/UTTHITA HASTA PADANGUSTASANA

.01   .02   .03

1. Stand in Mountain Pose. Breathe in and lift your right leg, taking hold of your big toe with the forefinger and middle fingers of
2. your right hand.
3. Breathe out, straightening your right leg.
4. Energise your standing leg. Focus on a point in front of you, and draw both of your shoulder blades down.
5. Be aware of keeping the posture as a clean line of energy, taking care not to collapse your shoulders or lean over to one side.
6. Balance and poise is everything in the Standing Leg Raise.

MODIFICATIONS Take hold of your right knee firmly with your right hand. This is one expression of the position. Another alternative, and perhaps more satisfying, is to hold your right foot with a strap, which will enable you to experience the full leg extension if you cannot do this others. Yet another variation is to press your raised foot against a wall in front of you.

ADVANCED When you are stable in the posture, inhale and lift your right foot higher to bring your nose to your right shin.

SEATED VERSION Lift your leg whilst seated in a chair, raising the leg as high as you are able whilst keeping your hands to the side or on your hips.

TREE POSE/VRKSASANA

.01

1. Stand in Mountain Pose. Inhale.
2. Bend your right knee to place your right foot on your right inner thigh, so that the foot is facing directly downwards and
3. properly aligned with your leg.
4. Open your hips so that your right knee points outward to the right, without compromising the position; i.e.,
5. your left hip should still be facing forwards.
6. When your foot is secure, inhale and open your arms to the side.
7. As you exhale, raise your hands above your head and push your palms together.

.02

DANCER'S POSTURE/NATARAJASANA

1. Stand in Mountain pose. Inhale and with your right hand, take hold of your right ankle from the inside, so that your shoulder and palm are

2. open towards your right, with your thumb pointing backwards.

3. Exhale and extend your right leg back, pushing your right foot upwards, which will deeply stretch your right shoulder. Be careful to keep the

4. right hip on a level plane, flattening your sacrum.

5. Inhale your left hand high, with the palm facing forwards.

6. Exhale and lean forwards, maintaining the energy through your left hand and right foot, continually pushing each in opposite directions.

7. Ground your left foot and intensify the backbend, continually raising your sternum.

MODIFICATIONS Bend your right knee and take hold of the foot, with your knee pointing towards the floor. Raise your left hand, and work on your balance while maintaining a basic sense of opening. Alternatively, take hold of your right foot with a strap and continue the pose as described above. A third variation is to do the full pose but while resting your left hand against a wall for support.

SPHINX POSE/BHUJANGASANA

The photograph shown is Sphinx Pose which is a preparation for Cobra Pose. Both are known in Sanskrit as *Bhujangasana*. In the full posture, both arms are straightened and the upper back is arched.

1. Lie flat on the floor. Place your hands beneath your shoulders, facing forwards. Take your legs hip-width apart which will reduce pressure on your lower back.

2. Push your quadriceps into the flower and point your toes back. Push your little toes into the floor.

3. Lift your upper chest and press your forearms into the group. Lift your chin and arch your upper back.

4. Open your shoulders, rotating them outwards.

5. Push your tailbone downwards, whilst keeping your hips off the floor. Ensure the tops of your feet are on the ground and engage the muscles in your thigh. Your thighs will remain in contact with the ground.

CAT–COW/MARJARASANA

The yoga posture is a simple "cat-cow meditation." Joseph is interpreting dreams of cows, so this is a good pose for us to explore here.

.01

.02

1. Go into an all-fours position on the floor.
2. Inhale and lift your head and pelvis upwards, dropping your chest to the floor (Cow).
3. Exhale arching your back, curling your head inwards towards your pelvis (Cat).
4. Continue this movement, arching back and forth.
5. Listen to your breathing, and see what your body is directing you towards. You may need to stretch your legs, your back, your shoulders. Meditate on realising your inner power—and trusting.

BOW POSE/DHANURASANA

1. Lie on your front and inhale, taking hold of each of your ankles with the respective hand, from the outsides.

2. As you inhale, lift your chest upwards and push your feet backwards whilst holding onto them.

3. The shape you form looks like a bow. The idea is to keep your body tense like the string of the bow. Continue to push your feet backwards, which will in turn open your shoulders and lift your chest higher.

4. This is a backbend, so ensure you are lifting your chest upwards and away from the lower back, to get the deepest backbend possible.

MODIFICATION Hold a strap around your ankles. An alternative is to do Side Bow/Parsva Dhanurasana, the same pose but lying on your side.

BRIDGE POSE/SETU BANDHASANA

1. Lie on your back in semi-supine position, bending your knees to bring the soles of your feet on the floor in front of your buttocks.
2. Place your hands facing down on the floor by the sides of your thighs.
3. Inhale and lift your hips, pushing into the balls of your feet.
4. Hold the position with your hips as high as possible.
5. Exhale, and slowly come down. Repeat three to five times.
6. Hug your knees into your chest and roll gently on your back, massaging your back muscles and releasing the lumbar spine.

VARIATION Place cushions or blocks underneath your lower back to support you in the posture.

CAMEL POSE/USTRASANA

.01 (MODIFIED)

1. Come up to a kneeling position with your shins in parallel position behind you. Your torso will be perpendicular to the ground/your shins (i.e., as though you were in a kneeling Mountain Pose). Tuck your toes underneath.

2. Place your palms on your sacrum and inhale your chest upwards, stretching your head to look back. Think of lengthening your cervical spine and opening the front, rather than squeezing or tightening your back.

3. Slowly exhale, dropping backwards, and take hold of your ankles.

4. Continue to keep the energy flowing through this position.

5. Eventually, on an inhale, come up to a straight position, taking care of the neck as you do so.

.02
(FULL VERSION)

When you've completed the posture between three and five times, move into Child's Pose.

WHEEL (BACKBEND)/URDHVA DHANURASANA

1. Lie on your back semi-supine, i.e., feet are hip-width apart and on the floor with your heels up near your buttocks.

2. Place your hands by the sides of your head, fingertips facing towards your feet.

3. Inhale, and lift your hips in the air so that you have moved into a modified Bridge Pose.

4. Exhale, and straighten your arms, opening your sternum towards the wall (or area) behind you.

5. Push into the balls of your feet whilst keeping the heels on the floor, making sure your feet are in parallel position. Draw up the muscles on your thighs, and raise your hips yet higher.

DOWNWARD-FACING DOG/ADHO MUKHA SVANASANA

1. Ensure your hands and feet are hip-width apart.
2. Aim to get your body in the shape of an upside-down letter V.
3. Tuck in your abdomen, engage your thigh muscles, and rotate your shoulders outwards, thereby elongating your neck.
4. Inhale and exhale through your nostrils.
5. Focus your eyes on your navel (the only officially sanctioned time for navel-gazing!).

HEADSTAND/SALAMBA SIRSASANA

Yogic writings call this the King of the Postures. Although it can take a while to master, it is immensely fulfilling once you have got it. Injury can be avoided if you go into the pose gently. Technically, you don't really balance on the head that much at all but rather create a tripod from the two upper arms, the head just below the apex.

1. Kneel on the ground, and place your forearms on the ground parallel to the front of the mat, one in front of the other.

2. Keeping your elbows in firmly in place, interlace your fingers in front of you. Your forearms effectively create the top two sides of a triangle.

3. Bring your feet up into the equivalent of Downward Dog, hip-width apart.

4. Place the crown of your head on the ground, cupped by your hands.

5. Walk your feet forwards, lifting your perineum as much as possible.

6. Inhale, bending your knees and bringing your hips directly above your head.

7. Raise your right leg first, followed by your left.

8. Keep the legs straight, and take 10 breaths.

9. To exit the headstand, slowly lower your legs towards the ground so that you can hover them just above the floor.

10. Practice Child's pose as a counter-posture to release the neck and upper shoulders.

SUPPORTED SHOULDERSTAND/SALAMBA SARVANGASANA

Mr. Iyengar points out that the crown of the head is usually the first part of our body to emerge into the world when we are born, and it encases the vital organs that control the functioning of the rest of our being. The head is likened to a king because it rules over the actions of the rest of our body and is home to our thoughts and our organs of speech. Regular practice of headstand can carry on into our old age, and there are examples of yoga practitioners who do the pose well into their 80s and 90s.

The pose brings extra blood down towards the brain, which refreshes the mind, brings a better supply of blood to the pineal and pituitary glands, and increases overall energy. There can be benefits to people suffering from insomnia and loss of memory, and the pose is also known to be good for relieving colds, foul breath, and palpitations. The list goes on; headstand is the ultimate posture recommended for achieving all-around balance.

1. Lie on your back and inhale to bend your knees in so that they are above your chest.
2. Place your hands on your rib cage and move them as close to the floor as possible.
3. Push/thrust your hips forward so that your torso is perpendicular to the floor.
4. Straighten your legs and engage the thigh muscles.
5. Leave space between your chin and clavicle so that there is space for your throat and no tension in your neck. Point your toes towards the sky.

VARIATION Try the pose leaning against a wall. You can also just do the first four stages of headstand and pause there; this is another variation of the pose.

ADVANCED When you are in headstand, take your legs into Eagle Pose/Garudasana (one leg bent around the other, foot behind), and hold.

EXTENDED CHILD'S POSE/BALASANA

1. Sink onto your knees. Place them hip's width apart and sit on your heels.
2. Stretch your hands out in front of you, with your arms lengthened.
3. Place your forehead on the ground.

VARIATION You can make the posture more comfortable by placing a cushion or pillow above your heels (i.e., to "sit" on) and placing a folded blanket beneath your forehead that it may rest on.

SEATED VARIATION Sitting in a chair, lean forwards to bring your chest on your knees, or place a cushion on your thighs and lean forwards onto that.

SHABBAT POSE/SAVASANA

There is lots one say about this pose but, briefly: Savasana is not "relaxation pose." It's a dynamic posture that is part of a very important yogic tradition. Often translated from the Sanskrit as "Corpse Posture," this pose serves as a reminder that our bodies are temporary and that we should appreciate this relatively brief sojourn on earth.

Shabbat Pose looks easy, but it is all about concentration. We completely release the breath in this pose and devote all of our resources to be conscious of our being. Focus on the inside of your body, and even mentally scan through every part of your body from your toes upwards.

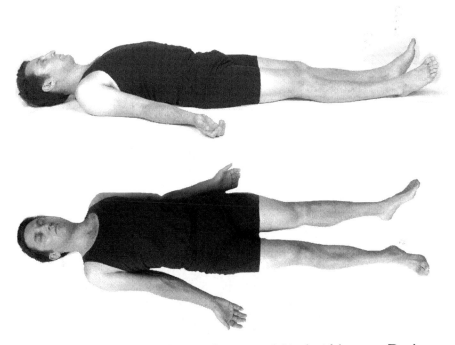

1. Lie on your back with your feet around hips' width apart. Don't spread legs too widely.
2. Place your palms facing upwards, by the sides of your hips.
3. Close your eyes.
4. Breathe. Be present. Discover the pose.

YOGIC BREATHING IN EASY POSE/PRANAYAMA IN SUKHASANA

One of the challenges of sitting cross-legged on the ground is to sit up straight for a long period time, because the pose as such lacks a firm three-point base. Lotus Pose does provide that base, but can be challenging and require our building up to it. Easy Pose is a good alternative to full Lotus Pose. If Easy Pose is challenging at first, continue to practice it to increasingly open and rotate the hip, which will allow you to maintain the posture for a long period of time. Personally, this is my favourite meditation posture, because I can get straight into the pose first thing in the morning without first doing the hip-opening routines usually necessary to prepare for a comfortable Lotus. Most important of all, make sure that you don't feel any knee pain whatsoever! If your hips are tight, you can prop pillows or blocks under your knees for support.

1. Sit on the ground and place your right foot so that it is resting on your left shin.
2. Place your hands on your knees with the palms facing upwards and press together your thumb and tip of your forefinger, on each hand.
3. Look forwards and close your eyes.
4. Breathe through your nostrils for 25 breaths, listening to the sound of the air. The breathing should be gentle and just loud enough to hear.

VARIATION You may find it easier to get into the posture by sitting on a cushion or a pillow.

ADVANCED Full Lotus, but only if you comfortably can hold it for a long period of time (without pain)

PRANAYAMA BREATHING

Here is a basic introduction to pranayama. Ideally it would be learned with a teacher physically present who can offer direct instructions to improve your breathing practice and conscious flow of energy.

1. Inhale through your nostrils and exhale through your mouth, imagining that you are trying to mist up a piece of glass held in front of your mouth. You can place your hand there to feel the warm air on the exhale. Listen to the soft "sssh" sound as you breathe out.

2. Attempt to make a similar sound as you inhale.

3. Continue this for several breaths, inhaling for a count of five and exhaling for a count of five. Aim to keep the throat relaxed and the breath soft.

4. Close your mouth, and continue the same motion through your nostrils, warming the air as you breathe in and controlling your breath in this manner.

SINGLE NOSTRIL BREATH/SURYA BHEDANA PRANAYAMA

1. Inhale through your nostrils, and exhale through your mouth, imagining that you are trying to mist up a piece of glass in front of your mouth. You can place your hand before your mouth to feel the warm air on the exhale. Listen for the soft ssshh sound as you breathe out.

2. Attempt to achieve a similar sound as you inhale.

3. Continue this for several breaths, inhaling and exhaling over a count of 5, and aim to keep the throat relaxed and the breath soft.

4. Close your mouth and continue the same motion through your nostrils, warming the air as you breathe in and controlling your breath in this manner.

PRANAYAMA BREATHING, COUNTING BREATHS

Pranayama is the yogic art of breath control and the conscious direction of energy. The most common form is inhaling and exhaling through the nostrils. This Kosher Sutra's recommended practice is to take a series of breaths and pause briefly at the point of the complete exhale (the "bottom" of the breath) and at the end of the inhale (the "top" of the breath). Notice the gaps between the breath, and allow your breathing to calm and your consciousness to expand.

LOTUS POSE/PADMASANA

Lotus is one of the classic yoga poses ideal for meditation. I caused myself lots of unnecessary pain for the first three years of doing this posture, because I forced my knees before they were truly ready, and they would ache for a couple of days afterwards. Such forcing should be avoided at all costs! Take your time, don't rush into it, and if it's not right for your body, either just take Easy Pose or simply sit cross-legged.

1. Sit on the floor cross-legged and take hold of your right foot, bending the knee and placing it on the top of your left thigh with the heel pressed into your abdomen.
2. Take hold of your left foot. Repeat Step 1, but with the left thigh.
3. Place your hands on your knees, with forefinger and thumb touching (on each respective hand).
4. Straighten your back.
5. Lower your chin towards the clavicle bone, at the top of the chest.

VARIATION Try sitting on a folded blanket or pillow. Begin by taking hold of one shin with both hands, wrapping one elbow around the knee and the other around the sole of the foot. Work on rotating your hip and opening it as much as possible before getting into the pose.

ADVANCED Continue to work your knees closer together so that your thighs are eventually parallel to one another.

MINDFUL WALKING MEDITATION

Walking meditation helps to ground a wandering mind. We specifically choose to walk back and forth along a direct path because it helps focus our mind; this way we do not have to negotiate finding a specific pathway.

1. Choose a straight path which is anywhere from 20-40 feet long.

2. Slowly walk back and forth along the path, looking down or with your eyes half-closed.

3. Allow your mind to settle into the route and bring your awareness to the lower part of your body.

4. Remain present to the sensations in your legs, and continue the walking meditation for 15 minutes.

ANJALI MUDRA (THE LOTUS OF THE HEART)

Sit with hands your in "Prayer Pose," (hands pushed together, thumbs on the heart chakra).

THANK YOU FOR HANGING OUT

Come and join us again!

GENESIS

DOWNWARD-FACING DOG/ ADHO MUKHA SVANASANA

"You shall be a blessing"

GENESIS 12:2

BREISHEET

A WHOLE NEW WORLD

KOSHER SUTRA: "In the beginning, God created..." (Genesis 1:1)
SOUL SOLUTION: Get the most out of every moment
BIBLIYOGA POSE: Yogic breathing - easy pose/*Pranayama in Sukhasana*, (p.90)
BODY BENEFIT: Increase calm and build energy

We can be standing in front of an awe-inspiring sunrise, but if our minds are experiencing chaos, we may as well be staring at a brick wall. The very essence of Hatha yoga is using asana (physical postures) to stabilise our body and make our mind calm and focused.

The Ishbitzer Rebbe[1] brought a new insight to the first phrase of Genesis. He taught that the word "created" also means "strengthening." According to this understanding, the first thing that God did was to allow His breath (*ruach*) to rest on the chaotic waters, to strengthen the earth that it would be a strong foundation on which to house the wonders of creation.

Similarly, our yoga practice leads us to calm the chaos in our minds through strong physical poses. Many people say, "I can't do yoga because I can't focus". However an inability to focus is actually a fine mental state in which to begin doing yoga, that we might learn these tools of strengthening the mind.

The masterful Baal Shem Tov taught that "where a person's thoughts are, that is where his entire being exists." Have you ever been eating a mediocre meal, noticed that it tasted only

---

[1]   Rabbi Mordechai Yosef of Ishbitz, in the Mei HaShiloach, Breisheet.

mediocre, but were with such great company that the meal seemed actually to taste better for it? Similarly, as with the beautiful sunrise mentioned earlier, we can be in a beautiful location and feel awful if our mind is elsewhere.

We need to strengthen our foundations, body and soul. Invigorating physical exercise will get our body strong, but by breathing, focusing on our breath, and allowing our ruach-breath to settle the chaos, we can have a strong mind as well as a strong physique. It all depends on where we choose to place our focus.

Mental focus and physical stability is not something that can be bought or paid for, and we cannot get someone else to go to the gym on our behalf. If you are reading these words then you are blessed with an incredible gift at this very moment, namely, the gift of life. The majority of us were not given a Life Instruction Manual as we grew up, but the discovery of meditation and yoga came later on. If you want to get the most out of every breath, every sunrise and ever moment, it is critical to train the mind and body.

God created the world and we can now co-create the quality of our life with every waking breath.

BREISHEET
RE:CREATION

KOSHER SUTRA: "Let Us Make Man" (Genesis 1:26)
SOUL SOLUTION: Transform a critical area of your life
BIBLIYOGA POSE: Extended Mountain Pose/ *Tadasana*, (p.51)
BODY BENEFIT: Experience the expanse and potential of your physical body

The human condition is driven by change. Few people are entirely happy with their body and mind. Whether you would like to be stronger, thinner, faster or happier, you are in the right place. The process of transformation can happen in a single moment, as soon as we make the decision to change.

One of the great fallacies of modern times is that we can achieve lasting change from an external source. Marketing gurus would have us that buying a certain mobile phone will magically reorganise our life, but how many times have you paid good money and received minimal results at best?

When the first human was created, God said "Let us make man" (Genesis 1:26)[1]. This is helpful because it allows us to look into the very fabric of creation; every other act of creativity began with "Let there be light"[2], "Let there be a firmament"[3], "Let the earth sprout vegetation of plants"[4] and so forth. There was a clear decision not to say "Let there be man".

---

[1]   We do not have space here to discuss what it means by God 'speaking', but let us assume it is a helpful metaphor

[2]   Genesis 1:3

[3]   Ibid. 1:6

[4]   Ibid. 1:11

Yoga is a story of self-empowerment. The terms yogi and yogini are the masculine and feminine nouns for people who have chosen to pursue the path of self-development and self-refinement. These are students who are dedicated to the path of cultivating themselves so that they are no longer at the mercy of anxious thoughts that arise in the mind and they do not exclusively rely on physicians to bring about healing for physical ailments. The yogi is ready to use a toolbox of asanas (yoga postures) as the first option for remedying aches and pains, and they will employ the various yogic meditation methods (such as pranayama, dharana and dhyana) to address psychological ailments. When they go to a doctor, they are entering a partnership to bring healing, rather than relying exclusively on the clinician.

Rabbi Shlomo Itzhaki (1040 –1105) was a medieval French scholar, who is considered one of the greatest Biblical commentators of all time. Known by his acronym Rashi (Rabbi Shlomo Itzhaki), he explained that "Let Us make man" was referring to a conversation between God and the angels, almost as if the creation of humans was a group effort.

Every day of our life, we have the ability to create and recreate ourselves. We can strengthen our body, calm our mind and train ourselves to think differently. Yours is the path of the yogi and the Bibliyogi; to practice these teachings and transform your life. Choose an area of your life where you feel that change is a 'must' and begin seeing yourself as a co-creator. Set your sights high, practice hard and do not stop until you have arrived at your goal.

NOAH
MORALITY BITES

KOSHER SUTRA: "All in whose nostrils was the breath of the spirit of life..."
(Genesis 7:22)
SOUL SOLUTION: Find meaningful spiritual connections
BIBLIYOGA POSE: Yogic Breathing / *Pranayama*, (p.92)
BODY BENEFIT: Calm, poise, and focus

The story of Noah is none too cheery: a tale of immorality and destruction—but ultimately one of rebirth. Whilst many of us may enjoy the occasional trip to Sin City, literal or metaphorical, the original inhabitants of earth took it one stage too far and brought upon themselves a world-changing flood. Noah, however, was different. He "walked with God". He was "perfect in his generation", top of the class.

The flood was all-immersive, and although we know that everyone died if they were not in the ark, the phrase used is that "all in whose nostrils was the breath of the spirit of life, of everything that was on dry land, died" (Genesis 7:22).

Rashi gives us a clue as to the ultimate body-soul connection. He explains that having the "spirit of life in your nostrils" means to be breathing (the Hebrew words for "breath" and "soul" are spelt with the same letters - *neshima/neshama*). This is an important Bibliyogic concept. We note that one of the most important rabbinic masters of all time directly connects the soul with the breath[1]. Understanding this allows us to experience a soul connection on a regular basis. Our breath allows us to

---
[1]   Rashi in Genesis 7:22

connect with God. The flood victims denied God through their behaviour and lost their breath-of-life as a result.

Breathwork is a core foundation of yoga, although *pranayama*, the practice of connecting our breath within the body, is far deeper than the mere act of inhaling and exhaling. *Prana* is understood as life force itself, and some teachers strongly recommend against the more powerful breathing-meditation techniques until our bodies are strong enough to hold the energy that those techniques unleash[2]. One purpose of *asana* is to make our bodies strong vessels in which to hold the life force, and when the *prana* is engaged, we begin to reach our physical-spiritual potential.

---

[2] The College of Purna Yoga, Aadhil Privhalipaka, teaches that "There can be asana without pranayama but there cannot be pranayama without asana". This statement might be disputed by other schools, but the reasoning is explained above.

NOAH
ALL AT SEA

KOSHER SUTRA: "And the water pushed on the earth..." (Genesis 7:24)
SOUL SOLUTION: Calm the chaos
BIBLIYOGA POSE: Boat/ *Navasana*, (p.42)
BODY BENEFIT: Strengthening the abdominal and thighs

There are days when we feel as if we are all at sea; chaos reigns and stillness eludes us. Sometimes it seems impossible to do everything we need to do, in the way we'd like to do it and in the time frame we'd like to get it done.

The Yoga Sutras remind us that "yoga is achieved when the mind's fluctuations are stilled" (Yoga Sutras 1:2). The sage Vyasa described five states of mind, beginning with the internal chaos of *kshipta*, which is a restless mind. The less severe versions are, sequentially, an infatuated mind *(mudha)* and a distracted mind *(vikshipta)*. Eventually we focus into the one-pointed state of mind *(ekagrata)* and, finally, a mastered mind *(nirodha)*. Today, yoga seems more important than ever to help us find equilibrium[3].

Our Kosher Sutra speaks of how water flooded the earth for 150 days. The world was returned to a primal state, much like the sheer chaos that preceded creation. The rabbis explain that this utter disorder, the *tohu vavohu* (Genesis 1:12), is more than just a physical formlessness. Rather, it is the state of confusion that is found in the mind of a child[4].

---

[3]   Gregor Maehee. *Ashtanga Yoga: Practice and Philosophy*, p. 142. The five states are also discussed by Vyasa in Yoga Sutra 1:32, as explained on Swamij.com's discussion of Sutra 1:4 (http://www.swamij.com/yoga-sutras-10104.htm).
[4]   Sfat Emet, Parshat Noach 5639

The purpose of yoga, according to the Yoga Sutras, is to bring order to the chaos and to still the inner craziness that some meditation systems call "monkey mind." I recently heard a friend say that she wouldn't even begin to attempt yoga because she can't focus her mind. But as I've said earlier, this is a prime state in which to begin a yoga practice! Though we may be pumped high on caffeine and constantly distracted with multiple mobile devices, we can always find a way to peace to the chaos in our lives.

Join me in five boat poses and let us sail these waters in peace.

NOAH

GO WITH THE FLOW

KOSHER SUTRA   "God's breath calmed the waters" (Genesis 8:1)
SOUL SOLUTION Deepen the breath trust in one's strength
BIBLIYOGA POSE Boat Pose / *Navasana*, (p.42)
BODY BENEFIT   Calms inner chaos, strengthens the abdominal muscles

There is a famous poster of the bearded guru Swami Satchidananda riding on a surfboard with a slogan along the lines of "You can't stop the waves but you can learn how to surf. Learn to meditate". Reading the Book of Genesis, we are reminded of the monkey mind, the *tohu vavohu* ("chaos and confusion") from which the world was created. Many of us experience this inner mental turbulence on an all-too-regular basis.

I am comforted by the calming verse the breathspirit of God "surfs" or "rests" *(merachefet)* on the surface of the water (Genesis 8:1). In case we missed the message in the first reading of Genesis, a similar action takes place in the story of Noah, where the earth is flooded and the Divine breathspirit floats once again on top of the once-wild waters.

The Taoists have a form of meditation that involves imagining our mind as water and using it to gently melt inner blockages, whether undefined emotional issues like pent-up anger or anything else standing in our way. This "water method" of Taoist meditation has us visualise water slowly sinking from the top of our brain down through the body until it reaches a blockage, and then slowly melting that block as if it were a chunk of ice.

113

In our yoga postures, we can apply a flowing movement similar to the quality of water; this is an essential element of *vinyasa* (sun salutes).

We can take our Bibliyoga practice to ever more subtle levels, bringing a deeper awareness to our daily lives. We can ask ourselves: When do we find ourselves suddenly overwhelmed with inner chaos? When are we revisited by old worries or ancient neuroses that seem continually to plague us, year after year? Now is the time to catch our mind, before it heads into the chaos: to take on this quality of water, to calm the wildness with our breath, and to unblock our energy so that we can flow once again.

LECH-LECHA
WE'VE GOT TO GET OUT OF THIS PLACE

KOSHER SUTRA "Get going from your land... to the land which I will show you" (Genesis 12:1)
SOUL SOLUTION Clarify your personal mission
BIBLIYOGA POSE Sun Salute A / *Surya Namaskar*, (p.30)
BODY BENEFIT Warms and invigorates muscles

Life is about journeys. We travel every day, whether it is to and from work on the literal journeys, or moving forward on life's path towards some greater ideal, or frantically running from harsh truths that are pursuing us (and we'd rather not face).

Hasidic mystics have often remarked on the internal aspect of this journey. *Lech-lecha* means "get going," but it also means to journey within, or, literally, to "go to yourself." We can sit still and take the internal voyage to our true self, to pass through the external layers we hide behind and get back to our inner being. When we have stillness within our mind, we find it easier to tune in to our ultimate personal mission.

The *Yoga Sutras'* early verses are almost entirely concerned with internal balance. The opening statement explains that yoga is achieved when the mind's fluctuations cease[1]; it goes on to explain that there are five types of mental disturbances[2] and that the aim is for us to correctly perceive the world around us[3] rather than engage with illusions that cause us to become upset and confused.

---

[1] *Yoga Sutras* 1:2
[2] Ibid. 1:5
[3] Ibid 1:7

The Meshech Hochma, a rabbinical commentator, takes this counsel one stage further. He suggests that Abram was being told to journey towards his true inner potential, to cast off the limiting beliefs of his environment, the attitudes of his childhood friends, and the restricting thoughts of his family. Then, and only then, would Abram be revealed to himself; then would he be shown his true inner greatness, and in turn, that potential would be shown to the world.

Do you ever sit at your desk and think, "I could be something more. I could be elsewhere. I'm better than this. I've got more to give"? This Kosher Sutra is a call to action, to go within and rediscover your potential greatness.

Go to yourself. Take the first step. Break beyond the limitations of your surroundings. Only then will the next stage be revealed to you. Be fearless. *Lech-lecha.*

LECH-LECHA

WALK TALL

KOSHER SUTRA   "You shall be a blessing" (Genesis 12:2)
SOUL SOLUTION Extend more blessings into your life
BIBLIYOGA POSE Downward Dog/*Adho Mukha Svanasana*, (p.83)
BODY BENEFIT   Elongates spine and extends the body

Although it has been years since I stopped exaggerating my true height on my acting resumé, the title of an article I once came across still grabbed my attention: "Yoga makes you taller". The claim is actually true: many of us don't stand at our full height, due to our contracting our shoulders or slumping into a day's weariness. Yoga addresses these misalignments.

Our Kosher Sutra was spoken to Abraham when told that he would literally become a blessing to others. In Chassidic thought, a blessing is an extension of God's will. Rather than thinking of blessings as brand new creations of goodness, the mystics see blessings as energies already extant that we but channel into earthly form[1].

The Iyengar approach to yoga focuses on physical alignment and on healing many of the ailments we all suffer as a result of poor posture and bad habits. I recently experienced something amazing whilst practising Downward-Facing Dog hanging from ropes on an Iyengar yoga-therapy wall: my spine seemed to elongate, creating more length throughout my body. I felt myself

---

[1]   The concept of Avodat Hashem is that our actions draw blessings into the world, whereas the notion of Yehi Ratzon is that our prayers influence the will of the Creator.

117

getting taller, and I was able to stretch what felt like an extra 10 centimetres after five minutes in the posture. It felt terrific.

Today's posture is Downward-Facing Dog, which focuses on the arms, shoulders, spine, hips, and legs. Try extending yourself, creating more space in your heart and increasing the flow of blessings through your body. If done it correctly, when you stand up you should feel some extra height.

Walk tall.

LECH-LECHA
OCCUPY YOGA, OCCUPY YOUR LIFE

KOSHER SUTRA   "Go inside for yourself..." (Genesis 12:1)
SOUL SOLUTION Begin the process of internal transformation
BIBLIYOGA POSE Easy Pose for 15 minutes/ *Sukhasana,* (p.90)
BODY BENEFIT   Grounding and internal peace

We are living in times of economic frustration, with "Occupy" protests having been organised in over 100 cities across the world[1]. These tented mini-cities have captured the imagination of people wanting a redistribution of wealth, but whether the occupations will achieve their ultimate aims is yet to be seen.

When I walked through the City Hall protest at Occupy Los Angeles, one thing became clear to me: a lack of clarity in intent. At least 20 different causes were being supported, from the more obvious "Cut the bankers' massive bonuses" to the more liberal "Free love" to more controversial and even anti-semitic protests.

There are two things that the entire Occupy movement is united on. The first is that organisers want change. The second is that they want other people to change.

Abraham's journey is one of extreme transformation. He was told to leave his country, his birthplace, and his family. It is no coincidence that the instructions came in that particular order. We can leave our country by getting on an airplane. We can get away from our birthplace by learning different languages and

---

[1]   Written during the first "Occupy Wall Street" campaign in 2011, which spread across the Western World.

119

customs,; which is somewhat harder. If we are incredibly strong, we might also free ourselves from the thought patterns and negative behaviours that we have inherited from our upbringing. Even those who may have had the most wonderful and loving parents in the world would most likely say, "I'll do some things differently from my parents." But how many of us ever really manage to do this?

Abraham is told *"Lech-lecha,"* which again translates as "go inside for yourself" or the more meditative "go to yourself" (Genesis 12:1). Reach deep inside. Do the work that is needed to change.

The yoga mat and the meditation cushion are places from which we journey towards change. Do not be fooled into thinking that transformation is accomplished by sticking your arms and legs into funny positions or just sitting still for a few minutes. Change happens with time, methodological application, and effort. It takes a lot of effort to make things look truly effortless.

Where would you like to see a revolution in your life? How would you like to see the world change? Become that change. Don't dream it. Be it. Occupy your mind, occupy your body, occupy your future, and occupy your yoga mat.

VAYERA

HEART N' SOUL

KOSHER SUTRA   "Strengthen your heart" (Genesis 18:5)
SOUL SOLUTION Heal the heart
BIBLIYOGA POSE Pyramid Pose / *Parsvottanasana* , (p.62)
BODY BENEFIT   Opens the chest and improves digestion and balance

How often are we completely reckless with our own hearts? How often do we put ourselves in situations where we could get hurt, or fail to look after our own needs? It is all very well to quote advice of the sage Hillel (200 BCE) who said that we should love our neighbours as ourselves, but what if we don't actually love ourselves in the first place?

The *niyama* (ethical) principle in the *Yoga Sutras* is *ahimsa*, the doctrine of nonviolence. We can practice this by acting kindly towards our own bodies, shutting off the voice of inner criticism and negative, self-destructive thoughts. But it can take a serious effort to replace our inner critic with an inner friend.

Today's Kosher Sutra is spoken by Abraham as he is feeding guests. He suggests that they "strengthen their hearts" with food; except we know that these guests are angels who don't actually eat. It is possible that Abraham knew that, too, and that he was focused on strengthening their hearts with friendship and hospitality. A commentator called the Baal HaTurim connected this phrase with other mentions of fortifying the heart: "Mark well in your heart her ramparts" (Psalms 48:14), and "You will see and your heart will rejoice" (Isaiah 66:14); he suggests that

Abraham felt pain in his heart when he didn't have guests to entertain.

Abraham was vitally aware of the needs of his heart. He was driven by the desire to reach out and connect with other people. Known for his quality of *Chesed* (lovingkindness), Abraham knew the clearest way to express his love for humanity. In the book *The Five Love Languages - How to Express Heartfelt Commitment to Your Mate*, Gary Chapman outlined five primary ways of connecting with our loved ones, which includes the methods by which we like others to show their love to us. These include words of affirmation, gifts, acts of service, quality time and physical touch. The better we know our primary language, he suggests, the more equipped we are for giving and receiving love in successful relationships.

Today's posture is a heart-opener: an opportunity to literally lift the heart, open the chest, and allow more oxygenated blood to flow through this vital organ. We begin by opening our heart on the yoga mat and in doing so we open our hearts to other people. We may offer them food, gifts, service or more. These actions begin with our hands but end up strengthening our hearts.

VAYERA
REVELATION

KOSHER SUTRA   "He lifted his eyes and saw three men standing before
                him" (Genesis 18:2)
SOUL SOLUTION   See enlightenment before your eyes
BIBLIYOGA POSE Triangle Pose / *Trikonasana*, (p.54)
BODY BENEFIT   Opens up legs, hips, shoulders; new possibilities; relieves
                anxiety; aids digestion

The male of our species is equipped with the unique capacity to ignore items directly in front of his eyes. "The pickles are in the fridge next to the butter," the female may say. "I can't see them," replies the baffled male. "Here," says his mate, pointing at the object he was looking right past. If only the gentler gender realised that male DNA may be primarily equipped for tasks such as throwing medium-range spears at tonight's dinner rather than foraging for berries and gathering their nuts.

Perhaps it all started with Abraham. God does *vayera;* that is, He "appears" before Abraham, who was sitting in his tent (Genesis 18:1). Or was the Divine presence in front of him all along? Abraham then lifts his eyes and sees "three men standing before him" (Genesis 18:2). But why hadn't he seen the men walking up? Shortly afterwards, God considers "concealing" Abraham's forthcoming fortunes and the City of Sodom's misfortune (Genesis 18:16), but He reveals that as well.

How often is the answer standing in front of our eyes but we fail to see it? My yoga teacher Edward Clark once said,

"Enlightenment is around us all of the time. All we need to do is to see it". More can be achieved when we become still and become present. The world itself can be revealed to us in these moments of stillness. Mindfulness leads to our seeing more opportunities before our eyes, to seeing the truth about certain relationships, to listening to the messages our body is sending us.

Abraham was present, aware, and tuned-in to the Divine voice within. He received immense rewards as a result. By focusing on the process of mindfulness, we can unleash the immense happiness that is always in front of our very eyes. Perhaps it was next to the pickles all along.

CHAYEI SARAH

CAMELS

KOSHER SUTRA   "And Isaac went out and meditated in the field"(Genesis 24:63)
SOUL SOLUTION   Ultimate spiritual and physical strength to sustain you for
the long term
BIBLIYOGA POSE   Camel Pose / *Ustrasana*, (p.80)
BODY BENEFITS   Strengthens the spine, shoulders, and legs; releases
tension from the back

Sometimes we can feel as though we are lacking energy and depleted by the challenges of life. The patriarch Isaac was facing in a difficult time when his mother passed away and we are told that he went out to walk in a field. Some translations say that he was meditating, and Rabbi Hirsch taught that this meditation was "... the inner growth of spirit and feelings, gathering thoughts", as if Isaac was gathering strength.

When Isaac is standing in the fields, he happens to see camels approaching that are carrying his bride-to-be, Rebecca. Interestingly, the first thing he notices is not his future wife but the camels.

There is a play on the word 'camel', from an earlier verse, when Isaac grew up "and was weaned" from his mother's breast (Genesis 21:8). The Hebrew word for weaning is *vayigamal*, which contains the word *gamal*, which in turn sounds like its English equivalent of camel. It is almost as if Isaac had supped the wisdom of life from his mother, stocked up on this spiritual strength as if he were a camel, and headed out into the desert of the world with his full provision inside.

Rav Matis Weinberg points out that this *sedra* (reading) has 15 mentions of the word camel—more than in the remainder of the entire Torah. In moving away from the reliance on his mother's milk, Isaac might be said to have become a camel, of sorts. The camel is the ship of the desert. With only a little meal it can keep going for days. Its mouth is strong enough to find sustenance in the most seemingly dry of vegetation: thorny plants, wild flowers, and cacti. The camel makes a dessert of the desert. It can carry people despite the heat or the terrain. A camel has the power to go the distance.

Consider the camel as a metaphor. Torah (spiritual wealth) is often compared to water. My friend Eric Rosen has said, "A little spirituality goes a long way." Let's think about it: What spiritual teaching means the most to you? Most of us have at least one phrase, belief or teaching that we have often repeated to ourselves over the years. Perhaps this is how Isaac lived, enriched by the teachings of his mother and father, infused by the words of the Divine, enlivened by the latent enlightenment all around him, and empowered with the ability to draw spiritual connection from the "cactuses" of everyday life.

Connect with your inner power and meditate on a spiritual teaching that means something to you. This is the "water" that carries you through the desert. And then spend the rest of the day seeing the spiritual potential in your everyday life.

Be a camel, and if someone annoys you today, try and carry them. Don't get the hump; they are probably just thirsty for some wisdom.

CHAYEI SARAH
TWO WEDDINGS AND THREE FUNERALS

KOSHER SUTRA   "And Isaac was comforted for [the loss of] his mother"
(Genesis 23:67)
SOUL SOLUTION Soul healing through loving relationships
BIBLIYOGA POSE Camel Pose / *Ustrasana*, (p.80)
BODY BENEFITS Stimulates kidneys, opens the psoas, opens the heartspace

A few years ago, there was a news story about a woman in middle America who held a solo marriage ceremony in which she walked down the aisle alone and expressed her commitment to herself. There are many unfair pressures placed on us by modern society that call us to be completely self-sufficient, finding all of our happiness from within. This is a tough call for any human being, as we are programmed to give and receive love.

Our Kosher Sutra is from the narrative that includes a death (Sarah's), a marriage (Rebecca and Isaac's), another marriage (Abraham and Ketura's), and two more deaths (Abraham's and Ishmael's). From a kabbalistic perspective, there is great similarity between these two motions of death and marriage. In the first, our soul becomes one with the creator, and in the second, it becomes one with another human being. When Isaac's mother passes away, he is consoled through his marriage to Rebecca, and he forms a solid unit with her that will last the rest of their days.

A popular focus for contemporary yoga practice is to bring attention to the heart, which stems from an early yogic text, the Chandogya Upanishad (~1500 BCE): "The Self is hidden in the lotus of the heart. Those who see themselves in all creatures go day by day into the world of Brahman hidden in the heart" (192–193)[1].

Although this text is more aligned with the Hindu tradition (given the reference to Brahman as the all-powerful God), there is an idea of locating our own heart-centre as a route to developing compassion for others and as a foundation for strengthening our relationships. In the school of Purna Yoga, the heart-centre focus is the centre of the chest, rather than the anatomical heart, per se.

Yoga is a tool for bringing healing, health, and balance through aiming for a state of oneness in our body. Camel Pose is most appropriate for this: it resonates with Isaac's "camel test" that proves Rebecca is the ideal wife, when she demonstrates her kindness by offering water to his camels. As we come into Camel Posture, we focus on lifting and opening our hearts to move into this gentle backbend, and we can visualise bringing healing into our body. Now is the perfect time to bring a body-mind focus to receiving some love and giving some love.

---

[1] From The Lotus of the Heart: A Summary of the Upanishads.
http://www.sunandmoonstudio.com/Articles/upanish.html

TOLDOT
REBECCA'S QUESTION

KOSHER SUTRA "The children struggled within her; and she said, 'Why am I thus?'" (Genesis 25:22)
SOUL SOLUTION Existential happiness, align with our true purpose
BIBLIYOGA POSE Sun Salute 'A' / *Surya Namaskar*, (p.30)
BODY BENEFIT Achieves a sense of stillness in motion

Internal struggles abound. True, there are always external struggles: Europe and the Euro, Israel's secularreligious JewArab troubles, Penn State's internal denial and reluctant acceptance of sexual-abuse scandals, the American elite's struggles with the so-called 99% and the dismantling of "Occupy" camps. Meanwhile, US news stations are fascinated with the conjugal struggles of reality TV stars (as I write this, the current media flavour is Kim Kardashian, and by the time this book is published, the celebrity media focus will have changed again).

Isaac marries Rebecca. During her pregnancy, she discovers that the twin babies are "struggling" within her (Genesis 25:22). She immediately asks, "Why am I thus?"

We have all experienced the symbolic equivalent of two children fighting within our stomach. Sometimes it is two ideas we are wrestling with, two possible jobs to pursue, two courses of action, or a choice about whether a relationship should be nurtured or let go. Some people have strong decision-making muscles; other people just freeze, unable to make the call due to overwhelming fear.

129

Nachmanides (1194–1270) compared Rebecca's struggle to that of Job. In the midst of Job's depressive struggles, he exclaimed, "If only I would be as though I was not born!" (Job 10:19).

This phrase is very important. In a seemingly shameless world, our society still holds as a huge taboo the subject of mental health. Although many people experience thoughts of suicide at some point in their lives, however fleeting, there is still much shame in discussing this. Yet almost everyone is beset with the difficult existential questions at some point or other - "Why do I exist ?!" - and the aim of our meditationyoga practice is to help us regain the inner balance and joy that are our birthright.

The 15th century treatise *Hatha Yoga Pradipika* explained that a state of yogic balance will be destroyed by six things: "overeating, overexertion, talking too much, performing needless austerities, socialising, and restlessness" (1:15). If we find ourselves experiencing inner struggle or turmoil and asking Rebecca's question, "Why am I here?", it is simply a sign that we need to stop for a moment—that we need to slow down, breathe, and introduce some quiet reflection.

Our meditation and yoga practice must lead us along the path of peace and bring us into alignment with our true purpose. Yoga means "oneness" or "unity," but we can also translate it as "clarity" or, better, "existential clarity." We become still, we start listening, and then we get clear. We hold variations of Rebecca's question during our meditations. "Why am I thus?" becomes "What is the point of my life?" or "What is my purpose?".

When we stop struggling with ourselves, we can truly start living.

TOLDOT

WE SHALL OVERCOME

KOSHER SUTRA   "And his hand was grasping Esau's heel" (Genesis 25:26)
SOUL SOLUTION Overcome obstacles
BIBLIYOGA POSE Forward Bend / *Uttanasana*, (p.68)
BODY BENEFIT   Lengthens the hamstrings, relieves lower backache

The very nature of being human is that we are each born with weaknesses in some area—although we have the chance to overcome them. Shortcomings differ from person to person: a hot temper, predilection for abusing drugs, moral flaws, or physical frailties. We can allow nature to dictate how we are going to live our lives, or we can strive to overcome weaknesses. This is the kabbalistic idea of *tikkun*, that is, identifying an area that we are going to improve.

There are two classical heroes who were born with a weakness related to their heels. Greek mythology tells the story of Achilles who was virtually invincible because his mother had dipped him into the River Styx when he was a baby. Unfortunately, she'd held him by his heel in doing so, which was the only part of him that remained unprotected and that would become the target for the arrow that eventually killed him.

Our Kosher Sutra tells of Jacob, born grasping his brother Esau's heel. Although Jacob was the physically weaker of the two, he used other strengths to pursue his goals, and his powerful spirit led him to succeed in overcoming his natural disadvantage. The

Rabbi of Levov taught that we can learn from Jacob's strength and be inspired to overcome obstacles that stand in our way.

Our bodies all suffer from some weakness, and we all have our own Achilles heel, but we can apply a yogic practice for healing (no pun intended): if our bodies are injured, we can focus on using the stronger muscles that work, and there are many remedial asanas that fortify the weaker muscles.

I wrote this chapter whilst in New Orleans, a city that has overcome immense struggles since Hurricane Katrina and the flooding of 2004. There are examples all around us of people who refuse to take "no" for an answer when they are faced with problems. Life is what you make of it.

TOLDOT

CLOSE YOUR EYES AND SEE THE TRUTH

KOSHER SUTRA   "When Isaac was old, and his eyes too dim to see, he
                called Esau..." (Genesis 27:1)
SOUL SOLUTION See more clearly and improve general clarity
BIBLIYOGA POSE Seated Forward Bend / *Paschimottanasana*, (p.38)
BODY BENEFIT   Greater flexibility and mental calm

Although it is a huge blessing to have the gift of sight, sometimes our eyes can mislead us. There are times when we see what we want to see, focusing on somebody's good qualities if it suits us even though other people around us might only see the bad in that person; or we focus on negativity and ignore the many abundant blessings before us. This Kosher Sutra is all about closing our eyes to see what is really going on.

The *Yoga Sutras* discuss the concept of *pratyahara,* a kind of sensory deprivation that allows you to get into a deeper space of meditation. At its most practical level, it can be experienced by closing your eyes when performing an asana. Eventually it extends to your becoming so enwrapped that your other senses are virtually shut off and you become entirely focused on stillness—that is, you have a one-pointed focus *(ekagrata)* and achieve the state of yoga.

This is akin to the reports of Biblical prophets who would completely shut down their outer physical senses when communing and communicating with God[1].

---

[1]   From *The Lotus of the Heart: A Summary of the Upanishads.*
      http://www.sunandmoonstudio.com/Articles/upanish.html

Isaac was giving the firstborn blessing to his eldest son Esau and it was significant that the elderly man could not see that he was actually giving the blessing to his younger son Jacob who had dressed up in disguise as Esau. The commentator Rashi suggested that, on some level, Isaac actually allowed his eyes to be dimmed, allowed himself to be fooled, because he knew on a deeper level that his younger son was his actual true heir and disciple.

When we enter an asana with our eyes closed, we can "see" things differently. It becomes possible to be more acutely aware of the ground beneath you, to feel the way your clothes brush against your skin, to feel the soft touch of the air on your face. Try it for a moment, in whatever position you are in, and begin to notice how you can "see" with other parts of your body, becoming aware of the space in the room around you and the more-subtle things you might otherwise miss if you were only looking with your eyes.

Yoga teacher Max Strom describes the skin as hundreds of tiny eyes, all increasing our sensitivity and acting as tiny teachers. Skin is the body's largest organ and its massive surface area allows us to increase our perception.

When you next face resistance or difficulty, close your eyes and notice how you are feeling. Whether you are faced with a challenging email, text message, or face-to-face conversation, listen to your intuition and allow it to reveal your next action. The truth is in there, if you choose to see it.

VAYEITZEI
STAIRWAY TO HEAVEN

KOSHER SUTRA   "God was standing over him" (Genesis 28:13)
SOUL SOLUTION Bounce back from setbacks
BIBLIYOGA POSE Shabbat Pose / *Savasana*, (p.89)
BODY BENEFIT   Rejuvenates, and strengthens inner vision

I was once looking at a shiny new wooden floor of a church, in the Temple of Zion congregation in the infamous Lower 9th Ward of New Orleans. Half of the building was submerged by the floodwaters that followed Hurricane Katrina. We were listening to a presentation from a member of Avodah, the Jewish service corps that has been helping rebuild the community, and it was inspiring to see how the locals regained their sense of belief after such devastation. With a new floor to stand on, they are now able to stand tall and move forwards.

Our Kosher Sutra is dramatic. Jacob lies down and has a meditation dream about angels ascending and descending a ladder. The 11th century commentator Ramban explains how this dream was a form of prophecy. On a symbolic level, Jacob was able to pierce through the surface layer of physical reality and see how his physical body was completely connected to the higher spiritual realms.

The process of yoga is to continually connect our body with our soul, through the unification that takes place in all of the flowing postures *(asana)* and movements *(vinyasa)*.

The sleep-like posture is a key penultimate pose in many yoga practices, certainly in both Ashtanga and Iyengar sequences. The yogi lies back-down, palms open, feet gently falling out to the sides, whilst aiming to remain as focused and present-minded as possible. For beginners and particularly exhausted advanced practitioners, the aim is also to stay awake during the pose.

Life is full of unexpected hurricanes and tornadoes. We always have the choice to take it lying down and find ourselves beaten into submission. Alternatively, we can use challenges as opportunities to find a deeper spiritual strength and, in so doing, overcome the slings and arrows of outrageous (mis)fortune, so that we bounce back stronger than ever before.

VAYEITZEI

AWESOME

KOSHER SUTRA   "How awesome this place is! This is...the gate of the heavens" (Genesis 28:17)
SOUL SOLUTION   Increase your ability to focus and concentrate
BIBLIYOGA POSE   Mindful walking meditation, (p.98)
BODY BENEFITS   Focuses the mind and body

A Kentucky man made big news when he went shopping, packed his three children and groceries into the car, and drove away from the supermarket parking lot before realising he'd left behind something in his shopping cart: his six-month old baby.

It is easily done. Not abandoning babies, but forgetting to be mindful. We are easily distracted by a myriad of, well, distractions. Our thoughts are in the past, in the future; on a phone call, an email, an errand—anywhere but the present. The breakthrough of Professor Jon Kabat-Zinn's Mindfulness-Based Stress Reduction techniques was that they taught people how to reduce stress through being mindful. Simple? Only if we actually do it.

Our Kosher Sutra recounts a flash of mindfulness. Again, the patriarch Jacob sleeps and has a dream about a ladder connecting earth and heaven, upon which there are angels ascending and descending. Jacob notices God standing over him. His response, as Californian natives might put it: "Awesome." We read how Jacob awakes, realises that Divinity is present, becomes frightened, and says, "How awesome this place is! This is none other than the home of God and the gate of the heavens" (Genesis 28:17). Awesome, indeed.

When we are able to keep our minds in the present moment we can tune in to a completely different reality. There is no past, no future, no stress, no worry, no pain, and no problem—only the moment. We've all heard this a million times. So why is it so difficult to realise? Have you ever done the equivalent of forgetting the baby, whether walking around the house looking for sunglasses that were on your head (ok, I confess...), or otherwise forgetting something else important?

Of course, psychoanalysts and writers would have something else to say about the topic. In *Confessions of an Opium Eater*, Thomas De Quincey wrote, "There is no such thing as forgetting possible to the mind" (2:67), and it was Sigmund Freud who introduced the idea of memory suppression, or "motivated suppression," whereby we forget things because we want to. This could be anything from an abuse victim's suppressing a traumatic memory to a husband forgetting to buy something for his wife because he feels that he can't afford it. Either way, suppressed memory or not, there is a lack of conscious thought matching unconscious action (or inaction).

Perhaps answers are to be found in the 15th century *Hatha Yoga Pradipika*: "When the breath is unsteady, the mind is unsteady. When the breath is steady, the mind is steady, and the yogi becomes steady. Therefore one should restrain the breath" (2:2). The breath "restraining" can involve various *pranayama* (yogic breathing) practices, whether inhaling and exhaling through the nostrils or holding the breath for short periods of time. Either way, the aim is to steady our thoughts and increase our level of consciousness.

Returning to the Kosher Sutra with Jacob, who merely laid down for a sleep and had a sudden flash of consciousness through his dream, Rashi (11th century) explains that the comment "How awesome is this place" was akin to a level of understanding. Jacob suddenly saw through the physical veil of his surroundings and was able to connect with the deeper spirituality around him.

The word for "awesome" was given an Aramaic translation (through Onkelos) similar to "understanding." No doubt Dr. Freud would have some comment about his great-great-great ancestor Jacob's reaching a deeper level of understanding through the dream state.

I sometimes moan about the overuse of the word "awesome" (particularly common in California), but wonder if there's also a positive aspect to it. Maybe people are genuinely finding awe in everyday events. Wishful thinking, perhaps, but if we could really breathe in every moment and understand the magnitude of what is around us, maybe we would all be seeing the awe every few minutes.

Right now, try counting your blessings. How many fingers and toes do you have? How much food is in your fridge? How many relatives do you have who love you? How many friends do you have (both real and on Facebook)? Awesome. Right

MINDFUL WALKING MEDITATION

*"How awesome this place is! This is…
the gate of the heavens"*

GENESIS 28:17

VAYISHLACH

SORE HIPS AND BLESSINGS

KOSHER SUTRA "Jacob wrestled until dawn—and his thigh was strained"
(Genesis 32:26)
SOUL SOLUTION Overcome the difficulties of a true spiritual connection
BIBLIYOGA POSE Bound-Angle Pose / *Baddha Konasana*, (p.47)
BODY BENEFIT Greater hip flexibility and thigh strengthening

In previous chapters we considered how Jacob felt light and his "feet were lifted" when he went through a deep meditation. We have also noted how he grabbed onto his brother's ankle when he was born. Here, Jacob faces the ultimate leg problem, as it were: a damaged hip. It is only when he has finished his bout in the ring that Jacob walks off limping and reaches spiritual fulfilment at the same time.

Jacob has had an all-night wrestling match with an unknown man. Some say it is with an angel. Others say it's with the alter ego of his brother Esau. The painful truth is that spiritual accomplishment can hurt. And if you're not careful in your pursuit of spiritual truth, it can leave you injured.

The ancient yogis talked of the notion of ahimsa, again, "nonviolence," in the yogic pursuit for spiritual fulfilment[1]. This seemed at odds with the extremely violent battle scenes described in the ultimate yogic reference poem, the *Bhagavad Gita*. The contradiction was resolved in the explanation that if a warrior has the correct intention of fulfilling his destiny (in

---

[1] *Yoga Sutras* 2:35. "The practitioner will cease to encounter hostility from others by practising nonharming and nonviolence (ahimsa)."

Hebrew this would be described as *kavanah*), then the violence was purely a means to an end. In other words, throw the spear but do it without internalising the violence. This is not dissimilar to the description of King David's battles where he fought with the sole purpose of gaining peace for his people, rather than to satisfy any urge of his ego.

Spirituality hurts for most of us, at some time or other. We all have different sources of pain, whether it be the childhood teacher who bullied you into accepting a certain dogma, a fury at God for taking away a loved one, or a general dissatisfaction with your life situation that leads to lack of belief. It is understandable. We have all been there. The challenge is this: Are you willing to go the distance, to fight it out, to lose sleep, in order to connect with the Great Unknown, and to spend all night doing so?

Jacob stayed with his fight throughout the night and eventually won against the angel. As a result he was given a new name, meaning "the one who has wrestled with God and overcome"; in Hebrew, the name is "Israel"[2]. This title is available to anyone willing to truly engage on their spiritual quest, to truly connect, and to battle it out.

Spiritual accomplishment can be painful, and whilst it is important to acknowledge the source of your pain, it is also important to keep going forwards. There is so much to enjoy about this life on earth, and every day can become more colourful when we find a deeper meaning. So get on your yoga mat, start opening the hips, and push yourself to your limits. Just make sure you don't walk off with an unfixable limp.

---

[2] There is a rabbinic idea that when someone takes on a new name, they can become that name. "Israel" is indicative of being upright (*yashar*) and bringing down the blessings of God (El). See Rashi on Genesis 32:28 to explore further.

VAYISHLACH

HEAL YOUR LIFE, HIPS, AND BANK BALANCE

KOSHER SUTRA   "The angel struck Jacob's thighbone on the displaced sinew" (Genesis 32:26)
SOUL SOLUTION Heal long-standing pain and regain inner balance
BIBLIYOGA POSE Triangle / *Trikonasana*, (p.54)
BODY BENEFIT   Better balance whilst walking, and stronger strides

There is this really incredible piece of machinery that has been developed. It has a built-in feedback system that tells you when it needs fixing, the software is continually upgraded, and the hardware has a lifetime guarantee. The technology is called a "body."

We are creatures of innate balance, whether we realise it or not. If we need food, we eat. When we are depressed, we try to cheer up. Should our skin get torn, it tries to repair itself. Even "bad" things like cancer cells are merely the body's misguided attempt at rebalancing itself in some way.

Our Kosher Sutra features the patriarch Jacob, who provides an interesting model of spirituality. He doesn't sit on a hill and meditate, nor does he withdraw from the world to "be spiritual." His spirituality is hands-on, dirty, and downright messy.

Spirituality is not about being separated from worldly influences but in choosing how we respond to them. Jacob's father-in-law lies to him, his brother dislikes him, and in this Kosher Sutra, we

143

find him in a place of sheer fear that meeting his sibling after 20 years could lead to a physical attack on his household.

The notion of karma is that there is cause and effect: every action has a reaction, and if we push something out of balance, then we essentially need to fix it. In the book *The Energy of Money: A Spiritual Guide to Financial and Personal Fulfillment*, author Maria Nemeth recommends healing one's "money karma" by doing a careful accounting of outstanding energetic debts. This means any promises we have made to buy someone a gift, any pledges to charity that we haven't fulfilled, or even any volunteer time we have promised and not delivered. She teaches that as soon as we say we will do something, we create a contract that must be completed. If we don't complete it, we create an energy block that needs to be healed, much like leaves stuffed into a drainpipe that then stop rainwater from flowing though.

Jacob has a seemingly awful time of it. He was tricked into giving up 14 years of his life to marry the woman he loved, and he's now fearful that his brother will kill him.

He doesn't ask, "Why is this happening to me?" because he knows full well. Twenty years earlier, he tricked his brother Esau out of his birthright, and now the time has come for payback. Jacob is so scared that Esau will kill him that he sends wildly extravagant gifts and splits his household into two, with one wife in each camp, so that if one half of his life is totally decimated he will at least have something left to rebuild with.

Spirituality is about meditation and prayer, but it is also about practicality and doing everything we can to build an incredible life on earth.

There is one specific part of the body that helps us keep our balance and enables us to move forwards in the world, but it can also hold us back: the hips. In Caroline Myss's outstanding book *Anatomy of the Spirit*, she explains how the hips and pelvis can be storage points for fear, blame, and guilt about power, control, creativity, and money issues. Her thinking is immensely developed around this area, but one basic idea is that when we suffer hip problems, it can be because there is a part of us that does not want to move forwards. Myss explains that we can heal our body when we can truly listen to what our body is telling us and that most physical pains can be related to emotional issues. This whole area of study is known, among other names, as "energetic anatomy."

Immediately before meeting Esau, Jacob has the wrestling bout with an unknown figure who is revealed to be an angel. Jacob leaves with an injury deep within his hip socket, which eventually heals once he has made peace with his brother. From an energetic perspective, this makes complete sense. Jacob has to get everything back into balance within his body and within his world. His physical pain is deep, affecting his muscles, tendons, and bones. To this day, the sinew of the leg muscle is considered a non-kosher piece of meat "because [the angel] struck the ball of Jacob's thigh bone on the displaced sinew" (Genesis 32:33).

When Jacob meets Esau, everything goes better than imagined. "Esau ran towards him, embraced him, fell upon his neck, kissed him, and they wept" (Genesis 33:4). Perhaps the meeting went so well because Jacob had already done the internal work, accounting for all of his actions and completing a full physical and emotional healing.

The yogis discussed five layers or sheaths to our body, which are mainly energetic. The "top" two layers are the physical and the energetic sheaths, known as the *annamaya kosha* and the *pranamaya kosha*. When we go into a yoga posture, we start with the physical level and work from there.

Jacob got deeply into the anatomy of his hip, healing his femur, hip socket, piriformus, sartorius, gluteus medius, gluteus maximus, psoas, and who knows what else. The Kabbalists associate Jacob with the sefirah-quality of *Tiferet*, which stands for compassion and inner balance.

Many of us have unresolved issues and unresolved pains, but healing is within our hands. We can maintain and "upgrade" our software by listening closely to our hardware. Rebalancing begins today.

VAYISHLACH

SAFE ARRIVALS

KOSHER SUTRA   "And Jacob arrived safely" (Genesis 33:18)
SOUL SOLUTION   Total healing, body and soul
BIBLIYOGA POSE   Bound-Angle Pose / *Baddha Konasana*, (p.47)
BODY BENEFIT   Strengthen hips; prepares women for childbirth

The saying goes that 'what doesn't kill us makes us stronger', but it's not much fun to hear when you're writhing with pain. We can all get stronger when we recover from injuries, but that does not mean that old war wounds don't still ache from time to time.

There is a beautiful image, or so I thought, of Jacob who walks away after he has spent the night wrestling with an angel. He's uplifted, inspired, had his name upgraded to Israel ("the one who struggles with God and man and overcomes")—but despite his spiritual enlightenment, he still carries a bit of pain and walks with a limp.

Yoga can be transformational although the physical-spiritual encounter that takes place on a yoga mat can cause injuries for many people. At some point or another plenty of serious yogis will push themselves too far, allowing their ego to overcome their breathing and causing themselves an injury. The bad news is that this hurts at the time but the good news is that a good practice and a great teacher can help you heal from many physical pains so that you become stronger than ever.

Jacob walking with a limp is poetic but it isn't pretty, and there's nothing beautiful about an exquisite, spiritually-induced pain. If we read a little further in this story, we see that Jacob's true graduation to become the man called Israel (in a Luke-Skywalker-becomes-Jedi sort of moment) happens only once he has healed various relationships. Things improve with his father-in-law and his estranged brother, and when he meets his sibling Esau, he "arrived safely."

The Hebrew word is *shalem*, meaning "complete" or "whole," and Rashi explains that JacobIsrael was completely healed with regards to his body, his emotional pains, his financial difficulties.

Be strong, be healed, be happy.

VAYEISHEV – CHANUKAH

JOSEPH'S TANTRIC DREAMCOAT

KOSHER SUTRA   "His master's wife said, 'Lie with me' and he refused"
(Genesis 39:7)
SOUL SOLUTION Overcome unhealthy temptation
BIBLIYOGA POSE Warrior II / *Virabhadrasana II*, (p.61)
BODY BENEFIT   Develops physical strength through resistance

Temptation makes us ache with desire, whether for bad food, too much drink, or great sex with the wrong person. This Kosher Sutra is specifically about overcoming misdirected passion. Sexual attraction is natural and healthy but it can be highly destructive when acted upon with the wrong person. Most people are sexually tempted at some point or other to such a person (work colleague, professor, or best friend's ex) but the main issue regardless is how to beat temptation. Our Kosher Sutra centres on the story of Joseph who has become the servant of the overlord Potiphar. Joseph finds himself regularly propositioned by Potiphar's wife, who tries to seduce him seemingly in every way possible; and she becomes one dangerous lady when her desires are not fulfilled.

One theory of yoga is that it is all about the movement of energy inside the body—what the Vedic writings referred to as *prana*. Prana is often mistranslated as "breath," but the broader idea is that we can harness this pranic energy through both breath and movement, and channel this life force. The closest Hebrew translation to prana is Ruach or Neshama. Tantric yoga is about focusing this energy inwards, rather than releasing it to the world, and becoming stronger and more powerful as a result.

We are told that Joseph is "handsome of form and handsome of appearance" (Genesis 39:6), and even though the woman asks him to lie in bed beside her (even without touching, according to Rashi), he still refuses. Just A leads to B leads to C, it is as if he knew what could happen, so he stopped himself before D led to E led to F.

The rabbis have provided more tales of Joseph's erotic temptations. One midrash says that the temptress changed her clothes three times every day so that she'd grab Joseph's eye, while another goes further to say that she invited around her Egyptian girlfriends, gave them each a citrus fruit to cut up and enjoy, and then asked Joseph to parade in front of them. He was so attractive that they cut their hands, which formed small, sensual bleeding scars. Oy.

According to the text, Potiphar's wife attempted to seduce Joseph every single day. She grabbed his clothes. She teased him. The commentator Rashi suggests that Joseph was at fault for the habit of curling his hair and preening himself when he should have been thinking and praying for his father (who thought Joseph was dead); hence Joseph's being tested by this raunchy wench (I say, if your hair isn't naturally curly, then enjoy it au naturelle, but that's beside the point.)

Yet another midrash says that Joseph saw his father's face outside the window, which is how Joseph resisted Potiphar's wife. It's entirely possible that Joseph summoned this image himself as a way of keeping himself cool, in a meditational equivalent of a cold shower, so to speak. Either way, he found the strength to say, "No." Now that is impressive.

The sages have asked, "Who is strong?" The famous reply is, "He who can control his desire." This is true whether your desire is for unhealthy food, unhealthy sex, or unhealthy hair treatments. True strength comes from inside. It produces the ability to keep going through difficult situations, through sheer force of will. Another way of translating the Hebrew is, "Who is a [true] warrior? The person who is in full command of their passions."

WARRIOR II / VIRABHADRASANA II

"His master's wife said, 'Lie with me' and he refused"

GENESIS 39:7

VAYEISHEV – CHANUKAH
KOSHER SUTRA HOLIDAY SPECIAL

KOSHER SUTRA   We were binding sheaves in the field (Genesis 37:7)
SOUL SOLUTION   Spiritual growth and physical growth
BIBLIYOGA POSE   Sun Salute A/ *Surya Namaskar A*, (p.30)
BODY BENEFIT   Increases strength and stability in the body

What do the following things have in common: jelly doughnuts, female assassins, massage oil, and good old-fashioned hard work? Switch on the kettle, make a cup of caffeine-free herbal tea, and join me by the fireside for the Kosher Sutra Holiday Special. It all boils down to three topics: food, sex and money. Is there anything else?

MONEY

There is a universal law that all musicians know: the more you practice your instrument, the better your chance of becoming a musician. A similar law applies to sports, which is why Tiger Woods spent countless hours practising his swing, and David Beckham put in his time honing goals. Of course, this applies to everything in life, which begs the simple question: Why do so many of us get frustrated at our getting poor results when we have not put in the work?

My yoga teacher Edward taught me how to do handstands, inverted eagles, and backbend kick-overs, but he always maintains that the hardest yoga move is this: putting on your shorts and standing at the front of your mat in the morning.

It is easy to sit and write New Year's resolutions but a lot harder to start—and continue—doing them. For some reason, we find it much easier to write them down. And while actions speak louder than words, we often prefer to talk rather than act.

There are many epithets that point in this same direction.

- How do you get to Carnegie Hall? Practice, practice, practice.

- Luck is where preparation meets opportunity.

- It is not talking about it (*midrash*) but doing it (*ma'aser*)[1].

- You reap what you sow.

- [Add your own here.]

Our Kosher Sutra begins with the dream-interpreting prophet Joseph who meets the King of Egypt. Pharaoh has had a dream of seven sickly sheaves and seven healthy sheaves standing next to one another. Joseph also had a dream of sheaves, that he was working in the field to bind. The Lubavitcher Rebbe points out the difference between the two dreams, in that Joseph dreams of working while Pharaoh dreams of wealth that just happens: the former is a model of spiritual and material growth: we put in the hours, we get results.

"This highlights the fact that all matters of holiness require effort, ensuring that what we receive from God in return should

---

[1] Ethics of the Fathers 1:17

not be unearned 'bread of shame' (Jerusalem Talmud 1:3). When a person dedicates himself to serious work, he has the promise of success that 'you laboured [and therefore] you discovered' (Megillah 6b). In fact, a person is capable of achieving success far beyond the proportion of effort invested—following the pattern of 'always ascending when dealing with matters of holiness'"[2]

The *Hatha Yoga Pradipika* mentions the importance of regular yogameditation practice. If we are truly honest with ourselves, surely we know all of this already?

FOOD

The winter holiday season in the West means Christmas cake, Chanukah doughnuts, and a whole lot of lip-smacking, high-cholesterol snacking. My father refers to the typical Chanukah foods as "heart-attack alley." He has got a point.

The festival of lights recounts how the Greek-Syrian empire invaded ancient Israel and set up foreign idols in the temple. A group of fighters known as the Maccabees ("hammers") staged a guerrilla-warfare campaign, stormed Jerusalem, and reclaimed the capital. The menorah, a ceremonial candelabrum, was almost out of oil, but a miracle occurred, and one day's supply of oil ended up lasting for eight days. Hence the eight nights of Chanukah.

Oh, and there is one more thing. The rabbis teach how it is customary to eat oily foods during Chanukah. That means oily doughnuts, oil-fried potato patties known as latkes, and any other

---

2   Likutei Sichot, Vol 3. p819ff, in Gutnick Chumash

artery-busting grub we can get our hands on. But is tradition always right? Would the Maccabees have said to themselves, "Hey ho! It's time to go on a sortie and invade Jerusalem. Let's have a plateful of doughnuts!"? I've yet to hear a spiritual leader stand up and say that Chanukah should be celebrated by a week of eating salads with high-quality first-pressed olive oil, coupled with organic fish rich in omega-3 oils, or that husbands should massage their wives with flaxseed or sesame oils.

Back to our "regular practice" principle of spiritual growth. We spend our days eating stodgy, oily foods, consuming high-fructose corn syrup and processed sugars, and then get surprised when our bodies finally start developing problems. We reap what we sow.

SEX

The universal principle of regular spiritual practice also applies to relationships. This is something we know instinctively, in that we need to put time into building our relationships rather than just taking them for granted. There was a famous medieval law known as *Droit du Seigneur*, whereby a feudal overlord was permitted to take the virginity of the new brides of the men under his rule, by sleeping with the brides on the nights of their weddings. Few are aware that this also took place during the Greek rule of Ancient Israel. The Kitsur Shulchan Aruch tells how the daughter of the High Priest Yohanan put a swift end to this custom when it was her turn to get married. She cooked a dairy meal for the governor, which made him sleepy, and during his slumber, she cut off his head and took it to Jerusalem as proof. Hence the widespread custom for women not to work whilst the candles are burning[3]. Whoever said that Jewish princesses couldn't cook was clearly mistaken!

TODAY...

The principle is straightforward; If we go to a meditation class only to complain that our minds are racing, we are not giving it a chance. We would not sit down by a piano for the first time and expect to be able to play one of Mozart's piano sonatas right off. We should be patient with our meditation practice.

We do not need New Year's resolutions. We just need to make a simple list of our priorities and take action. Where do you want to be this time next year, and what do you need to get there? Whether it's losing weight, saving more money, or becoming more organised, most things are within our reach if we can remove the blocks to achieving them. We can dream of sheaves of corn being gathered within our storehouse, but the dreams are a lot more likely to come to fruition if we start planting seeds right now.

---

3   Kitsur Shulchan Oruch, 3:1 and 3: 3

SUN SALUTE A/ SURYA NAMASKAR A

"We were binding sheaves in the field"

GENESIS 37:7

VAYEISHEV
TURKEY DAY

KOSHER SUTRA   "Go and see how your brothers are doing" (Genesis 37:14)
SOUL SOLUTION Inner peace and to banish depression
BIBLIYOGA POSE Pigeon Posture / *Eka Pada Rajakapotasana*, (p.48)
BODY BENEFIT   Opens hip flexors, lengthens the groin and hamstrings, improves flexibility in the back, opens the chest

Every day brings new teachings. I recently learned that, once a year, the leader of the free world, the President of the United States of America, spares the life of a turkey. It's all part of the American Thanksgiving festival, and although Queen Elizabeth II would be unlikely try a similar process due to the likely sardonic reprisals of the British tabloids (regardless that we do not have the death penalty), Thanksgiving is taken very seriously over here in the US. People even update their social media statuses during the lead-up to Thanksgiving, listing daily the things for which they give thanks.

This Kosher Sutra is the instruction given by Jacob to his son Joseph. The latter has previously upset his brothers after he gave a bad report about their behaviour, and he is now being given a second chance to see the good in them. The siblings were further upset when they heard about Joseph's famous dreams of his ultimate leadership, and he is now invited to revisit them and make amends.

We can read the whole passage from an internal, metaphorical perspective. How often do we cause depression through our telling ourselves old, negative stories? We have the ability to make ourselves disheartened when we summon negative reports into our mind about how our body is behaving, about what we should be achieving, about how we could have acted in a certain situation.

The Yoga Sutras discusses a principle, *santosha*, which translates as "contentment"[1]. Rather than criticising our body during a yoga practice or reinforcing negative thoughts, the Yoga Sutras suggest that we can cultivate an attitude of contentment in order to achieve satisfaction and "unexcelled happiness".

Jacob tells Joseph to see the *shalom* of their brothers, to literally see the goodness or the rightness of their work. According to the Radomsker Rebbe, Joseph is being encouraged to return to the scene of the crime and focus on positive aspects rather than negative aspects. He is being told to see the good and to talk about it. The Rebbe connects this with what I present as a Kosher Sutra, in Proverbs 34:12, and understands it as this: "Who is the person who has a great life? The one who loves their days and sees the good"[2].

We can begin our Bibliyoga practice by giving thanks for all of our limbs that are working. Count our blessings, one by one. There is a lot to give thanks for. Today's posture is Pigeon Pose (Eka Pada Rajakapotasana). Peacock Pose would have been another option but it is a fairly advanced practice and it is sometimes easier to be grateful for things that feel accessible. To the best of my knowledge, there is no Turkey asana so the instructions for Pigeon Pose are below. But if you should be reading this during the Thanksgiving season and find yourself too full from eating Turkey, then you are officially pardoned—at least for today; it's the least I can do.

[1] Yoga Sutras II:42
[2] Huge thanks to my teacher, Rabbi Dovid Ebner who related this teaching, that comes via Reb Elimelech of Lizensk.

VAYEISHEV
DREAM BIG OR GO HOME

KOSHER SUTRA   "We will see what will become of his dreams" (Genesis 37:20)
SOUL SOLUTION   Reconnect with your dreams, re-envision your future
BIBLIYOGA POSE Tree Pose / *Vrksasana*, (p.72)
BODY BENEFIT   Grounds the legs and expands the upper body

Some performers have a bad habit when they receive compliments. They reply, "Oh, I wasn't that good," or even worse, "Really? I was awful tonight." Rather than showing humility, they display an ironic arrogance and reject the verbal gift of the one who is commending them.

One of my former acting teachers, Janet Alhanti, has something very strong to say about this. Her client list has included plenty of accomplished people, including the likes of Robert Downey Jr., Salma Hayek, Tobey Maguire, Meatloaf, and Keanu Reeves. Meanwhile, the teachers she herself has studied with included Phillip Burton (Sir Richard's father), Sanford Meisner, and Lee Strasberg. Janet says, "When someone compliments you on talent, just say, 'Thank you,' and smile, because it's not about you. The talent is given by God. It flows through you, and you're only the guardian of it. This is why it's also your job to nurture and take care of talent so that it isn't wasted." I've paraphrased a little, but I love the idea!

Most of us are familiar with Joseph's dreams. First, he dreams that he is working in the field with his brothers binding sheaves, that his sheaf stands up, and that his brothers' sheaves bow down to his. He then dreams of the sun, moon, and eleven stars bowing down to him. There is one major question, though. Why did Joseph deliberately upset his brothers by sharing the dreams? Why did he not stay quiet?

Some commentators have said that Joseph mistakenly thought that sharing the dreams would appease the brothers, because it was only the sheaves and stars that were bowing down, rather than the brothers themselves. How wrong he was.

There is a fascinating opinion brought by a commentator who explains that when you are given a prophecy, you are obligated to share it with others *(Rosh)*. Wouldn't it be interesting if it were this way with talent; if, when children discovered their abilities, whether to sing, dance, paint, debate, or create, they would have to find a way to use their God-given skills?

At the beginning of the *Bhagavad Gita,* we are introduced to the notion of *dharma,* or purpose. In some ways, we only have one challenge in life: to discover our purpose and follow it.

Many people avoid try to avoid following their calling, a notable example being the prophet Jonah. In this Kosher Sutra, we are given an opportunity to consider how to serve our purpose with humility. *Dharma* is not about goals, ambitions, or ego-fuelled ideas. It is about seeing reality for what it is. We are all born with a talent (at least one), and there is a way to use it for good in the world. We just have to figure it out and do it.

A beautiful sutra was recently being displayed around Los Angeles. Posters for the HBO television series, *How to Make It in America*, have the tagline "Dream Big or Go Home." As the grateful recipient of an artists' working visa from the US Department of Homeland Security, I find this a poignant daily reminder!

In her book *A Return To Love: Reflections on the Principles of A Course in Miracles*, spiritual teacher Marianne Williamson, has this to say about fear: "Our deepest fear is not that we are inadequate. Our deepest fear is that we are powerful beyond measure. It is our light, not our darkness that most frightens us. We ask ourselves, Who am I to be brilliant, gorgeous, talented, fabulous? Actually, who are you not to be? You are a child of God. Your playing small does not serve the world. There is nothing enlightened about shrinking so that other people won't feel insecure around you. We are all meant to shine, as children do. We were born to make manifest the glory of God that is within us. It's not just in some of us; it's in everyone. And as we let our own light shine, we unconsciously give other people permission to do the same. As we are liberated from our own fear, our presence automatically liberates others".

There is a difference between humility and arrogance, and if we have been given a gift, we can use it for serving the world with a humble and upright spirit. How does it feel if we give someone a gift and they put it on the shelf to gather dust? I wonder how God feels about people who ignore their natural talents.

Joseph's natural talent was to interpret dreams, something still practised today by psychotherapists. In *The Interpretation of Dreams* (1913), it was Sigmund Freud's genius that taught us how we can use dreams to understand the workings of our subconscious. Freud also uncovered the idea of a "paraprax," where we unconsciously reveal a piece of information through language (commonly known as a Freudian slip). The difference with Joseph is that, more than delving into his own subconscious, he reveals prophecies through dreams. A more rational approach might describe Joseph as Jungian, given that Carl Jung (1875–1961) taught that dreams can help us tap into the "collective unconscious" through the use of archetypal symbols. A Jungian reading would suggest that Joseph tapped into the greater reality and could interpret the future because he knew how to read the archetypal symbols.

When Joseph uttered his prophecy, his brothers said, "We will see what will become of his dreams" (Genesis 37:20). I once heard the Chief Rabbi Lord Sacks describe this as a "prophetic slip." In other words, Joseph's brothers were eventually going to see what would become of Joseph's dreams but they didn't realise it when they said it! I love the Chief's brilliant phrasing of this.

Our waking mind is often full of ego and distraction, which is why the unconscious mind has to find creative ways to communicate with us. One way to get in touch with our purpose is through meditation and yogic stillness, and perhaps another way is through sleep.

During Chanukah, the festival of lights, there is a custom of lighting candles either on the front porch or just inside a window that they can be seen from the street outside. We can use this idea as a reminder to focus on how we can share our own light with the world.

May you be blessed today with peaceful sleep and very clear dreams. May your dreams come true for the good. Dream big... or go back to sleep for a little longer.

The choice is yours.

.01   .02

TREE POSE / VRKSASANA

"We will see what will become of his dreams"

GENESIS 37:20

VAYEISHEV
NEW YEAR – A NEW YOU

KOSHER SUTRA "The chief butler did not remember Joseph, but forgot
him" (Genesis 40:23)
SOUL SOLUTION Ride through stormy thoughts and chaotic events
BIBLIYOGA POSE Boat Pose / *Navasana*, (p.42)
BODY BENEFIT Core stability; strengthens stomach and back muscles

When being told a dramatic story, we all love a surprise "reveal" at the end. Darth Vader removes his mask to disclose, "Luke, I am your father." Russell Crowe spins around to say, "My name is Maximus Decimus Meridius, commander of the Armies of the North…".

In this week's Kosher Sutra, the prophet Joseph reveals to his brothers that the effective leader of Egypt is none other than himself: "I am Joseph." Today's Kosher Sutra is about revealing our true selves and our own potential in the coming year.

One reason humans love being told stories is that they reflect how our minds work. We go to sleep and use internal movies to process our deepest thoughts and desires, in a technique called dreaming. Psychologist Carl Jung identified that we dream in a three-act structure, with a beginning, middle, and end, which explains why the majority of films and plays follow this idea. David Mamet's excellent book *Three Uses of the Knife* explores the difficulty of constructing the perfect story and the need to keep on building the tension with a well-crafted Act II.

The middle of Joseph's story, his Act II, is a complete mess. We are all familiar with his Act I: he is the favourite son, he has some dreams, he is given a coat, and then everything goes wrong. He is sold into slavery, stuck in jail, and falsely accused of rape by his master's wife. Nonetheless, Joseph manages to stay on track, and rather than getting beaten by depression and giving up, he keeps his self-belief and belief in a Higher Power and eventually achieves immense success by the end of his drama.

The world we live in appears to be experiencing difficult challenges. Often it seems that things aren't getting better. We are told that Joseph had an overwhelming bitachon ("trust in the Divine"). We too can assume this quality to ride out the dark times and create space for light to follow. The rabbis teach that Joseph had a brief loss of faith when he was in jail, asking the butler to do him a favour rather than praying to God, and that he was subsequently punished with an extra two years in jail because of this brief lapse of focus (Rashi; Genesis 40:23).

The whole essence of yoga is told by means of the dramatic story, the *Bhagavad Gita*. If you have not already done so, I highly recommend you read it.[1] Try not to get hung up on the whole Hindu-god thing, and let's not go down the "Is yoga a religion?" route. It isn't! (See my notes in the FAQ section of www.jewishyoganetwork.org for more information!) One essence of the story is *dharma*, the idea of staying true to oneself and staying on mission. We can be swayed from our mission at any time, whether by well-meaning friends or family who imbue us with fears or by our own minds when we lack faith in our abilities.

---

[1]   Here is a link to a free download of the entire text of the *Bhagavad Gita*, as well as other great yoga classics: http://www.yogavidya.com/freepdfs.html

These are the times to pray, to get back onto the yoga mat, to meditate, or do whatever gets you back with the programme.

I once saw some beautiful Turner paintings at the Getty Museum in Los Angeles. Joseph Mallord William Turner is one of my favourite artists, and I have regularly enjoyed visiting his other masterpieces at the National Gallery in London. In *Long Ship's Lighthouse, Lands End* (1834–1835), he depicts a stormy scene where the coastline is obscured, the sea, chaotic, and the sky, dulled. The writer and aesthete John Ruskin commented that the painting captured "the whole surface of the sea...undirected, bounding, and crashing, and coiling in an anarchy of enormous power". We can also view this painting as a metaphor: when our thoughts are clouded or we seem to be in the middle of a stormy sea, it may seem as if the skies will never be blue again and that dry land has disappeared. If we can simply recognise such times are part of a cycle—accept that there are times of feast and times of famine—while keeping faith in our Divine essence, then we can ride out the storm.

May you be blessed with the strength to ride out any storm, the vigour to fulfill your purpose, and the insight to perceive the Light that is all around us.

BOAT POSE / NAVASANA "

"The chief butler did not remember Joseph, but forgot him"

GENESIS 40:23

MIKEITZ – CHANUKAH
IN THE PITS

KOSHER SUTRA   "I don't have the answers within me" (Genesis 41:16)
SOUL SOLUTION See the light that is all around us
BIBLIYOGA POSE Cat-Cow / *Marjariasana*, (p.77)
BODY BENEFIT   Spine flexibility

Joseph answered Pharaoh: 'I don't have the answers within me. God will respond to Pharaoh's welfare'" (Genesis 41:16)

When was the last time that you felt like you were in the pits, that things just were not looking good? Have you ever you felt as if you had been betrayed by your family, sold into slavery, falsely accused of sexual wrongdoings, locked up in a dark jail, and left to rot? Hopefully things will never get this bad for you, but we can often feel as if life has its moments of such utter darkness. This Kosher Sutra is about trusting that things will work out and discovering our inner power.

Our Bibliyoga practice is about transformational living and elevating ourselves. The whole essence of yoga is to come into the moment 100% and to be fully present in every limb and with every breath. This is a lot easier said than done, which is why one aspect of yoga, namely, *pranayama* (the yogic energy-breathing practice) focuses on closing the epiglottis so that we can listen to our breath and concentrate on the smoothness of the sound.... rather than getting seduced by the craziness of our thoughts. Just as certain forms of meditation ask the practitioner to focus on an external object such as a candle or a flower, the yogi uses the sound of breath for focus. This leads us towards *eka-grata*, the one-pointed focus, with an eventual view to *nirodha*, a stilling of the mind.

As we become centred and become at one with our body and mind, we begin to develop our physical power and also our mental power. Yoga means "oneness". When we are truly at one with the moment, we cannot worry about the future, as we are totally absorbed in the present. It is at these moments that we begin to realise our deepest power.

Joseph is sold into slavery. You know the story: coat, brothers, desert traders, Egypt. But what Joseph does with all this is truly remarkable, in that he keeps going through the dark years, trusting in a Higher Power. Joseph could have crumbled at any moment, focused on the darkness surrounding him, become obsessed with the things he didn't have, allowing everything to collapse. Instead he believed with a passion and fervour to such an extent that when opportunity came calling, he was ready.

When we completely trust in God, committing to the principle of *emunah* (faith), we can be free from stress and worry, and free to fully experience the moment. God can be understood as complete presence of mind and body[1].

Joseph was so trusting in God that he was freed from unnecessary stress, completely humble and able to use his powers confidently. He had such absolute conviction in his ability that when he met Pharaoh and was asked about his talent for dream-interpretation,

---

[1] Based on the verse of God's own self-description, "I will be what will be" (Exodus 3:14)— in other words, complete present-moment awareness

his first words to the king were, effectively, "I can't actually do it myself. It's God who's doing it". Ironically, in this humility came absolute power.

How do we find our personal power? How do we truly discover what we are good at? How do we connect to this sense of God within? Meditation is an excellent gateway, and yoga is a powerful form of physical meditation.

I remind here that my yoga teacher Edward has said that enlightenment is all around and that we just have to see it. The great Kabbalist Rabbi Yitzhak Luria taught that the Light is all around and that we just have to reveal it. The Kotsker Rebbe explained that God is everywhere, and He's waiting for us to find Him. When we light Chanukah candles, it is a reminder of spiritual light and spiritual potential for everyone.

Almost all ills are cured by trusting in God. This leads to the disappearance of worry and the ability to be fully present in the moment. At that point, once fully present, you can acknowledge, accept, and access your powers and talents.

SINGLE NOSTRIL BREATH/SURYA BHEDANA PRANAYAMA

"*They couldn't hear Moses because of shortness of breath*"

EXODUS 6:9

MIKEITZ

HEY, HEY, HEY, JOSEPH

KOSHER SUTRA "Pharaoh dreamed he was standing by the Nile" (Genesis 41:1)
SOUL SOLUTION Find balance, spread your light
BIBLIYOGA POSE Splits (preparation)/ *Hanumanasana,* (p.49)
BODY BENEFITS Flexibility in legs and groin

Do you ever find yourself having one of those weeks when everything gets busy at once? It never rains but pours, and you find it almost impossible to get back to balance. Such a week can seem good or bad but nonetheless one of extremes.

Pharaoh was a man of extremes. He had the ability to grant life or death, his word was law, and he was elevated to the status of a deity. In the dream that he related to Joseph, Pharaoh was standing by the River Nile, which was considered to be another Egyptian god. Even Pharaoh's dreams were extreme: seven fat cows, seven thin cows, healthy corn, and thinning corn. Joseph had arrived to restore balance.

Our yoga practice is destined to bring balance to the body. We become aware of the way we are standing and notice if we are balancing evenly on our feet during standing postures. We bring attention to the shape of our body and whether we have struck a healthy line in our eating and exercise habits. As we focus on the alignment of our hips, torso, and shoulders, we can bring healing to physical pains that would otherwise recur throughout our life.

Pharaoh saw only the physical aspects of the world, which is why his dreams are rooted in agriculture and animals. He stood by the river that was the symbol itself of physical wealth in Egypt. Joseph's dreams began in the fields but rose to the stars because he had such strong spiritual alignment, which supported him through difficult times.

As King David wrote at the beginning of Psalm 121, "I raise my eyes to the mountains; from where will my help come?" Our Bibliyoga practice is intended to heal our body and our soul, to bring healing and balance through our physique by continually remembering that we are more than just our body. Yoga can be understood as "yoking", and we are using this method as a tool for yoking or connecting with God.

VAYIGASH

GOODWILL TO ALL MEN

KOSHER SUTRA   "His soul is bound up with [his father's] soul" (Genesis 44:30)
SOUL SOLUTION   Support, love, and friendship
BIBLIYOGA POSE Communal yoga
BODY BENEFIT   Stronger body, soul, and mind

When was the last time that a friend or a family member was there to help you out in a time of need? When were you there to help out someone else? It is often times of adversity and challenge that show us who our true friends are, and we emerge stronger as a result.

The physical process of yoga is about going to the edge of our physical stamina and flexibility, almost flirting with the limits of endurance to see how far we can safely go. In *Moving into Stillness*, Erich Schiffman called it "playing the edge", when we challenge ourselves during our yoga practice but stop before we cause any injury. This leads to an increase in our personal power as we build in strength. We fortify our body but also empower our mind and spirit by testing our limits.

The story of Joseph and his brothers is dark and challenging, especially with regards to the episode between Judah and Benjamin. One of the various themes in the story is that of personal transformation, and here, Judah is put in the spotlight. Maimonides' famous definition of true change, or ultimate teshuva, is to be in the same place where we failed before but to behave differently[1]—to face a situation where we previously fell short of our potential but to act differently this time. This takes great courage and strength.

We demonstrate such strength every time we step on a yoga mat and try a posture we previously found difficult. We can either give up when we get tired—or go back to the edges of our limits and hold the pose longer and more deeply, or even keep going with a longer practice session. BKS Iyengar teaches that the benefit of an asana truly begins at the point when we want to give up.

When Benjamin is imprisoned on a false charge, Judah immediately jumps in and offers to put himself in slavery rather than let his youngest brother take the hit: "We are ready to be slaves to our Lord" (Genesis 44:16). This is utterly different from the moment when Joseph was sold into slavery and Judah did nothing. So Judah has now moved into an age of responsibility, an era of growth, and proven that his personal transformation has taken place. This is but one of the reasons why Judah merited to be an ancestor of King David.

One of the most powerful arguments that Judah uses to persuade Joseph that Benjamin should be free is that "his soul is bound up with [Jacob's] soul". This statement of oneness is absolute. It builds on Judah's previous statement of oneness, when he said that all the brothers would stand or fall together, as slaves or free men. The sense of unity in yoga, of being *Echad* (i.e., oneness), is what enables the family to rebuild, to grow, and to heal.

---

[1]   Hilchot Teshuva

The Talmud says that "all Israel are responsible for one another"[2], which is the ultimate statement of holistic living. Just as our right hand is aware of the fact that our left hand might be injured because our body is clearly connected, so, too, are we encouraged to feel concern if another member of our community is in pain. The repeated Biblical injunction to care for all humans around us, regardless of race or religion, is the battle cry for communal care and holistic living[3]. Judah's call for responsibility is a call for us all.

One principle behind the 2009 Copenhagen Conference and accompanying Kyoto Protocol to the United Nations Framework Convention on Climate Change is that if one country wrecks the ozone layer, everyone suffers. Similarly, our souls are indeed bound together. The concept takes us back to the rabbinic example of a person who drills a hole in a ship, defending the act by arguing that the hole is in their own personal space, but of course, all passengers are affected.

One of the most powerful things about practising yoga in a large group is that it seems easier, because we all seem to move as one large organism. Even if you feel tired or uninspired, it becomes possible to be uplifted and motivated by the person next to us. Again, it is as if our souls are bound together.

We can reread the Kosher Sutra to reveal an extra level to this notion. The word for soul, *nefesh*, is related to the word nashaf, which means "exhale" or "breath". In other words, our breaths are bound together.

---

2   BT Shavuot 39a
3   "Divide your food with the hungry, bring the moaning poor to your home, when you see the naked, cover him..." (Isaiah 58:7)

Today's Bibliyoga practice is to do some yoga—any yoga—with other people. Get thee to a yoga class! Be together, share together, care together, bond together, and grow together.

The writer of Proverbs noted that a brother is there for times of adversity[4]. Through strong bonds and refined sensitivity, we can truly be there for others in times of need, safe in the knowledge that people will be there for us when we need them.

Be strong, happy, and inspired—together.

---

[4] "A friend is always loyal, and a brother is born to help in time of need" (Proverbs 17:17)

VAYIGASH

DESTROYING FEAR

KOSHER SUTRA   "The spirit of their father Jacob revived" (Genesis 45:27)
SOUL SOLUTION Banish fear, revive the spirit
BIBLIYOGA POSE Extended Child's Pose/*Balasana*, (p.88)
BODY BENEFITS   Reduces anxiety

A challenging aspect of human life is that we all experience fear at some point. Many people hide it well. Although it changes over the years from a child's terror of the monster in the closet, fear can still reside in our hearts. Whether about financial worries, social concerns, or of death itself, no person is completely immune to fear.

Our Kosher Sutra is from the narrative when Jacob discovers that his son Joseph is alive *("Od Yosef Chai")*. Jacob instantly resolves to reunite with his son. Whilst on the journey, Jacob is catapulted into a nighttime state of prophecy wherein God tells him not to fear. Jacob is scared for his family and people, that they will never escape the new country to which they are headed. When the Jacob-Joseph reunion finally takes place, the exhausted parent effectively says, "I can die now".

We utilise the tools of yoga to revive our spirits and banish fear. Fear is one of the five types of psychological pains that the *Yoga Sutras* describe as "troublesome" (1:5). Child's Pose is an effective *asana* for slowing the body's flight-or-fight system, for releasing melatonin into the system as we prepare for a night's rest, and for reducing anxiety. Additionally, standing poses help lift our spirits and strengthen our resolve.

Jacob was fearful for his legacy and was only willing to let go once he knew that his favourite son was safe. That was the point when his *ruach* (his breath or spirit) was renewed with a powerful force. Each of us have the inner means to find the peace, strength, and faith to overcome our fears. When fear is truly overcome, we can sleep without worrying about the monster under the bed and live the life we are meant to lead.

VAYECHI
TOUCHA-TOUCHA-TOUCH ME

KOSHER SUTRA   "Place your hand under my thigh...with kindness and
              truth" (Genesis 47:29)
SOUL SOLUTION Get in touch with your eternal potential
BIBLIYOGA POSE Staff Pose /*Dandasana*, (p.36)
BODY BENEFITS Strengthen thighs and back, improves posture

On his 80th birthday, BKS Iyengar described how he started every day with a 30-minute handstand. As I write this chapter, he has just turned 93 and is still going strong. This gives us something to look up to. But how does he do it?

In a lecture given in the US several years ago, Iyengar explained how he taught his late wife how to adjust him in yoga postures. The key is to use your energy to help someone else, and the aim of every great teacher is to leave the pupil feeling more balanced and healed.

Jacob is in the last days of his life when he gives Joseph an instruction: "Please, do me a favour. Place your hand under my thigh and do this to me with loving-kindness and truthfulness" (Genesis 47:29). Taken at face value, Jacob is requesting the first-ever recorded hands-on yoga adjustment. On a deeper level, he is asking Joseph to make an oath on the eternal covenant[1], but let's consider how he makes his request. The relationship must be based on *Chesed*, i.e., loving-kindness, but also *Emet*, which is "truthfulness," "balance," or "integrity".

---

[1]   i.e., the point of the Brit Milah, the circumcision which is in lieu of a holy item that signifies
      connection to God

The yoga teacher Baron Baptiste once told me that our bodies are often in pain when we are not acting with integrity. We use these postures to find truthfulness, to ask ourselves the questions, "Where in my life am I not being more honest to myself? How can I act with more integrity in my key relationships? What do I need to change?" Above all, according to Jacob, we need to do this with loving-kindness and to answer these tough questions with gentleness.

Jacob's thigh was the place of an old injury. Although he was completely healed by this point, it tells us that memories can still blight us in the present, preventing us from fully moving to our future. The yogis referred to these long-held "injuries" as *samskaras* – wounds that need to be healed. If we treat our bodies with kindness and continually work on our integrity, we can move one step closer towards fulfilling our potential.

VAYECHI
WALK LIKE A MAN

KOSHER SUTRA   "The ruler's sceptre shall not depart from Judah" (Genesis 49:10)
SOUL SOLUTION Internal stability, regardless of external factors
BIBLIYOGA POSE Staff Pose / *Dandasana*, (p.36)
BODY BENEFITS Strengthens the back, lifts the heart, grounds the body

In his biography *Long Walk to Freedom*, Nelson Mandela recounts a rite of passage that was essential for members of his tribe in Africa. When a male turned 16 years of age, he was expected to take on the guise of a warrior and go through a public circumcision ceremony, without anaesthetic and without expressing pain or resistance. Jewish males have to go through a similar form of public torment in order to become a man: upon turning 13 years, we gather all of our family and friends, musicians are hired, and he must then dance in public with his mother. Only then is he truly considered a man. Is it any surprise that Freud was Jewish?

This week's Kosher Sutra is based around the reading of Vayechi, my bar mitzvah portion (and dedicated to my wonderful parents).

The sene is Egypt. The elderly patriarch Jacob gives his deathbed speech and addresses each of his children. The most powerful speech goes to Judah, who recently showed a depth of maturity and responsibility when he stood up for Benjamin. He is told:

"Judah, your brothers shall acknowledge you; your hand will be at your enemies' nape; your father's sons will prostrate themselves to you. A lion cub is Judah...The rod shall not depart from Judah nor a lawgiver from between his legs..." (Genesis 49:8-10).

The essence of this blessing is stability. Unlike his elder brother, the first-born Reuben, Judah is solid. Reuben is described as "hasty like water" (Genesis 49:4), which is a fluid element. There are many positive qualities to water but hasty fluidity is not one of them.

Internal balance is essential for all spiritual practice, and the *Hatha Yoga Pradipika* states that "living...free of all anxieties, one should earnestly practice yoga as taught by one's guru. Yoga perishes by overeating, overexertion, talking too much...Yoga succeeds by...enthusiasm, openness, courage"[1]. For some time now, I have been practising meditation to reach a state of inner evenness, which is the midway point between extremes.

What does it mean to be an adult? This is a question I ask every year on the anniversary of my bar mitzvah. Perhaps it is about achieving a state of emotional stability, being able to see the seasons come and go without being flustered. Perhaps maturity is the ability to appreciate pleasure and endure pain without over-identifying with either.

Who knows what the coming life will bring? Ultimately what goes on outside is not within our control. We can find stability through the "enthusiasm, openness, [and] courage" mentioned by the yogis. We can emulate the leonine qualities of Judah and stay grounded. If nothing else, we might be comforted by this thought: however bad things get, most of us will never face such horrors as a public circumcision. There are many reasons to find strength in our lives exactly as they are, whatever may arise.

---

[1] *Hatha Yoga Pradipika* 1: 14–16

EXODUS

YOGIC BREATHING / PRANYAMA

"With the blast of your nostrils...
you exhaled with your wind"

EXODUS 15:8-10

SHMOT

FREEDOM FROM FEAR
AND FEARLESSLY FREE

KOSHER SUTRA   "He made for them houses" (Exodus 1:21)
SOUL SOLUTION   Freedom from fear and fearlessly free
BIBLIYOGA POSE   Easy Pose (Sitting Cross-Legged)/*Sukhasana,* (p. 90)
BODY BENEFIT   Allows the body to feel more grounded and stable

Tightrope walkers are mesmerising. They are seemingly fearless. What is fear? It has been explained as the acronym "False Evidence Appearing Real". In other words, it is often the ideas that we have about something that hold us back from reaching a specific goal or objective. There are few things more frustrating than living in regret for avoiding the path we were too scared to tread. This Kosher Sutra is about smashing through fear to live in a state of true freedom.

Our tale picks up in deepest Egypt where a new Pharaoh is in control. The first officially recorded anti-Semitism is in full swing, and midwives are busy saving freshly circumcised boys from being drowned in the Nile. These brave women feared God more than they did the political authorities, and we are told that "houses" were created for them as a reward. Rashi (12th century) explains that "houses" means that they were granted ongoing family dynasties, but the Ishbitzer Rebbe, Rabbi Mordechai Yosef (1800–1854), takes us one stage further. "It is the nature of human fear that when one experiences it, his mind is unsettled", he explains, "for fear is the opposite of a settled mind. However, with the fear of God, one experiences confidence and comfort"[1]"Houses", further writes the Rebbe, "teach of an organised, settled mind". The phrase "as safe as houses" has a literal meaning here, in that, when we are feeling solid, have a good foundation, and feel positive, we resemble a house. When we have this extra spiritual dimension and are truly connected with the awesome wonder of creation and the Godly aspect, then we really become this metaphorical *bayit*: a house that is able to withstand the slings and arrows of outrageous misfortune.

A major principle within the Kosher Sutras is freedom and becoming truly freed in all aspects of our lives—emotionally, spiritually, and physically. The ancient yogis had various Sanskrit words for liberation, including *moksha* ("freedom") and *jiva* ("liberation while living"). The eighteenth chapter of the *Bhagavad Gita* is entitled *Moksasamnyasa-Yoga*, or "the yoga of freedom and enunciation." We can start with freedom from attachment, whether to physical or spiritual outcomes. When we can let go of the result of our actions, e.g., to say a kind word without expecting anything in return or to begin a creative project without being overly concerned about how it is going to be received, then we are well on the path to freedom.

We can begin on the yoga mat by taking a posture and freeing ourselves from the outcome. See if you are able to sit for a good long while cross-legged, in half-lotus, or in full-lotus. If you feel mild discomfort, just try to stick with the pose. If you find you still feel genuine discomfort, then try elevating your buttocks onto a cushion or folded blanket—but give yourself an opportunity to stay with the pose (although you should ensure that your knees are not hurting, as these pose variations are

---

[1] From his commentary, the Mei HaShiloach, Parshat Shmot/Exodus, p.115

primarily about opening the hips). Keep your stomach tucked in, and stay in the position for at least 70 breaths, if possible.

The physical practice of yoga is a great spotlight on the internal workings of our mind. It is precisely when we attempt to hold poses for longer periods that the ego goes into overdrive. The ego is that wired voice that might scream, "I'm your body! Get me out of here!" or "Doughnut time!" or "It's too cold! Too hot!" or, indeed, anything else that will get you out of the pose.

Stay with it.

EASY POSE / SUKHASANA

"He made for them houses"

EXODUS 1:21

SHMOT

AN OFFER YOU CAN'T REFUSE

KOSHER SUTRA   "And [Moses] struck down the Egyptian and hid him in
the sand" (Exodus 2:12)
SOUL SOLUTION Freedom from emotional disturbances
BIBLIYOGA POSE Warrior I/*Virabhadrasana*, (p. 60)
BODY BENEFIT   Strengthens the legs

As human beings who are full of passion, we can easily become overwhelmed with joy, consumed with lust, or provoked to anger. The *Yoga Sutras* identified these mental fluctuations *(vrtti)* as the objective for a yoga practice, as we aim for a freedom in our body and mind marked by a state of psychological calm.

This Kosher Sutra is very Mafioso: Moses kills an Egyptian man and buries him in the sand. The commentaries (Rashi) describe how the Egyptian man was a slave master who was beating up a Jew and who had previously raped his victim's wife earlier that day. What is interesting is that the text describes Moses' actions very plainly as free from emotion; there is absolutely no indication that he acted out of spontaneous reactive anger.[1]

The practice of yoga is the pursuit of psychological freedom, which we achieve through physical application *(asana)*. Patanjali named five afflictions *(kleshas)* that affect us: ignorance *(avidya)*, egotism *(asmita)*, attachment *(raga)*, aversion *(dvesha)*, and fear

---

[1] 'Moses is giving a thought-through response. The Hebrew verb is in the present tense, i.e., "hitting," which implies that the Egyptian taskmaster's assault had been going on for some time, so presumably Moses was watching from the sidelines (Maskil LeDavid).

193

of death *(abhinivesha)*[2]. We practice the postures so that we can find internal stillness and inner calm, building our physical strength and psychological self-control so that we are not thrown into chaos by the chaotic world around us. Yoga teacher Baron Baptiste stated it well in a Twitter feed: "Do not wait for somebody else to set you free".

So what should we do when somebody else deeply upsets us, when they catch us off-guard and do something that seemingly has power to throw our world into utter disarray, or that messes up our plans and/or otherwise provokes a strong internal reaction?

We have to work harder. These are mental disturbances, emotions over which we can become the master. The 2nd Century sage Ben Zoma asked, "Who is strong? The one who is in control of their passions"[3]. Ben Zoma was taking inspiration from the proverb: "The person who is slow to anger is better than the mighty, and the one who controls their passion is more powerful than the conqueror of a city"[4]. Powerful words.

Moses eventually lost his temper, at the end of his life, but he displayed self-control in facing this current situation of watching an innocent victim under attack. Yes, Moses killed the oppressor. But enlightenment does not mean that we sit on a mountain and separate ourselves from the world. In Moses' case, it was the right time for carrying out retributive justice.

---

[2] These afflictions, or kleshas, are explored in the *Yoga Sutras*.
[3] Ethics of the Fathers 4:1
[4] Proverbs 16:32

Our opportunity is this: to use these transformational tools to strengthen our body and mind through a conscious Bibliyoga practice. In so doing we can set ourselves free from the emotional disturbances that are simply part of life on earth.

Wishing you inner strength.

WARRIOR I/Virabhadrasana

"And [Moses] struck down the Egyptian and hid him in the sand"

EXODUS 2:12

SHMOT

FLOW

KOSHER SUTRA   "A new king arose over Egypt who did not know about Joseph" (Exodus 1:8)

SOUL SOLUTION   The flexibility to respond to change and go with the flow

BIBLIYOGA POSE Tripsichore Sun Salutes / *Surya Namaskar*, (p. 24)

BODY BENEFITS Openness and flexibility to increase flowing movements

Humans put extraordinary energy into resisting change. We have the ability to stay in jobs we do not like or to live in apartments with annoying neighbours, remain in unhealthy relationships, or chronically carry out several other activities that drain our energy.

The Children of Israel faced a sudden change in Egypt; we are told that "a new king arose over Egypt who did not know about Joseph" (Exodus 1:8). There is one view that this was the same Pharaoh who suddenly changed his character and rejected Joseph. Another view explains that the king died and was replaced by a new one[1]. Either way, it was the beginning of slavery for the Jews, and the transformation was harsh.

How can we best respond to sudden change? One strategy is to stay present. Things get a lot worse when we add our own narrative: "This shouldn't be happening. It isn't right. I don't deserve this". The purpose of all yoga and meditation is to strip us of the story we tell ourselves and bring us instead into the present. Yoga is the single focus of ekagratta, the end of the

---

[1]   As explained by Rashi on Exodus 1:8

mind's fluctuations (*Yoga Sutras 1:2*), achieving a deeper state of unity within.

The great sage Hillel taught a powerful lesson when he uttered the words, "If I am not for myself, who will be for me?" (Pirkei Avot 1:14). When times are rough, we are responsible for our own well-being, and when difficult changes descend upon our life, we do have to attend to our needs. This can mean quieting our mind, centering ourselves, and smoothing our breathing. This is the essence of vinyasa—the sun salutes—in yoga. We literally practice moving with the flow, trying to keep our movements and breath as smooth as possible.

Change is inevitable in good times, let alone when the world is in environmental, financial, and social turmoil. The secret to successfully resisting change is simple: just allow it to happen! Life can be a lot less stressful, and we will fare a lot better if we just go with the flow.

VAYEIRA
THREE STEPS TO FREEDOM

KOSHER SUTRA   "Pharaoh...hardened his heart" (Exodus 8:11)
SOUL SOLUTION   Break the ties that bind us
BIBLIYOGA POSE   Staff Pose / *Dandasana*, (p. 36)
BODY BENEFITS   Increases flexibility in the back, strengthens, clears
                     tightness and toxins

"It's a plague," said a panicked Haitian being interviewed on the news. "I pray God will open the love for Haiti. I don't know why. Why He do this to us?" [sic].

The 2009 earthquake in Haiti was shocking. Sheer devastation was brought to one of the world's three poorest countries. I watched the news footage from a very comfortable bed in a hotel room. At that time, it was not clear whether international rescue crews would be able to get through easily, as planes were finding they could not land properly and unload, and rescuers were even dying in the aftermath. At times of such humanitarian disaster, those of us distant can send money, but it's not always clear if these donations make any direct impact in the short term or even ever reach those in need of immediate aid. We can but try. At the same time, we can at appreciate, bless, and be thankful for the blessings we experience and for the comparative stability in our own world.

This Kosher Sutra is about taking three steps positive towards freedom. The concept of *moksha* is central to yoga, with every breath and every posture taking us in that direction.

Here we will focus on three different tools for spiritual and physical liberation. We have all felt the sensation of being restricted in one way or another, whether through having tight muscles and a sore back or feeling emotionally squashed by another person. How do we break free?

Yogic practice is so much more than just exercise, as we use asana to identify points of pain and begin to heal. Rather than merely stretching a muscle to feel better, we consciously meditate through a pose, employ breathing (*pranayama*), focus (*drishti*), and energetic awareness (*dharana/dhyana*). More than just a stretch, a new and deepened posture moves us beyond prior restrictions, going further than before, increasing personal potential, and pushing the boundaries of achievement.

Our Kosher Sutra takes place amidst human catastrophe and plagues. A corrupt ruler is bringing pain and destruction on to his land. Likewise, "Haiti has no discernible government", said a news reporter of the disaster, "and the people are in serious trouble". This Kosher Sutra scene takes place in Egypt amidst plagues. "Pharaoh hardened his heart", we are told. The ruler suffers from a lack of love and an absolute conceit that will eventually bring extreme pain on his household.

Freedom Tool #1: Heart-Softener, Heart-Opener (Body)

What is the easiest way to overcome a hard heart, to teach ourselves to empathise with the pain of others, and to become more sensitive to their needs? One way is to open our heart. The physical posture is embodied by none other than God, who is described as having "an outstretched arm". When we reach out our arms above our head or any open pose, we create more space around the internal organs, more room for blood to flow around the heart, and more freedom within the thorax.

Freedom Tool #2: The Gift of Emotional Flexibility (Mind)

Egypt, here, is symbolic of restriction, tightness, and reduced potential, and it is embodied in the image of a staff. Moses approaches the Egyptian ruler with a firm staff in his hand. If we sit in *dandasana*, the physical staff pose that involves rooting your buttocks on the ground and holding the torso at a strong 90° angle to the outstretched legs, we can experience this sense of restriction and "held-back-ness". We free the spine of tightness and experience a sense of freedom by holding a counterpose that release the spine. This is symbolised in Moses' next step, as he turns his staff into a snake. As we move into Cobra Pose, we can substantially loosen any tightness in the back, address any issues of physical restriction, and experience the pose. Cobra Pose is about literal flexibility, and we can use it as a metaphor for emotional flexibility.

Freedom Tool #3: Deus Ex Machina (Soul)

There was a ancient Greek theatrical convention called deus ex machina, which referred to the easy resolution of a play's plot by having Olympian gods pop out of the sky to fix the human characters' problems (the phrase deus ex machina literally means "out of a machine", referring to what was staged when the set allowed it). Nowadays the phrase is a kind of shorthand for lazy playwrights and novelists who come up with weak solutions to plot problems (e.g., having a character declare, "I woke up and realised that it was all a dream!").

The Bible was a revolutionary document because it recognised that true spiritual accomplishment involved work, commitment, and belief. Visual idols were banned because of the idea that a true God cannot be confined to a block of carved wood, a machine, or a picture. God was thus freed from the machine. The god of Egypt was embodied in the Pharaoh (and I highly recommend that you visit the amazing Tutankhamun exhibition if it should pass through your city, to see how this was played out). When Moses asks God how He should be represented, the answer was simply, "I will be what I will be" (Exodus 3:13); in other words, "Do not try to restrict me to the moment, to a confined idea. I am God. I am bigger than that—bigger than you can possibly imagine. But trust Me".

VAYEIRA
THE LONG BREATH TO FREEDOM

KOSHER SUTRA   "They couldn't hear Moses because of shortness of
                breath" (Exodus 6:9)
SOUL SOLUTION Internal liberation
BIBLIYOGA POSE Single Nostril Breath/*Surya Bhedana Pranayama*, (p. 94)
BODY BENEFITS Releases stress

We all do it sooner or later: we get into a panic. It is natural. It is the way that the human system is wired. Our fight-or-flight system takes over, the sympathetic nervous system kicks into play, and we are ready to run for our lives. Adrenaline floods our body, and we find we are either primed for war or to make like a tree…and leave. Worst of all, we forget to breathe.

In this Kosher Sutra, the children of Israel were *Kotzer ruach*, or short of breath. Some translate it as "impatient of spirit". Either is good. The Kabbalah[1] locates the *ruach* as the belly breath, the part of the breathing mechanism localised within the abdomen. Again, this description makes sense; these helpless slaves were taking short, panicked breaths that came as a result of exceedingly hard labour. According to classic texts, yoga is the pursuit of inner freedom. The Sanskrit word for freedom is *moksha*, and here is something that BKS Iyengar wrote over a decade ago: "*Moksha* means freedom from the bondage of worldly pleasures…this liberation is only possible if one is free from afflictions such as sickness, languor, doubt, carelessness, physical laziness, illusiveness, despair, tremor of the body, and gasping of the breath. It is also freedom from poverty, ignorance, and pride.

---
[1]   Zohar.

Emancipation sets in, and divine beauty shines only when one is free from all afflictions. This is *moksha*"[1].

The purpose of Bibliyoga is to find internal liberation through the combination of powerful physical yoga asanas and ancient Hebrew wisdom. Our Kosher Sutra reminds us of how people were unable to fulfil their potential when they were curtailing their breath in response to the pressures of slavery. Many teachers have reiterated how slavery is an internal process, and we are aiming to banish the internal slave master, which is an internal voice. By taking deep and guided breaths, using the yogic practice of *pranayama*, we can begin to find more balance and ultimate freedom.Nachmanide[2] commented that this shortness of breath was due to fear. Unsure of what was going to happen next, the Children of Israel went into a panic. The result was that they not only experienced restricted breathing but also could not hear the words of the incredible teacher standing beside them. The world is a narrow bridge, as Rav Nachman said, and the most important thing is to move beyond fear. Breathe deeply, release the pressures inside your mind, and listen closely to the people around you; they might just help to set you free.

---

[1]   Yoga Rahasya, Vol A. Iyengar Memorial Yoga Institute (RIMYI), p. 104
[2]   Ramban on Exodus 6:9

VAYEIRA

BE A CONTENDER

KOSHER SUTRA   "How will Pharaoh listen to me? And I have blocked lips"
                (Exodus 6:12)
SOUL SOLUTION Release blocked energy
BIBLIYOGA POSE Yogic Breathing/*Pranayama ujay*, (p. 90)
BODY BENEFIT   Opens the energy channels (nadis) within the subtle body

We have no shortages of ways to excuse our lack of success. "If only I had a better education", we say; "if only I had more money," or "if only I had been born into another family". A most famous lament is from the 1954 Marlon Brando film On the Waterfront, when he memorably complained, "I could'a had class. I could'a been a contender. I could'a been somebody".

Moses has a problem—or so he thinks. When asked to lead the people out of slavery, he explains to God that it is impossible; after all, "How will Pharaoh listen to me? And I have blocked lips" (Exodus 6:12).

Let's do a quick, deep re-reading. Moses is explaining to God something that seemed impossible to do on earth. But If God created the earth, surely He knew what was possible and what wasn't! In case we missed it the first time, it is repeated again that "Moses said before God, 'Behold! I have blocked lips so how shall Pharaoh hear me?'" (Exodus 6:30).

The yogis were well aware of the issue of blocked energy. They identified thousands of energy channels within the body—the nadis—with the three central ones being the *ida* (left column), *pingala* (right column), and *shushumna* (central column). Kundalini yoga focuses on unblocking these channels through the pranayamic yogic breath.

The yogis' ideas are reflected in the Kabbalah, with the three channels clearly demonstrated in the sefirot/tree of life—but as I mentioned, this is a quick reading, so we will not delve too deeply here into tangents.

Moses was convinced he wasn't up to the job. He described his mouth as *aral sefatayim*, which translates as "blocked lips", "sealed lips, or even "uncircumcised lips". The last image can be helpful as we consider that sometimes we have to "circumcise" our self-image, i.e., take out a metaphorical knife and cut away our excuses. This can hurt! It is much easier to stay clothed in the warmth of our own supposed reasons for not being successful.

The Bibliyogic challenge here is to clear internal blockages. A basic pranayama breath is to inhale and exhale through your nostrils. In so doing, consider meditating on how you might be using an excuse not to pursue an important goal.

The path is not easy. Moses faced challenges, but he was able to succeed when he stopped blocking his own success, that is, when "God spoke through Moses" (Exodus 9:35). When we are able to step out of our own way, we are well on the path to becoming a contender.

BO

AIN'T NOTHING BUT A HOUND DOG

KOSHER SUTRA   "And [Moses] left Pharaoh in hot anger" (Exodus 11:8)
SOUL SOLUTION Defeat powerful negative emotions and achieve state of peace
BIBLIYOGA POSE Downward-Facing Dog/*Adho Mukha Svanasana*, (p. 83)
BODY BENEFIT   Strengthens back, shoulders, and legs

Whoever said that Colosseum blood sports died with the final Caesar? They are still as popular as ever: the Ultimate Fighting Championship is one of the biggest sports in the USA; a plethora of gun magazines stocks the shelves in supermarkets for hunting enthusiasts; and the English love nothing more than a good on-field punch-up among football players.

Our Kosher Sutra is perplexing. Moses gets angry. It does not say what happens next, but I would like to conjecture a scenario: he deals with the emotion and gets over it. There are other matters on his mind, like, oh, the minor task of freeing a nation of slaves, splitting a vast body of water for the escape plan, and marching the Israelites to freedom via a few unexpected pit stops and skirmishes with hostile tribes. Moses is not always immune from acting out of anger, but on this occasion, he succeeds.

Yoga is often presented in a way that is very sanitised (all "peace and love"), but every aspect of both the theory and practice actually deals with real emotions. Few teachers acknowledge the thread of violence in the history of asana practice. The *Bhagavad Gita*, a yoga classic, tells of people who are fighting one another in a battle to the death and how the protagonist Prince Arjuna has to face his own family members in the ultimate fight. Where else do you think Warrior Pose comes from? These guys are hardly warriors of love, and the battlefield gets messy. The difference is that, although there is fighting, it is not out of anger but rather out of a sense of *dharma* or Divine Purpose. When Ecclesiastes says that there is "a time for war"[1], it is acknowledging that war can be underpinned with a sense of peacefulness, that sometimes there is a time to fight—when it is to achieve a purpose. One of my friends recently reminded me of the immortal line that I will misquote here, for purposes of modesty: "Fighting for peace is like having sex in order to become a virgin". But we get the gist of both the Gita and Ecclesiastes: peace is ideal, and war has its place, but acting out of anger is never an option.

Rabbinic literature periodically warns against the dangers of being overcome by anger, even going so far as to say that an angry person is actually an idolater[2], partially because they are effectively worshipping the whims of their own ego rather than accepting that the moment they are experiencing, however challenging, is part of the divine plan.

How can we overcome anger when we feel it? Perhaps there is a clue in the verses preceding the description of Moses' anger. This Kosher Sutra comes on the back of a curious phrase describing the ways that the Jews left Egypt: "that dogs will not sharpen their teeth". In other words, animals accustomed to becoming angry and acting on their anger were suddenly able to overcome their own nature. Dogs bark, dogs react; that's their job—they

---

[1] Ecclesiastes 3:8
[2] "One who tears his clothes, breaks his utensils, and destroys his money in his rage should be in your eyes as one who commits idolatry" (Shabbos 105b)

are dogs. The saying goes, "Leopards can't change their spots", but is the metaphor really true?

My meditation teacher, Dr. Gabe Goldman, author of *Guide for the Spiritually Perplexed: A Jewish Meditation Primer*, has written a thoughtful treatise on the creatures:"We [think that we] made dogs into 'man's best friend.' What a backward way of understanding what happened. In reality, dogs made man into 'dogs' best friend.' Dogs adapted. They learned to live with people. They learned to behave in ways that satisfied human needs for companionship and protection. Dogs learned not to bite the hand that feeds them and, instead, to lick the face. They learned to bark when someone approaches whether or not they are prepared to follow up on their bark. They learned to lie beside us when we do not feel well, to guide us if we cannot see, and to cheer us up when we feel depressed. In short, the hardwiring in dogs has dramatically changed because of their interaction with people.

"I am inclined to believe that dogs which go into burning buildings to save people are not exercising free will but rather are demonstrating the power of evolutionary forces to change their hardwiring. That is, I suspect the new hardwiring in these dogs makes it impossible for them to do anything but go back into the burning building!"[3].

Downward-Facing Dog is an excellent posture for reducing our ego and overcoming strong negative emotions. As we hold the posture for longer periods of time, we can feel the strain, and it's not inconceivable that the muscles in your hands and legs may

---

3   Dr. Gabe Goldman, unpublished paper

shake a little. This can be taken as a positive signal. It shows that you are working, and if it all becomes too much, then the ground isn't far away.

We've all felt overwhelmed by tough emotions at various times, but anger is one of the most challenging. Even if you're feeling great and generally enjoy a peaceful disposition, try Downward Dog for a good few minutes (or as long as you can last), and you'll begin to experience the wonders of your own inner strength, training sheer willpower to overcome your ego, and you'll be even more powerful than you already are.

BO

FREED FROM EGO

KOSHER SUTRA   "God killed every firstborn" (Exodus 12:29)
SOUL SOLUTION   Connect with the present moment
BIBLIYOGA POSE Shabbat Pose/*Savasana*, (p. 89)
BODY BENEFIT   Deeper relaxation and increased awareness

Being a firstborn is a unique experience. (I speak as a firstborn.) We are the children that our parents desperately wanted, or in some cases, the happy accident. We met our parents at the moment they first became parents, and we made them figure out how to "do" parenting. An hour after my sister was brought home from the hospital, I spoke up as a precocious two-year-old: "Can we take her back to the ho'pital now? [sic]. I'm bored". As children, we have to learn how to make room for others.

Pharaoh is a firstborn who refused to adjust[1]. Pharaoh's identity is then shattered to pieces. He thought his country would rule the world forever. He thought his land endlessly fertile. He thought his wealth immutable. But he would come to watch everything he thought he knew, collapse.

"The causes of suffering are not seeing things as they are, the sense of 'I'" attachment, aversion, and clinging to life... Attachment is a residue of pleasant experience"[2]. Our physical yoga practice makes us face harsh realities in our body. We can get upset for a number of reasons, and every reason is futile and

---

[1]   Zohar
[2]   Yoga Rahasya, Vol A. Iyengar Memorial Yoga Institute (RIMYI), p. 104

self-inflicted. Rather, we simply, powerfully, do what we can and let go of attachment to the result.

Although we cannot control the outcomes, we still need to begin things and try our best. "You are not responsible for creating the result", said the rabbis, "but neither are you free to resist from starting the job"[3]. We begin tasks, we work hard, but we cannot force the outcome. Attachment brings misery.

- What are you attaching yourself to, today?

- Where are you creating pain through fixating on a result?

- Where are you trying to force something to happen?

- What can you let go of?

We plant seeds and have high hopes that they will grow. As Deepak Chopra points out, there is no use in planting a seed and then digging it up five days later to see if it's growing. We do what we can, whether building a career, relationship, or trying a new yoga posture. And then we have to let go.

Firstborn or not, we all have a fixed idea of who we are. When we can let go of this idea, stop telling stories that inflict self-pressure, and just focus on our moment-to-moment tasks, we can truly know what it means to be free. Who knows what joys the present may hold, even if we cannot immediately see the benefits? It may have taken me a few years to fully appreciate my sister, but I am glad that they did not take her back to the hospital.

---

3   Ramban on Exodus 6:9

BO

NIGHT TERRORS

KOSHER SUTRA   "It will be a night of anticipation...a night of guarding"
(Exodus 12:42)
SOUL SOLUTION Reduce anxiety when it strikes at night
BIBLIYOGA POSE Lotus Pose/*Padmasana*, (p. 96)
BODY BENEFIT   Calms the mind and body, banishes doubt and fears

A couple of my friends were having trouble sleeping at night because their three-year-old son often woke them up. For a few months, around the 2 a.m. hour, the child would suffer from the "night terrors", screaming and scared, or be wide awake and in the mood for playing and singing. Many other people experience problems sleeping through the night, whether from anxiety, troublesome thoughts, or disturbing dreams.

The long, lonely night was a theme frequently visited by the Psalmist, and King David reported, "Every night I drench my bed, with my tears I soak my couch" (Psalm 6). His counterpose to this fear was for him to acknowledge that, "though I walk through the valley of death, I will fear no evil for You are with me" (Psalm 23). But how can we banish fear if we find ourselves awake in the middle of the night with anxiety? How do we jolt ourselves into a state of consciousness that is free from fear? If you have ever tried pulling out a yoga mat at 3 a.m. and trying to meditate or do a physical yoga practice, you know it is not always that easy to calm down and become present.

When the Children of Israel were preparing to leave Egypt amidst the ten plagues and escaping Pharaoh's wrath, they were told, "It will be a night of anticipation to God to take [you] out of the land of Egypt, this is the night for God, a night of guarding for all the Children of Israel for their generations" (Exodus 12:42). The Hebrew word for "anticipation" is *shomer,* which is also translated as "to observe", as well as "to guard".

A meditative reading of this passage can be deeply revealing. If our nights are beset with fear, the only way to banish the terror is to become aware of our fears and to understand that they are more intensified at night. If we can *shomer*—truly guard and observe our thoughts—then we can reach a state of peace. The idea here of "leaving Egypt" is akin to becoming free from oppression, and, once we become conscious, we are freed from enslavement to our oppressive thoughts.

Finally, we can even re-read the idea of "God" as becoming conscious to the Will of the Universe, to really internalise the notion that there is something bigger than ourselves. A nighttime worry is often based on the idea that we have to fix everything, that we are responsible, that we have created our problems. When we can relinquish this ego and remember that there we did not create the universe, our problems are shared and our problems halved.

So what can we do if night terror strikes? Does it work to roll out the yoga mat when the night is darkest, when "the country cocks do crow, the clocks do toll, and the third hour of drowsy morning names"?[4] Yes! That is precisely the time to meditate. It

---

4 Shakespeare, Henry V, 4:i.

is not always easy. It might take some while to calm. It probably will not feel like your favourite upbeat yoga class—but this is where the real meditation action happens. This is the time to create "a night of guarding": to guard your thoughts, guard your soul, and guard your well-being. Breathe deeply, commit to the practice, and enjoy your journey from slavery to liberation. If you want freedom, you have to realise that it is within you.

LOTUS POSE/PADMASANA

"It will be a night of anticipation...
a night of guarding"

EXODUS 12:42

BESHALACH – TU B'SHVAT
DON'T STOP MOVING

KOSHER SUTRA   "Be still…and get going" (Exodus 14:13-15)
SOUL SOLUTION Find stillness and calm in turbulent situations
BIBLIYOGA POSE Sun Salutation A /*Surya Namaskar A*, (p. 30)
BODY BENEFIT   Energises, and increases your physical stamina

What do you do when everything is going so fast that you just want to hit the brakes, or when life seems sluggish and you want to get moving? What about when your body is feeling great but you just cannot seem to focus on the important task? Or when you are just frustrated at having to wait for the action to begin? This Kosher Sutra is about achieving a balance of stillness and movement, getting your body and soul into harmony. It will help smooth out the kinks and show you how to use Bibliyoga to rebalance your life. The biblical scene resumes in Egypt. Moses is about to lead the people out of slavery and responds to their extreme doubts and anxieties by making a promise which is refuted by God: "But Moses said to the people, 'Don't be afraid. Collect yourselves and see the salvation which [God] will make for you today…[God] will fight for you and you will be still.' Then [God] said to Moses, 'Why do you cry out to me? Tell the Israelites to just get going'" (Exodus 14:13–15). This powerful translation was by the Zen Rabbi, Alan Lew, author of *Be Still and Get Going*. It speaks for itself, and rather than add a single word of explanation, I will encourage you simply to read the quote once again. The theory and practice of vinyasa yoga brings together movement and stillness in one great swoop. Vinyasa is the Sanskrit word that describes bringing together breath and movement, so that we achieve a rhythm in our body that synchronises everything. When we get it right—such as when doing a sun salutation—we inhale and lift our arms, matching the movement to the length of the breath and focusing our mind on this inhalation. Our body, mind, and movement come together in perfect unity, and this is why yoga is a form of moving meditation.

When our mind is furiously pacing in different directions, we can use a vinyasa yoga practice to get our body to speed up and our mind to slow down. When we are feeling sluggish and lethargic, we can kick-start our body and mind through this practice. What really increases the benefit is adding this Kosher Sutra as an intention, using Moses' injunction to "be still" and God's direction to "get going". There are elements of *vinyasa* even in standing poses, as we keep an internal sense of movement while our breath is powerful engaged. My yoga master Edward Clark points out that stillness is only ever an illusion: we might be standing in one place but we are on a planet that is spinning and revolving around a sun that is in a galaxy that is moving through the universe. We draw together these contradictions and live with the confusing paradoxes of life by engaging in a prayer that involves our body and our soul.

Tu b'shvat celebrates the new year for trees. Trees combine a sense both of movement and of stillness: they stand in one place but are continually moving, growing, transforming, and reacting to the environment around them. The wisdom of the Torah is described as a "Tree of Life" (Proverbs 3:18), and human beings are also compared to a "tree of the field" (Deuteronomy 20:19). We can take this quite literally in our standing postures, by rooting ourselves into the ground with our feet and using the breath and physical alignment to lift ourselves upwards. We engage with each pose to the absolute limits of our capability—our breath, body, and mental focus—and remain still whilst moving inside. It is not easy to maintain inner stillness when we are in a flurry or on a journey that contains surprises. This journey has a name: life. In *Autobiography of a Yogi*, Paramahansa Yogananda describes a rollercoaster of events, meeting the mystics and teachers who present themselves as he is open to receive them. The folk-saying goes, "When the student is ready, the teacher will appear", and if we can be strong-minded enough to take what life throws our way, by maintaining stillness in our movement, we can open to receive incredible gifts and outstanding teachers.I really like the comparison of humans to trees, as trees can give us something to aspire to. A tree has a unique capacity to give: it can produce fruit, provide shelter, offer oxygen to the planet, serve as refuge to animals, support a local ecosystem; and when we pulp it to pieces, it can make our Sunday newspaper. On a serious note, a tree is still but can go with the flow of life, bending and yielding to the winds and re-creating itself each year as a new season rolls around.Have a refreshing day as you try putting this Kosher Sutra into practice by locating the stillness within. See if you can maintain that sense of calm whilst moving through the yoga sequence and whilst moving through your day. The world has enough stress and anxiety, so let us do our bit to send out some goooooood vibrations.

SUN SALUTATION A /SURYA NAMASKAR A

"Be still…and get going"

EXODUS 14:13-15

BESHALACH
BE THE TIGER

KOSHER SUTRA   "With the blast of your nostrils...you exhaled with your wind" (Exodus 15: 8–10)
SOUL SOLUTION Find strength in times of challenge
BIBLIYOGA POSE Yogic breathing / *Pranayama*, (p. 92)
BODY BENEFIT   Unleashes energy and generates inner heat

Sometimes we all need to go to war. Once more unto the breach, dear friends! It may be an internal war 'gainst our own emotions. It may be for good reasons, to prevent ourselves from doing something we shall regret.

Our Kosher Sutra features the powerful exhalation from God's "nostrils". This anthropomorphism describes the seawaters piling up so that the Hebrew slaves can escape Egypt, and the Divine breath paves the way for freedom. In the 12th Century, Rashi confirmed the translation that this was indeed an exhalation, while Ramban connected it with a verse from Isaiah (40:24): "Even if He were to blow on them, they would wither". A powerful, connected breath achieves great things.

We can generate inner strength through this powerful breath, focused through the nostrils. Pranayama is the yogic science of energy control through the breath, and the focus here is Bhastrika breathing: a succession of quick exhales by "pumping" the abdomen.

Before the classic Battle of Agincourt in Shakespeare's *Henry V*, the King is rousing the English troops before they have the French enemy running to save their baguettes:

"In peace there's nothing so becomes a man

As modest stillness and humility:

But when the blast of war blows in our ears,

Then imitate the action of the tiger;

Stiffen the sinews, summon up the blood,

Disguise fair nature with hard-favour'd rage;

...Now set the teeth and stretch the nostril wide,

Hold hard the breath and bend up every spirit

To his full height. On, on, you noblest English"[1].

Our mind and body can be controlled and rallied through the breath of our nostrils. The Hebrew word for exhalation is *nashaf*, and the three consonant clusters, *n*, *sh*, and *f* rearrange to form *nefesh,* a Hebrew name for our soul.

Godspeed to you. Be strong in body and soul.

---

[1] Shakespeare, Henry V, Act III:i.

BESHALACH
GENERATION FLUX

KOSHER SUTRA   "Do not fear! Stand fast and see the salvation of God"
(Exodus 14:13)
SOUL SOLUTION Increase optimism and remain open to possibilities
BIBLIYOGA POSE Forward Straddle Bend /*Prasarita Padottanasana*, (p. 64)
BODY BENEFIT   Opens hip flexors and upper back, improves balance

There is a question as to whether the US economy is in a recession or has entered a full depression. One thing we can be certain of is that things have changed. Fast Company magazine led one issue with a story about "Generation Flux", the publication's name for the status quo population. Generation Fluxers could be 20 years old, 40, 60, or older, and are defined not by their age but by their attitude. "You don't need to be a jack of all trades to flourish now", the magazine wrote, "but you do need to be open-minded"[1].

Our Kosher Sutra joins the Children of Israel who are in a state of flux. They have been uprooted from the "comfort" of slavery and are being pursued by Egyptian forces as they escape towards the Sea of Reeds. Things have become so uncertain that their anxieties are running sky-high, and they are campaigning to return to a life of slavery rather than open up to the possibilities of a new and exciting world. Moses gives them a very simple and very yogic instruction: "Do not fear! Stand fast and see the salvation of God…[and] remain silent" (Exodus 14:14).

---

[1]   January 2012 issue: http://www.fastcompany.com/1802732/
generation-flux-meet-pioneers-new-and-chaotic-frontier-business

How can we stand still and remain silent when we are overcome with the fear and anxiety that are brought on by sudden change? What Bibliyoga tools can we use when we find ourselves longing to wind back the clock to the way things were?

On a trip once to China, yoga guru BKS Iyengar gave some helpful clues on how we can learn to stand fast, using the metaphor of a tree. He explained that "the movements for any asana should come from the root, not the shoot"[2]. For example, in a Standing Forward Straddle Bend *(Prasarita Padottanasana)*, the focus should be on spreading the legs from the groins ("the roots") rather than the feet ("the shoots"). While standing straight, we might also focus on keeping the front of the groin open and using gravity to bring our weight to be evenly distributed across our feet.

The world is going to change whether we like it or not, and it is our choice how much we want to suffer in response. We may feel like resisting the flux and turning back the clock. Some say, "Better the devil you know", but that does not need to be the motto by which we live our lives, especially if we desire liberation. Rather, we can stand up straight, get rooted, listen actively, and watch carefully for the miracles that are about to unfold before our eyes.

---

[2] Yoga Rahasya, Vol. 18, No. 3, 2011.

YITRO

THIS IS IT

KOSHER SUTRA "Do not make a graven image" (Exodus 20:4)
SOUL SOLUTION Tap into your vast, unlimited potential
BIBLIYOGA POSE Mountain Pose /*Tadasana*, (p. 50)
BODY BENEFIT Increases the stillness within

Society usually rewards and celebrates human beings who realise their ultimate potential, even though they may be flawed in their own life. Whether athletes at the top of their game, artists, or orators, there is something truly uplifting about people who reach beyond the realms of regular achievement.

One view of the 10 Commandments is that they are 10 statements of freedom, each a tool for liberation. In theory, if we are able to approach them with an open mind and an open heart, they can lift us up out of the challenges of everyday life and help us become the greatest possible version of ourselves. Bibliyoga is concerned with tools for transformation, and this Kosher Sutra is about touching the infinite potential within all of us.

Physical yoga practice—*asana and vinyasa*—is literally about expanding ourselves. We increase our breath capacity through engaging our abdominal, thoracic, and clavicular breathing, introducing more oxygen into our bloodstream, filling our body with more dynamic energy, sharpening our mental focus and clarity, stretching our muscles, increasing flexibility, and boosting our physical strength. A great physical yoga session will reconnect us with our true potential, and this Kosher Sutra's practice will guide us towards realising our spiritual potential.

The Kosher Sutra "Do not make graven images" is controversial because so many religions espouse statues, idols, icons, and other images of God. The problem with such images, in my understanding, is that it limits the idea of God. How could you capture the full power of a sunrise in a painting? How could you limit the beautiful feeling of love for your partner in a statue? How could you constrict the emotions of gratitude for your dearest friends within a mere icon? According to the 12th Century philosophical writings of Maimonides, every thought and emotion and physical object is an expression of God.

When we limit our view of the Creator, we limit our own potential. Think of the last time you were truly in touch with your own personal power. Think of the broad and fascinating aspects of your personality. Think of all of the wonderful character traits that your closest friends know about. Could you possibly sum that all up in a 140-character Tweet? Are you your Facebook profile photo? Of course not.

Maimonides is tough on idols. He would especially have a field day with the statutes that sit at the front of many yoga studios, even though the studio owners claim that they are all representative of aspects of God. Bowing before idols is expressly forbidden by Biblical law, and one reason for this is that any statue of God limits our understanding of the unlimited[1]. One of the most effective and inspiring ways to practice yoga is to close your eyes, focus on the sound of your breath, and just be aware of the sheer vastness within.

Take Mountain Pose, standing with your feet together, hands by your sides, eyes closed, and body alert. Focus on the sound of your breath, and be aware of the vast, unlimited space within your body. Bring your mind to the gap—the gap between thoughts, between breaths, between the atoms and neutrons and protons and quarks. Try taking your mind to outer space, even, imagining the breadth of the universe, the immeasurable limits that we still have not yet discovered. Then acknowledge the space and vastness within.

When we can get in touch with this every day, reminding ourselves how truly infinite The Infinite really is, we can begin to touch our greatness within. One of my friends wears a t-shirt that says, "God is too big to fit into any religion". And this is true. Can you really open up and allow your inner potential to flow forth? Try re-reading this Kosher Sutra, taking Mountain Posture, becoming aware of your vast potential and allowing your power to flow. This is it.

MOUNTAIN POSE /TADASANA

"Do not make a graven image"

EXODUS 20:4

YITRO

YOU CAN'T ALWAYS GET
WHAT YOU WANT

KOSHER SUTRA   "Do not be jealous" (Exodus 20:14)
SOUL SOLUTION   Feel calmer and meet your needs
BIBLIYOGA POSE   Mountain Pose / *Tadasana*, (p. 50)
BODY BENEFIT   Strengthens legs

There seems to be a flaw in the human design. At some point or other, we experience jealousy. We see that other people have things that look nice, and we want those things. Maybe it is their car, their income, their house, their holiday home, their spouse, their partner, their blinging jewellery. The thing standing between us and ultimate happiness seems simple: if we could change the "theirs" into "ours", then all of our problems would be solved. Or would they?

The Kosher Sutra takes us up Mount Sinai, to the last of the 10 Commandments: "Do not covet", sayeth the speaker. Do not be jealous of your neighbour's house. Do not be jealous of his wife, his male servant, his au pair, his ox, his donkey; do not be jealous of anything that belongs to him (Exodus 20:14). Compared to the more simply obvious commandments ("Do not kill"), this seems to be overkill. The verb "covet" (tachmod) is mentioned thrce times here, and there are seven categories of things that we should not be jealous of. Enough, already; we get the point! Or do we?

Everyone has to say something about jealousy. The *Yoga Sutras* referred to the *klesha* (affliction) of *raga* (attachment), which is one of the Top Five Mental Disturbances of All Time. Elsewhere the *Yoga Sutras* refer to the need for *aparigraha*, or non-coveting. On the yoga mat we practice not being jealous of someone else's posture, body, yoga clothes, or anything that is theirs—and we focus on our own practice.

Why does the Kosher Sutra introduce seven categories of items for non-jealousy? Possibly because we are human beings: seven is the mystical number that represents the human world, and we all have big ambitions. We all have desires, and it is through ambition that we create great things. But we can be far more successful when we recognise that there is enough sustenance on earth to fulfill everybody's needs.

We do not need the income of our neighbour but can earn our own. We do not need the house of our friend but can build our own. We do not need the partner who has just rejected us but can go and find new love.

Be free, be free, be free. Tap into the abundance around you, and use your desires to become great.

YITRO

SYNAESTHESIA

KOSHER SUTRA   "All the people saw the voices" (Exodus 20:15)
SOUL SOLUTION   Improve sense awareness (sight and sound)
BIBLIYOGA POSE Extended Mountain Pose/*Tadasana*, (p. 51)
BODY BENEFIT   Strengthens legs, heart, and mind

In the mid-1920s, the Russian journalist Solomon Veniaminovich Shereshevsky was reprimanded by his boss for not having written any notes during a meeting. But Shereshevsky did not need to; he had a photographic memory. He was later discovered to be a rare, fivefold synaesthete. In synaesthesia, one's neural pathways cross over, so that one sensory system affects others: when that person hears a musical note, they will see a colour; touching something will trigger a taste sensation; and so forth.

Our Kosher Sutra takes us to Mount Sinai where people "could see the voices" that were usually heard (Exodus 20:15). There was disagreement between Rabbi Akiva and Rabbi Yishmael over whether this was indeed a miracle. The former argued that it was supernatural, as it lifted humans up to a heavenly realm, whereas the latter suggested that it was merely an opportunity for everyone to experience the Divinity that is always around and within them[1].

When we stop to truly listen to that which is going on around us, we can quickly find ourselves in the realm of the supernatural, hearing things that we might otherwise have missed. We can "see" the anger in someone's voice even if they are speaking calmly, if we but quiet ourselves and look at their body language. We see the anxiety and depression in someone's voice if we stop listening to just the words they are saying and really listen to them in their entirety.

The journey of yoga and meditation takes us much deeper, and far closer, to our full potential. The book *Autobiography of a Yogi* describes someone having extrasensory experiences on a daily basis—but are these really miracles? Or are they merely touching the potential that we all have?

The excellent film *Limitless* portrays a man who takes a drug to open up the full potential of his brain. We do not really need such drugs to enjoy our brain to its fullest. We just need to slow down and listen.

The *Diagnostic and Statistical Manual of Mental Disorders*, also known as the *DSM-IV*, does not list synaesthesia as a neurological condition because it does not necessarily cause problems in everyday life. Many synaesthetics have begun to see this "condition" as a gift rather than a burden.

We have incredible abilities at our fingertips, and most of us have only just begun to scratch the surface of our body and soul's potential.

MISHPATIM
I DON'T WANT YOUR FREEDOM

KOSHER SUTRA   "If the slave shall say, 'I will not go free...'" (Exodus 21:5)
SOUL SOLUTION   Freedom from limiting thoughts
BIBLIYOGA POSE Chair Pose / *Utkatasana*, (p. 52)
BODY BENEFIT   Strengthens legs, shoulders, abdomen and builds stamina

Have you ever chosen a path of restriction rather than liberation? There are often compelling reasons to choose the route less free: "I don't want to leave this relationship because I don't want to be alone (even though I'm not happy with my partner)", "I can't leave my job although I hate my boss/colleagues/the work, because it's regular pay, and besides, you can't always get what you want—better the devil you know", "I can't possibly consider moving to a new apartment/city/country, because it's just too scary".

The French philosopher Rousseau (1712–1778) taught that all human beings have the possibility of freedom, but the ultimate declaration of human autonomy actually came thousands of years earlier.

The Book of Exodus depicts a peculiar scene of an Israelite slave who has served six years and is due for the mandatory release that comes on the seventh anniversary of being a slave. Our particular slave decides he would rather remain in servitude—perhaps because he likes the security of regular food, shelter, and routine, or because he has built a family in the master's

233

household with people who are also slaves, and he chooses to remain even if his boss is something of a slave driver.

The Biblical "punishment" for his choice is to have a nail driven through his ear as it is banged into the doorpost. The new earhole symbolizes his choice of forsaking freedom for slavery. According to Rashi (1040–1105), the ear was the organ that received the message of universal human freedom at Mount Sinai, and this nail becomes a piercing reminder that the slave has chosen a master other than God. Another idea is that the poignancy of the nail-through-ear symbol stems from specks of the slave's blood running down the doorpost, reminding us of the blood of the paschal lamb in Egypt that was smeared on the doors as the ultimate symbol of freedom during the 10 Plagues[1].

The practice of yoga is concerned with freedom (*moksha*, in Sanskrit). We aim to find physical freedom through the postures, psychological freedom through achieving stillness of thought, and spiritual freedom through reminding ourselves that our soul is eternal whilst our body is temporary. This is important, because much of our suffering comes from the illusion that this life lasts forever, so we try our best, ironically, to cling to things that will inevitably change. (If we really believed life to be permanent, would we cling?) Whether a relationship, a job, or an identity, change will surely come, be it in seven minutes or 70 years.

Yoga was preceded by *Samkhaya* philosophy, which states that "liberation occurs when one has understood this truth", that the body is temporary but the soul lasts, and that the goal is for us to reach a point where "the Spirit regains its original

---

[1] This idea was shared with me by Samuel Klein.

freedom"[2]. Only through experiencing this truth and realising that suffering comes from over-identifying with the body can we free ourselves from pain and touch our true potential. If we remind ourselves that we are a soul temporarily housed inside a body—and meditate on this truth—we will ultimately become free of suffering and experience true freedom.

For this yoga posture: Have fun. If you are feeling really brave, here is a difficult question to chew on: In which are of your life could you experience more freedom? Where are you holding back? Sometimes we are held back by other people's ideas of us, and it can be painful to say to them, "Actually, I'm not the person you thought I was. I've changed. I've moved on. Whether or not you accept me, I'm now living my truth and becoming free". The words of George Michael's song *Freedom '90* were a revealing message to the fans who wanted to force him to match their image of his former days in the band Wham!, when he rocked the 1980s pop scene with uplifting teenybopper hits:

> *"Heaven knows I was just a young boy*
> *Didn't know what I wanted to be*
> *I was every little hungry schoolgirl's pride and joy*
> *And I guess it was enough for me...*
> *But today the way I play the game is not the same*
> *No way...I won't let you down*
> *So please don't give me up*
> *Because I would really, really love to stick around "*

We celebrate the month of Adar as a time of joy and fun. Sing, play, dance, let your hair down, and feel free. If you're stuck for

---

[2]   Merce Eliade. Yoga: Immortality and Freedom, p 17-19, Princeton University Press: 1958.

ideas, do the Bibliyoga posture while playing *Freedom '90*. The Talmud says that "when we enter Adar, we increase in joy"[3]. So play hard, be free, and share your true gifts with the world.

---

[3] Babylonian Talmud: Ta'anit 29a

MISHPATIM
HEARTBREAK HOTEL

KOSHER SUTRA   "I love my master...I will not go free" (Exodus 21:5)
SOUL SOLUTION   Stop holding ourselves back
BIBLIYOGA POSE Backbend / *Urdhva Dhanurasana*, (p. 82)
BODY BENEFIT   Increases flexibility in the back

Sometimes we get so used to seeing ourselves in a certain way that we limit our potential; we stop ourselves from changing. Although we may be quick to blame others for our lack of progress, in truth we are the only ones holding ourselves back.

The Book of Exodus is the key story of human liberation that provided inspiration for many revolutions, including the American Civil Rights movement. It tells of a people who are no longer content with being slaves and who start the long walk to freedom after 400 years under the whip. We are revisiting the same verse as the previous sutra as there is much to reflect upon when one exceptional slave says: "I love my master...I will not go free", (Exodus 21:5).

We might imagine the master's response:

-- Excuse me?
— Yes. I want to carry on being your slave.
— Why?
— Well, because, it's comfortable. Better the devil you know, eh? Besides, my wife and kids are also slaves. I mean, I could get a job on the outside, buy them all their freedom

237

in a couple of years, but, well, you've got a really nice house.
Freedom's probably overrated.
– You sure about this?
– Yes.
– Ok. I'm going to have a bore a hole in your ear as a sign
that you've given up your freedom.
–That's fine. I've even brought a hammer and nail. Here you
go. – As you wish.

And so it went.

There were Hebrew slaves who actually chose to stay in slavery. We know that 80% of the Jews actually stayed in Egypt anyway, because they could not imagine life on the outside. This makes sense, in a way: it's a known phenomenon in Western society that a certain proportion of released prisoners will re-offend, however subconsciously, so that they can live out their days in prison, because it's what they know best. How are you holding yourself back from becoming free?

The first areas of study for Ashtanga Yoga are *yama* and *niyama*, the codes for moral behaviour. BKS Iyengar explained how "one becomes the slave of the senses of perception and organs of action" and that the process of yoga is gaining freedom through the practice of yoga[1]. We gain control over our behaviour, learn to control our desires, and realise our potential through this process.

---

[1] BKS Iyengar, Yoga—Freedom Through Discipline. Essay in Astadala Yogamala, Vol. 1, Allied Publishers Ltd., Mumbai, India, 2000.

We can tie ourselves to a bad situation through being scared of choosing something we don't know, and this might happen with our job, behaviours or relationships.

Shakespeare parodies this in *A Midsummer Night's Dream*, in which the lovelorn Helena follows Demetrius into the woods with the hope of enticing him. Despite Demetrius's continual insults and rejections, Helena still dotes on him, with painfully funny results:

DEMETRIUS:

Do I entice you? Do I speak you fair?
Or, rather, do I not in plainest truth
Tell you, I do not, nor I cannot love you?

HELENA:

And even for that do I love you the more.
I am your spaniel; and, Demetrius,
The more you beat me, I will fawn on you:
Use me but as your spaniel, spurn me, strike me,
Neglect me, lose me; only give me leave,
Unworthy as I am, to follow you.
What worser place can I beg in your love—
And yet a place of high respect with me—
Than to be used as you use your dog?

DEMETRIUS:

Tempt not too much the hatred of my spirit;
For I am sick when I do look on thee.

HELENA:
And I am sick when I look not on you[2].

How often do we do similar, aiming to get someone's respect when they are turning us away, or keep continuing to slave slaving away at a project that is fruitless? Sometimes it is just time to say that it's time to move on.

This Kosher Sutra yoga posture is an expansive backbend. Try looking at the world from another perspective, stretch yourself a little, and consider where you can free yourself from a limiting situation to experience the more expansive version of yourself.

---

[2]   A Midsummer Nights Dream, Act 1, Scene 2

MISHPATIM
FREEDOM ISN'T FREE

KOSHER SUTRA   "I will not go free" (Exodus 21:5)
SOUL SOLUTION Liberation of the spirit
BIBLIYOGA POSE Headstand /*Salamba Sirsasana*, (p. 84)
BODY BENEFIT   Increases blood flow to brain, calms the nervous system

One failing of the penal systems, as we have noted in other Kosher Sutras, is that some prisoners can become too comfortable with the lifestyle. Some people become accustomed to being managed by an institution, and the routine living inspires some ex-cons to quickly re-offend upon their release, that they might thrown back into jail.

Our Kosher Sutra centres on the Hebrew slave who has completed his term of service but tells his master, "I will not go free" (Exodus 21:5). These are not conventional slaves, according to the modern understanding, because they still have some human rights, albeit limited. Nonetheless, the owner is commanded to take the slave and drive a nail through his ear into a doorpost as a sign that he has voluntarily given up his liberty forever.

The Talmud explains that the mark must be made on the slave's ear because he has chosen not to engage with the proclamations of freedom that were heard at Mount Sinai and because he has also decided not to walk through the doorway that would be the first step towards his new life[1].

---
[1]   BT Kiddushin 22b

Shockingly, many of us behave similarly in our own lives. We complain about slavery in our jobs, relationships, body image, weight, fitness levels, psychological well-being—but we do not take any action. Rather than step through the doorway and make the journey towards freedom, we would rather moan and choose the path of restriction.

Yoga is the way of freedom, or *moksha dharma*, and it can lead the practitioner towards "liberation of the spirit"[1].

"Yoga was devised as the sovereign means to end all suffering"[2], but it takes daily practice to experience this freedom. It is much easier to find reasons not to practice ("I'm too busy, I can't afford it, I don't have the time, I don't have a teacher"), and it is far easier not to begin the work than to go through the "trouble" of putting in the time (really, are we not investing in ourselves?).

One song lyric sums it up: "Freedom isn't free…there's a hefty… fee"[3]. The question is this: We all want self-realisation, but are we willing to pay the price?

---

[1] David Frawley, Yoga—The Great Tradition, p 34
[2] Ibid, p 33 .
[3] Freedom Isn't Free from "Team America World Police". Lyrics by Trey Parker

TERUMAH
THE KARMA SUTRA

KOSHER SUTRA   "Those whose hearts motivate them, will give" (Exodus 25:2)
SOUL SOLUTION Joy
BIBLIYOGA POSE Karma Yoga (doing something for others)
BODY BENEFIT   Feeling good

The new-lunar month of Adar is a traditional time for bringing joy into our lives. Somehow, however, we don't always feel up to it. There are a million cures for feeling downhearted, and most have a price. Yet one cure for depression remains free.

"Those whose hearts motivated them" gave to the building of the key communal structure. It is an innate human desire to give, to share, and when we do so, we often feel better about ourselves. Why is this? Giving taps into our higher nature. The kabbalistic aspect of *chesed,* of lovingkindness, is the first impulse that is connected with our body, in particular, our right arm. We are designed to give. Think how frustrating it is when we pay someone a compliment and they refuse it. Likewise, sometimes we ought to thank other people for a present they have given but that we do not like, simply because they are benefiting from the act of giving. "Help me to help you", said Jerry Maguire to his protégée, in the eponymous film. The act of giving connects us with others and connects us with our source.

Karmic Yoga is the path of action, of doing, and of getting involved. "Action is greater than inaction: perform therefore thy task in life. Even the life of the body could not be if there were no action" (*Bhagavad Gita 3:8*). What's a great way to tap into the joy of life? Get up, get out of the house, and do something for others. "When you help others, you can't help helping yourself", says a song in the musical Avenue Q. This may sound counterintuitive, but it works.

Feel good.

TERUMAH

IF YOU BUILD IT, SHE WILL COME

KOSHER SUTRA   "Make Me a sanctuary, and I will dwell within them"
                (Exodus 25:8)
SOUL SOLUTION   Release, and increase the flow of blessing that you receive
BIBLIYOGA POSE Bound-Angle Pose/*Baddha Konasana*, (p. 47)
BODY BENEFIT   Opens the hips

Much has been spoken about how great it is to give, to volunteer time, to help others, but we rarely talk about the subtle art of receiving. Sure, the new-age spiritual market is full of chatter about manifesting your true desires, directing the flow of the universe, and so forth, but what about good old-fashioned receiving of gifts?

This Kosher Sutra is about opening up the channels to receive the ultimate blessing of all, ensuring that you do have everything you need. Bibliyoga is concerned with transforming our lives and becoming more enlightened through the combination of yoga and Jewish wisdom.

Yoga means "unity" or "oneness", and one aspect of the practice is using postures (*asana/vinyasa*) to unblock physical tightness, so that more of our life force (*prana/neshama*) can flow through our body and enrich our life. This Kosher Sutra's posture is Bound-Angle Pose (*Baddha Konasana*). We open the hips and chest to strengthen our thighs, become more emotionally grounded, and increase our sense of calm through a deeper and more connected

245

breath. Traditional yogic texts also say that the pose reduces fatigue and even eliminates disease.

Our Kosher Sutra refers to the construction of the Temple in Jerusalem and says, "they shall make Me a sanctuary, and I will dwell within them" (Exodus 25: 8). Many commentators have noted the linguistic problem herein, in the way that the verse's object switches from singular to plural, mid-flow. Although the verse is describing the construction of the main sanctuary, one interpretation is that the "them" is actually "us". In other words, we make ourselves into a sanctuary, and God will dwell within our bodies. One 19th Century rabbi equated parts of the Temple with the body[1], while an earlier Chassidic teacher explained how the heart corresponds to the altar[2]. The question is, how can we make our body like a temple or at least set it up to receive the presence of God?

It can be much harder to receive than it is to give. Think of the last time someone paid you a compliment or offered a massive present you were not expecting or insisted on buying you a meal when you were all set to pay. On the other hand, think of how you felt when you gave the first present to your very first boyfriend or girlfriend. Giving actually feels great, as it is satisfying and rewarding. And what happens when a gift is rejected? There are various Biblical examples of this, such as when Kayin's offering is rejected in favour of his brother Abel's (a story which certainly doesn't end happily ever after; Genesis 4:6) or when the two sons of Aaron try to present a spontaneous offering in the Temple and end up being barbecued by a heavenly fire (Leviticus 10:3). If you

---

[1]   R'Meir Leibush Malbim in Remazay HaMishkan ("Secrets of the Sanctuary").
[2]   Quoted in Basi Legani, discourse 1940, from the previous Lubavitcher Rebbe, Yosef Yitschok, as found in the shaloh "veshechanti betocham."

have ever had a gift rejected or been unable to lavish someone with love when you ready to give, you will know how painful it can be. Whilst it is not as bad as being incinerated, it can certainly be frustrating.

If giving is the greatest thing of all, then maybe we can help other people in their giving by actually becoming better at receiving. This actually fits with the core idea of Kabbalah, which means to receive, and is ultimately about turning ourselves into vessels to receive the ultimate kindness of the Creator (the *sefira*/energy of *chesed*). By taking this Kosher Sutra to heart and visualising ourselves as a Sanctuary, opening our hip and chest through the Bibliyoga Bound-Angle Posture, we truly focus on receiving the Godly energy. The verse refers to the Shechina, which is the caring, nurturing, female presence of God, but it can only be received; it cannot just be taken. We need to be open and ready.

As you take Bound-Angle Pose, reflect on this Kosher Sutra, become aware of how your body is feeling restricted or pained, remind yourself of the eternal nature of your soul and breath, and begin to open up to receive the Divine flow of blessings.

The next time you feel you are lacking something in your life, try taking this pose, reflecting on the Kosher Sutra, and meditating on making your body a Sanctuary, a dwelling-place for the feminine presence of God. The pose involves opening up the heart, which has a further resonance for the reading, in that everyone in the reading whose heart motivated them could make a voluntary contribution to the Temple (Exodus 25:2). People would begin by giving to the community, and before long they would be receiving far more in return. Bibliyoga is about transforming our lives to achieve peak performance on the physical and spiritual levels, and this Kosher Sutra's practice is an opportunity for upping our game to receive the ultimate blessing. It all begins by giving a little.

TERUMAH
SANCTUARY

KOSHER SUTRA   "Make Me a sanctuary, and I will dwell within them"
(Exodus 25:8)
SOUL SOLUTION Strengthen the body as a spiritual vessel
BIBLIYOGA POSE Triangle Pose / *Trikonasana*, (p. 54)
BODY BENEFIT Strengthens legs and arms, opens torso

"Oh Lord Prepare Me To be a sanctuary
Pure and Holy Kind and True With thanksgiving
I'll be a living sanctuary For You" (Gospel Standard)

Our Kosher Sutra reads, "Make Me a sanctuary, and I will dwell within them" (Exodus 25:8). As I have commented in this book elsewhere on this same Yoga Sutra, the rabbis teach that there is an apparent mistake within this verse, in that "sanctuary" is a single noun, but "them" is plural. The rabbis resolve the problem by explaining that every single one of us is a sanctuary and a dwelling place for God.

This is all nice and fluffy—but what does it mean? The context of the verse is at the beginning of a long passage that gives incredibly specific details for building the *mishkan*—the structure that will become a "house" for God. It describes beams, staves, joints, foundations, furniture, and accoutrements of all sorts.

The traditional purpose of asana is to strengthen our body so that we can sit and meditate for extended periods. Asana means "seated" (in Hebrew, it would be *yoshev* or *yeshiva*), and asanas

249

are supposed to be rigorously applied to bring strength and vitality to our body. This is so much more than using yoga merely as a flexible workout or relaxation practice. Although it offers all these benefits, yoga practice is really to focus the body so that it becomes a powerful dwelling place for *prana* (yogic energy).

In our modern world, spirituality is often described in very vague terms. Teachers talk about "doing what you feel is right", "following your heart", "listening to your intuition". These statements hold truth but they are incomplete if they are all that are taught. Spirituality takes a lot of work and continued application if it is to come to fruition.

Yoga postures are a very helpful tool for strengthening our body, which is the dwelling place of our soul. Standing poses help our feet and legs provide a firm foundation for the structure, backbends help open the upper cavities for the breath and create openness in the spine, while twists help cleanse toxins and clear blockages to keep the life force flowing.

Our reading begins with the saying that "everyone whose heart will motivate them" should get involved (Exodus 25:2), and it goes on to say how they should get involved. If we really want to create a dwelling place for the Divine, we have to work consistently to make a vessel that can hold the spirit of the universe. The stronger the vessel, the more light it can contain.

TETZAVEH – PURIM
THE VERSACE BREAKDANCE PARTY

KOSHER SUTRA   "Speak to all the wise-hearted people" (Exodus 28:3)
SOUL SOLUTION   Access your inner spirit and experience release from
                worldly pressures
BIBLIYOGA POSE   Headstand/*Salamba Sirsasana*, (p. 84)
BODY BENEFIT   Reverses flow of blood and gravity, releases tension in
                spine and body systems

Some people say that talking about clothes is shallow. They think that focusing on the externals is a superficial pursuit and that there is nothing to be gained by looking at the way we dress. Whilst there may be some truths to this, who has not felt better wearing a new pair of shoes or putting on a crisp new shirt for the first time? Doesn't it just feel great when you know that your new outfit is a stunner? Can't we all admit that sometimes an evening just seems to go better due to how we feel in our clothes?

This Kosher Sutra is about how we can use our external clothing to access our glorious inner spirit while yet releasing ourselves from the pressures of the outside world.

"And you shall speak to all the wise-hearted people whom I have invested with a spirit of wisdom and then shall make the clothes of Aaron..." (Exodus 28:3).

"And you shall speak to all the wise-hearted people"... begins a passage that instructs the Children of Israel to make the priestly

251

garments for Aaron, who was to be the High Priest of Israel. The narrative speaks of garments, which include a robe, a tunic, and a breastplate engraved with stones representing all of the tribes. It was very glitzy and glam-rock in its own way. A few years ago there was a marvelous Versace exhibit at the Victoria and Albert Museum in South Kensington, UK, but even the late Italian designer's outrageous creations did not include anything to match the diamond-encrusted uniform of the *Kohen Gadol* (High Priest).

Here is the paradox: although Aaron had to wear this outfit (which even included a golden headband and hem of pomegranate-shaped bells), it was not at all about the outside. Aaron was famous for his ability to bring peace between people, and when the entire nation eventually spent a month mourning for him, they certainly were not commemorating the loss of a great fashionista (the plot thickens, as do the layers of expensive fabric).

The festival of Purim is the only occasion when the rabbis actually recommended wearing fancy dress[1]. The whole essence of the Purim story is that there was no obvious mention of God, and despite the huge miracle of the Jewish people being saved, there were no obvious (flashy) miracles otherwise. We are told that God's face was hidden (*hester panim*), and by wearing a costume, we are actually hiding away a part of ourselves.

The origins of Greek theatre began with the wearing of masks so that the actors' faces would be hidden. The concept was that

---

[1] Shulchan Aruch, Rama 696:8. .

their external personality could fade away and blend into the characters they were portraying. The Greek audience could then watch the characters and see beyond the surface level; so the masks would actually, however counterintuitively, allow the actors to reveal the inner part of themselves.

We still see this today when actors use extensive make-up to portray different characters that are a far cry from their own selves (think: Dr. Evil, Goldmember, and Mr. Powers, three distinct Mike Myers characters that come to mind). While I was at drama school, my acting teacher and yogic inspiration Edward Clark taught us that the biggest compliment he could give to an actor is: "I didn't recognise that it was you on stage". Such a compliment would not be attributed to extreme latex or make-up but to the actor having managed to completely blend his or her personality into the role.

Yogic practice has the concept of *brahmacharya*, which is a kind of modesty, or celibacy. It is a holding back that allows us to be set free. The *Yoga Sutras* describe how "the practice of modesty/celibacy brings us to attain a great strength"[2]. This is true in the everyday practice of *asana and vinyasa*, where we discipline ourselves to move through postures and gradually strengthen our body and mind. Ultimately yoga is a purely internal practice, but we use the body to reveal our inner strength and allow the poses, to practice subduing our desires and make us stronger.

Before the High Priest put on his garments, he would dip in the *mikveh*, the ritual bath that is the original source of the Christian baptism. When someone steps into the *mikveh*, it is as if they

---

[2]   *Yoga Sutras*, 2:38

are washing away a part of themselves, and when Aaron put on the priestly garment, he became a spiritual conduit for the world, revealing his inner purpose through his outer clothes. We see people seem to change for the entire time they are wearing different uniforms (policeman, nurses, soldiers), and people can easily be seduced into becoming attached to external garments. The fancy dress of Purim is actually a form of modesty that can remind us that we are not our body and we are not our wardrobe but, rather, special and unique beings.[3]

This Kosher Sutra is about reminding ourselves of our internal wisdom, the hochmat Lev—only the truly wise could see that clothing could be an important tool to reveal the inner self. This Sutra's yoga practice is about turning everything on its head, which is the essence of Purim. I am talking about starting practising headstand!

It's best to practice Headstand in the presence of a qualified yoga teacher. You can, however, do as much as you're able on your own, but do be very careful of your neck, and do not move your head at all whilst in the pose. It still "counts" as a headstand if you place your head and hands on the floor with feet in Downward Dog, without actually taking the full balance. Do what you can. But know that age is no excuse for not giving this pose your best: BKS Iyengar has an outstanding yoga practice well into his 90s.

---

[3] This is also a reference to the character of Esther in the Megillah, who epitomised the quality of tzniyus (modesty): "In reward for the modesty that Rachel had, she merited to have Shaul as a descendent. And in reward for the modesty that Shaul had, he merited to have Esther as a descendent" (BT Megillah 13b). "Esther did not reveal her origins or her nationality, as Mordechai had told her" (Esther 2:20). Thanks to Rabbi Eric Goldman's excellent article that helped inspire this sutra, Behind the Mask: Internalizing Ourselves, http://www.yutorah.org/togo/purim/articles/Purim_To-Go_-_5770_Rabbi_Goldman.pdf

As you move into this yoga pose, reflect on the fact that the body is purely a conduit to the soul. Your body is a garment to see you through for a few years, but when we can acknowledge that it is purely temporary, we begin to deeply free ourselves.

HEADSTAND/SALAMBA SIRSASANA

"Speak to all the wise-hearted people"

EXODUS 28:3

TETZAVEH
THE SHMATTE GAME

KOSHER SUTRA   "All the wise-hearted people... with a spirit of wisdom shall make the garments of Aaron..." (Exodus 28:3)

SOUL SOLUTION   Improve patience, focus, and concentration

BIBLIYOGA POSE   Bound-Angle Pose/*Baddha Konasana*, (p. 47)

BODY BENEFIT   Opens hips, reduces sciatic pain

There was a time when three generations of my family were involved with the clothing business, or as my Dad calls it, "the shmatte game" (*shmatte* is Yiddish for rag or fabric). I remember my late Grandma Sadie in her 80s, sitting by her classic Singer sewing machine, patiently making dresses, doing alterations, and fixing hems. My Father was flying to and from fashion warehouses in Milan and Bologna to source new women's-clothing lines for London buyers, and my sister was weaving fine silks on the loom she'd bought after graduating from the famed Central St. Martins College of Art and Design.

Our Kosher Sutra centres on clothing production. We read about how "all the wise-hearted people whom I have invested with a spirit of wisdom shall make the garments of Aaron, to sanctify him" (Exodus 28:3). The designers, garment makers, weavers, haberdashers, milliners, and their colleagues all have full employment in the preparations for the *Mishkan,* the predecessor to the Temple.

One thing I have learned from watching family members at the sewing machine is that the task takes patience. This isn't mentioned in our Kosher Sutra, but it is certainly implied. If you have ever tried to sew something, you will know that it demands time and concentration. To this day, when my father works on the sewing machine, he is in a Zen-like state of focus. He lines up all the hems, threads the needles carefully, dutifully irons the seams, and all of this preparation goes towards creating a perfect result.

Spiritual growth takes patience, focus, and concentration. The *Yoga Sutras* teach *dhyana* (inwards-focused meditation) and *dharana* (outwards-focused, all-inclusive meditation), which are considered the fifth and sixth "limbs" of yoga, respectively. Whether our meditations are on a specific point or on the entire universe, it is through concentration that we can become one with the object of our focus. This oneness can be called yoga, spirituality, enlightenment, or many other names. In every form, though, it is characterised by patience and focus.

There are a million routes to stillness but if we want the "spirit of wisdom", the *ruach chochma* of the Kosher Sutras, then we need to be open to receive it. The idea of *vinyasa* yoga is that we are achieving a sense of stillness-in-motion, keeping a fluidity to our body and a fluidity to our mind. If you want to check whether you are achieving this, pull out a needle and thread and start sewing.

KI TISSA

DESERT BLING

KOSHER SUTRA   "The Israelites would see the radiant skin of Moses' face"
(Exodus 34:35)
SOUL SOLUTION Remove blockages and reduce stress
BIBLIYOGA POSE Cat-Cow / *Marjarasana*, (p. 77)
BODY BENEFIT   Improves circulation and makes skin more radiant

It is very easy to create something to blame for our problems and to look, for example, at astrological charts for the hope of good news. It's much harder to be in a state of not knowing. When the Children of Israel were scared because they thought they had lost their leader, as Moses had been missing on Mount Sinai for 40 years, they created a Golden Calf. Rather than holding onto faith, they forced an unnatural solution that only created more problems: in response to their actions, Moses ended up smashing the first set of Ten Commandment tablets, ground up the calf into powder, mixed it with water, and forced the worshippers to drink their so-called god.

The great American dramatist David Mamet explained how a self-created god limits our true potential: "The very arbitrary and mechanical choice of the Golden Calf, for example, reveals its meaning: I, the Worshipper, have created you. I have abstracted you from myself...The Golden Calf, similarly, frees us mechanically from consciousness of our own egotism. It possesses no qualities either to chide or guide us. We have given it life. Much like the person who creates an imaginary partner for his or her business firm—a partner on whom all blame can be placed for unpleasant decisions...At the foot of Mount Sinai, in Freedom (adulthood) for the first time, the Israelites desired desperately to return to their preadolescent state. Being deprived of a pharaoh (parent) to worship or fear—being deprived of childhood—they took matters into their own hands. They made a statue to allow them to worship the idol of any adolescent—to allow them to worship themselves"[1].

Yoga is intended to lead us to a state of *moksha*, of freedom, and this involves not knowing. When we unnaturally force our body into an asana, we create injury. Perhaps we will never be able to achieve certain postures, especially if we begin practising later on in life. That is not an impediment to reaching *samadhi* (enlightenment or ultimate peace), because asana is purely a tool to lead us from the outer body to inner stillness.

The Hebrews were desperate to find a spiritual connection and could not wait for Moses return from the mountain, so they built the Golden Calf. The problem with idolatry is that instead of making space for Divine inspiration, it tries to force it. Rather than allowing themselves to be made in the image of God, the Hebrews tried to make God in their own image. Moses was free and ascended to a new level. When he eventually returned from Mount Sinai, he had reached such an intensity of self-realisation that his face was glowing and he needed to wear a mask to protect other people.

We can experience so much more when we are open to what is rather than what we would like things to be. When we force our image on reality, we limit possibilities and block the opportunity for a higher spiritual connection. A committed yoga practice helps clear toxins in our body, creates more radiant and glowing skin, and enables us to connect to the Source. We cannot know where the path will lead us, but why limit ourselves? Reach high.

---

[1]   Make-Believe Town—Essays and Remembrances, David Mamet, p166.

KI TISSA

SUPER-8

KOSHER SUTRA   "When you take a census...everyone shall give a half-shekel" (Exodus 30:12–13)

SOUL SOLUTION To find peace of mind and inner joy at every moment

BIBLIYOGA POSE Still-pointed focus whilst spending time with other people; listening profoundly/*Ekagrata*

BODY BENEFIT   Cultivates inner calm and openness to those around us

There was a time when every second mattered. My childhood birthday parties were captured on Super-8 that my father carefully filmed before sending off the four-minute reel of tape for developing over a two-week waiting period. He then physically spliced the film for any edits, before closing the curtains, setting up the projector, and gathering the family for the long-awaited film showing.

There was a time when every shot mattered. We bought 35-mm film for our cameras and were careful about how we used the precious 24 or 36 photographs we would get from each roll.

There was a time when every friend mattered. We knew exactly who our friends were and physically wrote their names and numbers in a contacts book. Back then, the word friend held a higher linguistic currency; most people couldn't number their friends in today's Facebook thousands, and there was not the option to add, delete, or ignore friends at the click of a button. What is the impact of all of this digital rapidity on our time, our self-respect, our value?

Our Kosher Sutra recalls a system of counting people: "When you take a census...everyone shall give a half-shekel" (Exodus 30:12–13). Rather than being counted by their numbers, the community was counted by their contribution. Everyone had to give a half-shekel unit of currency towards the communal structure, and the money was then calculated, telling the leaders how many people there were. This was a simple but radical shift. What makes us matter is not how much we have (status, possession, friends), but whether or not we are prepared to give.

As I wrote this chapter, both the Girl Scouts of America and the musician Lady Gaga were running campaigns to help children improve their confidence and sense of self-worth[1]. If we look closely, many of us question our value at some point or other.

Yoga's overarching goal is for us to become *sukha stiram*, or "stable/secure and joyful"—to find peace of mind and inner joy at every moment. Although joy may be our birthright, it does not always come automatically.

Perhaps we can achieve more by accumulating a little less. Take shorter videos and fewer photographs, collect fewer friends, and instead focus on each moment and each person we spend time with. The paths of spirituality, yoga, and meditation may demand discipline, but the rewards can be immense.

---

[1] Articles in Time Magazine, March 2012, US Edition.

VAYAKHEL
YES, WE CAN!

KOSHER SUTRA   "They came, every person whose heart stirred them up"
                (Exodus 35:21)
SOUL SOLUTION Feel inspiration and re-tune with your true calling
BIBLIYOGA POSE Straddle-Bend / *Prasarita Paddotansana C*, (p. 66)
BODY BENEFIT   Strengthens legs and relieves tension in upper back

There is a classic moment in the movie The Blues Brothers. Jake & and Elwood Blues are wearing their trademark dark glasses and black suits, have succeeded in "getting the band back together", and proclaim that they are "on a mission from God". Their new-found blues enlightenment leads to a successful fund-raising concert and their saving an orphanage...even as these events are followed by the most spectacular cop-car chases in movie history straight after they finish singing Everybody Needs Somebody [To Love]. This Kosher Sutra is about utilising the tools of Bibliyoga to get in touch with our personal mission and get back in tune with our true calling.

The last readings from Exodus describe garments and other artistic items being prepared for the Temple and focus on the people who are driven to start creating: "And they came, every person whose heart stirred them up...Every man and woman whose heart moved them...every willing heart...every wise-hearted woman..." (Exodus 31:21–29). The theme of "heart" is unrelenting, and there are at least ten mentions of the Hebrew word lev (heart) during this sequence. There is a clear metaphor in play, using the idea of someone's "heart stirring them up" or "heart moving them" to describe someone's feeling motivated.

The heart is probably the most frequently mentioned organ in yogic practice, with teachers describing postures as "heart-openers" or telling people to "lift their hearts". Early yoga texts refer to the "lotus of the heart" as a focus for meditation:

"In the city of Brahman is a secret dwelling, the lotus of the heart. Within this dwelling is a space, and within that space is the fulfillment of our desires. What is within that space should be longed for and realised.

"As great as the infinite space beyond, is the space within the lotus of the heart. Both heaven and earth are contained in that inner space, both fire and air, sun and moon, lightning and stars. Whether we know it in this world or know it not, everything is contained in that inner space"[1].

There are many cardiovascular benefits to vinyasa yoga, but the practice is more than just a form of exercise to improve heart health. There are famous tales of yogis able to speed up and slow down their heart rate at will, the most recent being renowned Indian teacher Krishnamacharya, who could stop his heartbeat for two minutes. His students included BKS Iyengar, Patthabi Jois (founder of Ashtanga Yoga), and Indra Devi and his son TKV Desikachar.

---

[1] From Chandogya Upanishad, 191, c.1500 as quoted in "The Lotus of the Heart: A Summary of the Upanishads," http://www.sunandmoonstudio.com/Articles/upanish.html.

Yoga means "combining" or "unity", and there is a beautiful psalm that asks us to "unify our hearts in love and awe"[2]. We can take this unity on both a physical and metaphorical level. During an asana/vinyasa yoga sequence, we are attempting to bring our body into one unified whole, so that the breath matches the movement and we are able to maximise our physical potential during any one posture. There is also an internal aspect, as the yoga practice is ultimately about becoming completely present with the moment and with God through our breath-body-movement-mindfulness practice. On one level, yoga is just another form of prayer, and the body is really the most superficial aspect of the process—but it is the easiest place to start. (This is the real reason that yoga should never make it into an Olympic sport, unless the judges were to have the metaphysical capability to peer into the contestants' minds to see if they are fully unified...but that's a whole other conversation. The Woody Allen joke comes to mind: "I cheated on my metaphysics exam by peering into my neighbour's soul".

Back to the heart: our Kosher Sutra describes people who felt fully motivated and had the ability to create works of art, but the commentator Ramban (1194–1270) takes it one stage further. He explains that:

---

2   Psalms 86:11. This phrase appears in the morning service prior to the Shema. There's also a whole other drash (explanation) of the word Vayakhel, which is the title of the first parsha; the word means "and he gathered" or "and he congregated," and although it's talking about bringing the community together, we can also do a physical reading of this word as we bring together all parts of our body and mind through the asana practice. This reading would be backed up by the Zohar reference that explains how the Temple was a metaphor for the body (i.e., the heart corresponding to the Holy of Holies), but that's a whole other story. We've got time; there are at least another 50 years' worth of Bibliyoga teachings if everything goes to plan, so hang in there...

"The 'stirring of the heart' implies the arousing of their capacity to undertake the work. For none had ever learnt these skills before from any teacher nor had ever practised them before. But each one discovered his [or her] natural talent or aptitude for the task, his[/her] heart rising as it were to the Divine challenge enabling him to come into Moses' presence and say, 'I can do it!'"[3]

What a brilliant explanation! Ramban is telling us that when the whole Temple project began, all kinds of people suddenly felt motivated to start creating things and using talents that they did not previously have. They listened to their inner motivation, felt their spirit welling up, and discovered a new talent.

Carefully listening to your inner wisdom, the *chochmat lev* (literally, "wisdom of the heart") will help lead you in a direction that is ultimately prosperous and beneficial.

Wishing you a healthy heart and true joy in following your heart's calling.

---

[3]   Ramban on Exodus 35:21.

VAYAKHEL
THE HOW OF HAPPINESS

KOSHER SUTRA   "Everyone whose heart inspired them, and everyone who
               is generous of spirit" (Exodus 35:21)
SOUL SOLUTION Open your heart to others and increase happiness
BIBLIYOGA POSE Camel Pose / *Ustrasana*, (p. 80)
BODY BENEFIT   Releases tightness in upper chest, improves circulation
               around heart

Freud articulated it best when he explained the Pleasure Principle. Ultimately, we all want to be happy. Almost everything we do derives from that one basic desire, whether pursuing money, entertainment, love, or intellectual activities—we just want to experience joy.

In her book *The How of Happiness*, Professor Sonja Lyubomirsky suggests that up to 40% of our happiness quotient is within our own control. She outlined "a scientific approach to getting the life you want" and used research data to create a systematic method to help us feel better that included "happiness activities", such as Practising Acts of Kindness, Nurturing Social Relationships, Learning to Forgive, Savouring Life's Joys, Taking Care of Your Body, and much more. The book is very good indeed!

This Kosher Sutra is a repeated phrase about "everyone who is generous of heart" (Exodus 35:5), "everyone whose heart inspired them, and everyone who is generous of spirit" (Exodus 35:21), describing those who are motivated to help others and build part of the community. This can be understood as Karma

Yoga, something that has been explained as "selfless community service."

Karma Yoga is the exercise that takes place away from the mat for the direct benefit of others. Perhaps the puppets of the musical *Avenue Q* said it best when they sang, "When you help others you can't help helping yourself"[1].

---

[1] The Money Song, Avenue Q (Musical), by Robert Lopez and Jeff Marx.

PEKUDEI
PURPOSE

KOSHER SUTRA   "These are the accountings for the Temple" (Exodus 38:21)
SOUL SOLUTION Re-tuning with our higher calling
BIBLIYOGA POSE Lotus Pose (Seated Meditation Position)/*Padmasana*, (p. 96)
BODY BENEFIT   Brings calm and stillness

We all have a purpose on earth. When we are in tune with it, everything comes into focus, and we can achieve deep success. The challenge is that nobody can tell us what our calling is, and we have to figure it out for ourselves.

Our Kosher Sutra lists the items that were needed in the Temple. There is a list of objects, and the message is that every item counts when putting together the whole. The Kosher Sutra's accompanying reading of *Shekalim* demands that everyone donate an identical half-shekel coin to the Temple building project, which sends out the further message that every person counts. Finally, when we translate the Hebrew phrase *l'haper al nafsho* as an "accounting for our breath", we can deduce the subtle message that every breath counts.

How are you using this precious breath?

The royal path of yoga, Raja Yoga, leads us on the journey home to ourselves. Postures fine-tune our musculature, and *pranayamic* breathing leads us to a subtle inner calm through deep awareness of our inhalations and exhalations.

The word *tafkid,* usually translated as "accounting", can also be understood as "purpose". Self-acceptance leads to happiness, and we come into fruition when we perform those tasks that we do best.

This reading resonates with the month of Adar, whose paradigm is joy, and ultimately it is only with deep joy that we can find and pursue our life's purpose.

LEVITICUS

CAMEL POSE / USTRASANA

*"Everyone whose heart inspired them,
and everyone who is generous of spirit"*

EXODUS 35:21

VAYIKRA
BE BRILLIANT

KOSHER SUTRA   "If you bring from amongst yourselves a sacrifice to God"
                (Leviticus 1:2)
SOUL SOLUTION   Banish negative energy and be brilliant!
BIBLIYOGA POSE Downward-Facing Dog/ *Adho Mukha Svanasana*, (p.83)
BODY BENEFITS   Builds strength and stamina

What makes us appreciate great artists over reality-TV stars? Why do we love accomplished athletes and sports figures more than lottery winners? How is it that we are drawn to the stories of people who have positively fought and survived illnesses, whereas we get frustrated with those who continually moan and whine about their lot? Perhaps it is because deep down we respect those who have sacrificed a part of themselves to achieve something greater.

This Kosher Sutra tells a powerful secret. The Hebrew verse is usually translated as, "if any Man brings an offering of you to the Lord", but it can be read as "if any man brings an offering of you" or indeed, "if you bring from within yourself a sacrifice to God" (Leviticus 1:1)[1].

The notion of sacrifice is being willing to give up something that is important to us. It can be a physical object; in Biblical times, this was represented by an animal or a sum of money. In Kabbalistic thinking, this sacrifice is giving up a part of our ego.

---

[1]   Translation from the Lubavitcher Rebbe's Likutei Sichot, Vol 1 pp205-208

The idea of Karma Yoga is translated as the "discipline of action", as we perform positive actions without expecting any personal reward, similar to the Hebrew concept of *hesed* (acting with lovingkindness). The distinguished Indian yogi Swami Vivekenanda believed to have urged his followers, saying "forget about your own salvation" and to "see God in those who suffer, and for them sacrifice everything of yourself". This truly elevates this idea of sacrifice to the next level.

Every time we step on the yoga mat there is the opportunity to sacrifice part of our self-importance by being completely honest about who we are. Perhaps our mind is saying, "My backbend isn't as flexible as I'd like it to be, my body isn't as supple as it once was, my mind isn't as focused as it could be". If you try this Kosher Sutra's posture, Downward-facing Dog, whilst meditating on the Sutra, try staying in the pose until you literally cannot stay any longer. Watch any self-critical thoughts, and then "burn through" them. Breathe deeply and allow yourself to grow.

Once you have completed the experience two or three times, you might discover that your stamina has increased. Maybe you will have uncovered or reminded yourself about your inner strength and be reconnected to that vital sense of brilliant potential that has always been within you.

VAYIKRA
THE CALLING

KOSHER SUTRA   "And He called to Moses" (Leviticus 1:1)
SOUL SOLUTION Deep understanding of what we need to do
BIBLIYOGA POSE Pranayama Breathing, counting breaths, (p.95)
BODY BENEFITS Expands consciousness

The book of Leviticus begins with the word *Vayikra:* "And He called" (to Moses)[1]. Rashi explains that God's calling to Moses was an explanation of the entire body of wisdom but said in such a way that nobody else could hear it outside of the tent where Moses was standing. What is most interesting is that the information was delivered in bite-size chunks with small gaps in between so that Moses had the chance to understand and reflect (Hebrew: *l'hitbonen*).

My first real encounter with yoga began with the breath when my teacher Edward Clark explained that by slowing our breathing, we can slow down our thoughts.

The distracted mind, or monkey mind, is a common dysfunction that yoga seeks to redress, and when we can control our thoughts, we can have a much more powerful impact on the world around us. Slowing our thoughts allows us to expand our consciousness and reach a greater sense of understanding in any given activity. Edward once said in a magazine interview that "yoga can teach you anything," and by matching physical movement with breath we can enter this *l'hitbonen* space of understanding.

---

[1]   The Hebrew name, Vayikra, is so much more illuminating than the English Leviticus, the latter referring to the laws of the Levites that are listed later on.

We all have moments of wondering what to do, whether on a practical or existential level. Rather than reacting out of fear, we can find the space between the breaths, drop into the gap, and listen to the calling.

VAYIKRA
BURNING MAN

KOSHER SUTRA   "When you bring an offering to God...it shall be a male
without blemish" (Leviticus 1:3)
SOUL SOLUTION Clarity of heart, mind, and spirit
BIBLIYOGA POSE Extended Child's Pose / *Balasana*, (p.88)
BODY BENEFITS Calms, relaxes, dissipates stress

There is a pilgrimage that takes place every summer in the Nevada Desert. Fifty-thousand people head to the sandy wasteland and participate in a week-long festival that culminates with the nighttime burning of a massive effigy of a human being. Burning Man is a phenomenon that eerily connects modern living with the ancient phenomenon of sacrifice.

Our Kosher Sutra is stark: "When you bring an offering to God, you shall bring an offering of cattle, or even of herd or of flock. If the offering is a burnt-offering of the herd, it shall be a male without blemish..." (Leviticus 1:3). The Hebrew word for offering or sacrifice is *korban*, and the root of the word, *karev*, literally means "draw close". Through the process of sacrifice, humans come closer to God and closer to one another.

Sacrifice is a painful business. It hurts. It smells. It is visceral. When we talk about "making sacrifices" in our life, we usually refer to giving something up in order to transform something else. We might sacrifice the last drink of the evening in order to get to sleep so that we can rise early to exercise, or we might sacrifice some pride if we are to create a lasting sense of peace within the home.

The teachings of yoga refer to an idea of inner sacrifice, and it has been taught that "the sense organs, the tongue, etc., are the sacrificial vessels; the objects of the senses, taste, etc., are the sacrificial substances"[1]. The fire, or *tapas*, of a yoga practice heats us up and burns away our ego, wiping away the thoughts and behaviours that hold us back.

If we practice with commitment, we can end up with a purer heart, a clearer mind, and spiritual clarity. It just might burn a little. But allow yourself the gift of releasing into the burning.

---

[1]   Merce Eliade. Yoga: Immortality and Freedom, p. 111 fn.50

TSAV – PURIM
(LEAP YEAR)
IF YOU'VE GOT IT, FLAUNT IT

KOSHER SUTRA   "[Place it] on the altar" (Leviticus 6:2)
SOUL SOLUTION   See the world from a new perspective
BIBLIYOGA POSE Headstand/Salamba Sirsasana, (p.84)
BODY BENEFITS   Release stress and balance hormones

There are plenty of reasons not to be joyful, and life provides endless reasons to complain. American yoga teacher Max Strom once taught that most of our waking hours are spent in the pursuit of happiness.

One proven source of contented living is to connect to something greater than ourselves; rather than focusing on our own thoughts, we turn the spotlight on others. The ancient art of sacrifice was a visceral way to become connected with something greater, and when people brought sacrifices to the Temple in Jerusalem, they had their eyes on something higher than themselves.

Rabbi Elimelech of Lizensk (1717–1787) understood sacrifice as the act of eliminating our negative traits. Just as the priest changed his garments during the ritual, Rabbi Elimelech said we should change the behaviours that cover our true potential. Even if we are stuck in a particular way of thinking or behaving, we "place it on the altar", almost like a sacrifice, and start channelling the energy for a higher purpose. "If a person is easily angered or has other negative traits, one should break them and use them positively", he wrote[1]. If we are thinking negative thoughts, we should use our mind for creating positive plans, and if we display self-destructive behaviours, we can choose to use them instead for the good.

The yoga mat is an altar of sorts, a laboratory for changing behaviour and channelling energy. We use the *pranayamic* breath to drive our movements, travelling back and forth through the choreography of *vinyasa* Sun Salutes. Even if we begin with negative thoughts at the start of a practice, if the yoga session is successful, then the energy will have been transformed for the good. However chaotic the world outside, we aim to reach equanimity and peace. The *Bhagavad Gita* promised that "joy supreme comes to the Yogi whose heart is still, whose passions are peace...who is one with God" (6:71).

The Talmud teaches that we are all born pure and that we all have huge potential[2], but the challenge is how to focus our energy on the greatest good. The Book of Esther tells of heroes who utilised their natural strengths: Esther's beauty led her to a position of influence in the King's bedroom, while Mordechai's strategic intelligence helped him save the day. How are you realising your potential today?

There is a yogic moment at the heart of Purim. As the list of Haman's criminal sons is read, it is traditional for them all to be said in one breath. Sometimes we need to purge negative feelings or thoughts, and what better way than in a huge exhale. The yoga mat also takes us to the essence of Purim—the only

---

[1]   Mipeninei Noam Elimelech, translated by Tal Moshe Zwecker, p. 172. .
[2]   In the "Elokai Neshama" passage in Talmud Brachot, 60b

festival that does not mention God but instead is all about oneness, the celebration about connecting to our inner selves and bringing them to the outside (albeit with the help of alcohol and wild costumes).

We all have at least one powerful personality trait, and the challenge is to find the best way to express it for the greatest good. There is always a place for it in this world to help it serve a higher purpose. If you've got it, flaunt it. Use it to find inner peace and the deepest joy imaginable.

HEADSTAND/SALAMBA SIRSASANA

"[Place it] on the altar"

LEVITICUS 6:2

TSAV – SHABBAT HAGADOL
WE DIDN'T START THE FIRE

KOSHER SUTRA   "Fire shall be kept burning upon the altar continuously" (Leviticus 6:6)
SOUL SOLUTION Re-ignite endurance and passion
BIBLIYOGA POSE Warrior I /*Virabhadrasana I*, (p.60)
BODY BENEFITS Opens the hips, soothes sciatic pain; stretches the groin

"What I desire/Is man's red fire/To make my dreams come true" — King Louie, *The Jungle Book*

Fire is mesmerising. At some point or another all of us will have stared at a flame, watching the way it dances unpredictably, temporarily taking us beyond the realm of human experience. Flames hint towards greatness, almost as bridge between limited human potential and infinite possibility. Dancers have imitated fire, painters have drawn it, and singers have mused about it.

The fire on the altar in Jerusalem burned continuously, regardless of whether it was day or not, Sabbath or not, in states of purity or impurity[1]. The sacrificial fire had to be made visible to everyone by being placed on the external altar, and in some ways it reflected a heavenly fire that would come down to join the humans' fire[2]. The very idea of sacrifice is about giving up something so that we can connect with greatness.

---

[1] Jerusalem Talmud, Yoma, 4:6, as quoted by Lubavitcher Rebbe in Likkutei Sichot, Vol. 1 pp. 217–219, translated by Lord J.Sacks in Torah Studies.
[2] "Although fire comes down from Heaven, it is a commandment also for man to bring fire," Babylonian Talmud Yoma 21b

Shabbat HaGadol (literally, "The Great Shabbat") is all about gearing up for the cleansing of Passover and preparing ourselves for spiritual and emotional freedom.

Sacrifice is the process of giving something up. In Biblical times it was represented by money or the favourite cow in one's herd. When we sacrifice something, we create new space and open ourselves up to new possibilities. A mundane metaphor would be to imagine a garden full of weeds; there isn't much room for flowers to grow until you do some weeding. All gardeners need to have a bonfire from time to time (although it is best not done in the middle of a Sunday afternoon, which tends to be something of a well-rehearsed antisocial custom in the Home Counties of Great Britain). The burnt offering of Biblical sacrifice is akin to spiritual cleansing.

Yoga is all about internal fires and sacrifice. Words such as *tapas* (heat) and *agni* (fire) appear throughout early yogic literature, and when we hold a posture we burn away parts of our ego and aspects of our personality that limit us. I have seen people transformed by their yoga practice. This Kosher Sutra is about strengthening this internal fire and unlocking our potential and our yoga pose is Warrior I. Hold the pose for as long as you can, fan the internal flames, and follow your passions to greatness. We didn't start the fire, but we can keep it burning.

TSAV – SHABBAT HAGADOL

THE HOLY GRUDGE

KOSHER SUTRA   "A holy of holies" (Leviticus 7:1)
SOUL SOLUTION   Freedom from guilt through the power of forgiveness
BIBLIYOGA POSE   Warrior II / *Virabhadrasana II*, (p.61)
BODY BENEFITS   Strengthens the legs for moving forwards in life

There is a powerful field of medicine known as intuitive healing. Whereas traditional (allopathic) doctors focus on symptoms within the physical anatomy, intuitive healers are able to read a person's energy field. One of the most well known is Dr Caroline Myss, author of *Anatomy of the Spirit*. She explains that we can all bring about a huge amount of healing if we are able to forgive.

Forgiveness is not easy. We enjoy holding onto past pains and having something to complain about. It is easier to make our loved ones feel guilty about something they did in the past than to forgive them in the present. Ironically we never feel like forgiving someone until we have followed through and completely forgiven them! That is the point when we feel cleaner, purer, and lighter.

This Kosher Sutra speaks of the guilt-offering, a sacrifice that is described as "a holy of holies" (Leviticus 7:1). The process is sequential: a person feels guilty about something, then brings a guilt-offering; the offering is slaughtered, burnt, and eaten; and then the person will have reached this "holy of holies". There are no more guilt-trips and no more reminders, because everything is forgiven and truly finished. I think this points towards a radical idea, that when we arrive at a place of true forgiveness—whether forgiving ourselves or others—we are in the holiest place on earth.

The Kabbalists connected the Holy of Holies, the *Kadosh Kadoshim,* with the heart. Perhaps this is because when we truly forgive someone, it really has to come from our heart. Not only that, but the Holy of Holies is the place where the High Priest used to connect directly with God, and if we create space in our heart by forgiving someone else, then we really have the chance to establish a Divine connection. Meanwhile, the ancient yogis had absolutely no doubt about the need for clearing energetic blockages. This is also true of the Taoists, the Buddhists, and many other spiritual groups.

The yogis noted five levels of the body *(the koshas)* and viewed the physical body as only the most obvious manifestation. The driving idea behind yoga is to remove blockages within the body to allow healing to take place, so that the life force/*prana* can flow through the channels. When energy is blocked, cells and tissues do not get the life force they need, the body is ill-at-ease, or dis-eased, and this is what we call "illness" Myss teaches that one way to heal the body is to free up bound energy by forgiving people.

When the Torah states, "Do not take revenge, and do not bear a grudge against a member of your people" (Leviticus 19:18). We can do an instant Bibliyogic re-reading: "Do not bear a grudge against a member of your people" is an Imperative Universal Law, because to contravene this is actually to store that grudge in our own physical members, e.g., our limbs. If we do not forgive other people, then we are harming ourselves. When somebody says, "But I can't forgive X for what they have done", it just means there is a need to work harder to find that forgiveness and bring about closure. Otherwise, the energetic law states dictates suffering. Paradoxically, we will often feel a greater amount of joy if it has been more difficult to forgive someone. When we truly clear our hearts, we create a space for God.

In the next few days, try to forgive someone. You may not feel like it, but once the deed has been done, you are guaranteed to feel lighter. And if you don't, then blame me, and I will promise to forgive you.

WARRIOR II / VIRABHADRASANA II

"A holy of holies"

LEVITICUS 7:1

SHEMINI
LUCKY NUMBER 8

KOSHER SUTRA   "Aaron's sons brought foreign fire before the Lord" (Lev. 10:1)
SOUL SOLUTION Increase spiritual strength
BIBLIYOGA POSE Bridge pose /*Setu Bandhasana*, (p.79)
BODY BENEFITS Strengthens back and thighs

How can we reach beyond ourselves and touch the Infinite? The Beijing Olympics officially began at 8 seconds and 8 minutes past 8 p.m., on August 8, 2008. There are eight petals on the Buddhist lotus flower. There is a report of a group of men arrested in China for a street fight over the number plate "8888". Jewish boys are traditionally circumcised on their eighth day. There is clearly something going on with this number, if we can but figure it out.

Many cultures see eight as a lucky number. The rabbis saw it as a code for something bigger, beyond the natural. There are seven days of creation, and Day Eight represents the metaphysical, which is why the inauguration of the Temple—a bridge between man and God—took place on the eighth day of festivities. The day of joy turned to tragedy when two priests, Nadav and Avihu, began to improvise and paid dearly for their spontaneity, killed by a heavenly fire.

Why should there not be room for spiritual spontaneity? Ashtanga Yoga is a strict form of asana/vinyasa practice that aims to unite physical and spiritual aspects in its eight-part system (ashto means "eight"). If you practice with a traditional Ashtanga teacher, you will find that keeping to the system takes precedence over personal ideas and spontaneous movement. The majority of yogis will agree that even if you want to become creative with the sequence of postures, there are basic principles of correct alignment that ensure you get the full benefit from any individual asana. The Kabbalistic theme of *gevurah* means both "strength" and "discipline". One form of strength comes through holding back. Discipline can lead to freedom; it can mean that sometimes we have to pay a price to get that freedom.

Some say that Nadav and Avihu were killed because they were actually drunk[1]. Others say the two were arrogantly waiting for the older generation to die so that they could take the senior leadership[2]. Worse still is the charge that they were punished because they were unmarried:

"Nadav and Avihu were supercilious and never married. Many were the women who waited for them, wasting themselves as old maids. But they said, 'What woman could possibly be suitable for us?'"[3]

Talk about Jewish guilt!

The rabbis teach that, although there are many paths to God through the different spiritual traditions, there are also limits. When we keep to the physical limits in any yoga posture, through correct foot placement, alignment, and breathing, we use this power of gevurah-discipline to release our inner strength.

---

[1]   Vayikra Rabbah 12:1. "When He commands Aaron, 'Do not drink wine to intoxication, you or your sons, when you enter the Ohel Mo'ed (tent), that you not die!' (Leviticus 10:9). We come to understand that they died only because of wine." [translated by R Matis Weinberg].

[2]   "Moshe and Aaron walked along, and Nadav and Avihu walked behind them. Said Nadav to Avihu, 'When will these two old men die already, and you and I can lead the generation?'" BT Sanhedrin 52b.

[3]   Vayikra Rabba, 20:10 [translated by R. Matis Weinberg]

A powerful spiritual-physical connection doesn't have to be a matter of relying on lucky numbers, but channelling our physical energy so that we can connect with greatness.

BRIDGE POSE /SETU BANDHASANA

"Aaron's sons brought foreign fire before the Lord"

LEV. 10:1

SHEMINI
SILENT RETREAT

KOSHER SUTRA   "And Aaron was silent" (Leviticus 10:3)
SOUL SOLUTION   Overcome life's challenges through staying grounded
BIBLIYOGA POSE Pyramid Pose/*Parsvottanasana*, (p.62)
BODY BENEFITS   Strengthens legs, grounds the emotions

When were you last with someone who spoke a lot but said nothing?

Oftentimes, it can be a human tendency to speak as a way of letting out anxiety. Rather than acknowledging uncomfortable emotions, we chatter so that we can avoid feeling the discomfort. Few people take the time to retreat into silence, which is why very few discover the incredible rewards from this practice.

Moses' brother Aaron makes a powerful choice of words when faced with an extraordinarily challenging personal situation concerning a Divine punishment on his sons: he says nothing. Instead of wailing, blaming God, or anxiously talking through his problem, he chooses not to make it a problem and retreats into a contemplative, accepting silence.

The Hebrew word used is *dum,* which is a form of silence. It is a self-controlled, spiritually connected, completely aware, active silence. The word is used when Elijah hears the "still, silent" voice of God, and the same word also appears when King David wrote, "Be silent and know God" (Psalm 46:10). This is Aaron's form of silence; it is not passively accepting tribulations from heaven but acknowledging that there is a time to listen rather than speak.

Ayurveda is the primary school of yogic medicine that originated in India over 3,000 years ago. It is based on the five elements of earth, water, fire, air, and ether. One of my yoga teachers suggested that our society is engulfed by the air and ether elements, or what *Ayurveda* calls *vatta*. In other words, we have a tendency towards a flitting, airy nature that would benefit from grounding. How can we ground ourselves? We ground through holding the air within and using the tool of silence. Yoga postures good for grounding include all of the standing poses, such as Triangle, Mountain, and Pyramid.

In today's world it is harder than ever to "be silent", but the rewards can vastly outweigh the effort.

TAZRIA-METZORAH
SCRATCH THE ITCH

KOSHER SUTRA   "He shall dwell alone, outside of the camp" (Lev. 13:46)
SOUL SOLUTION Holistic healing for the body and soul
BIBLIYOGA POSE Thunderbolt / *Vajrasana*, (p.46)
BODY BENEFITS Reflective mind, calms the body, tones the spinal column

There is nothing funny about skin disorders. So I'm going to cut out the usual light-hearted introduction to the Kosher Sutras. There is nothing flaky going on here; it is a serious issue and an itch that I've wanted to scratch for a long time. I would have written about this topic earlier but just didn't want to do anything rash.

Most people get itchy skin at some time or other in their life. Doctors teach that there are two ways of dealing with this. Traditional Western medicine (allopathic) will usually approach the symptom by putting some kind of lotion on the skin to push the problem inside and make it disappear. Holistic medicine (e.g., homeopathic) works from the inside out, taking the entire physical and mental system into account whilst looking for a cause.

This Kosher Sutra can be seen as ancient, archaic, and arcane, with someone being banished outside of the camp to heal from a spiritually related skin affliction. The story tells of people who are suffering from *tza'arat,* a kind of blemishing disease that affects people's bodies, houses, clothes, and even their hair. There are various formulae for solving it, and one is for the sufferer to sit in isolation away from their community. This is a challenging text; how is it relevant to us today?

One of the key benefits of a yoga practice is the way it fine-tunes us to internal processes. A regular *asana* practice will ensure that the yogi knows how their body can feel on a good day and how to make adjustments when they are not feeling tip-top. BKS Iyengar prescribes different poses for physical healing and has achieved legendary results over the years. By heightening our awareness over body and mind, we too can often discover the roots of illness and suffering. An incredible example of this is Brandon Bayes, whose inspiring book *The Journey* charts her recovery from a life-threatening stomach tumour, through the use of a powerful yogic meditation.

The rabbis suggest that the *tza'arat* disease was a dysfunction that could be traced to various negative behaviours, such as speaking badly of others *(lashon hara)*[1]. The Talmud records how the command for the sufferer to dwell in isolation was so that they could reflect, repent, and restore their behaviour[2]. This is a visionary text, to describe a disorder that can be solved through truly holistic means. Although our current world is full of terrible diseases that still baffle medical science, perhaps this tale of holistic suffering can help us find healing in some parts of our lives.

---

[1]   "Tza'arat comes from loshon hara and from 'stinginess.'" Devarim Rabbah 6:8. (translated by: R Matis Weinberg).

[2]   He shall dwell alone, outside of the camp' (Leviticus 13:46). Why must the metzorah dwell alone? He utilised loshon hara to detach man from wife and people from friends—he too must be isolated." BT Arachin 16a.

This Kosher Sutra's posture is Thunderbolt/*Vajrasana*. A superb meditation pose, it can be used as an opportunity for journeying inwards and increasing healing. The pose is achieved by kneeling down with your back upright. A cushion can be placed between your shins and buttocks for increased comfort. Try sitting still, breathing deeply and smoothly, and journeying inside[3] to bring healing and calm into your world.

---

3   To take this meditation further, try focusing on a specific ailment. Imagine yourself journeying inside to that part of your body, "look around" inside your muscles at the problem, notice what shoes you are wearing (so to speak), and be aware if there is an unresolved emotional issue that comes to mind.

THUNDERBOLT / VAJRASANA

"He shall dwell alone,
outside of the camp"

LEVITICUS 13:46

TAZRIA-METZORAH
PAY IT FORWARD

KOSHER SUTRA   "When a woman gives birth to a male" (Leviticus 12:2)
SOUL SOLUTION   Heal the world, one step at a time
BIBLIYOGA POSE Backbend ("upright heart") / *Urdhva Dhanurasana*, (p.82)
BODY BENEFITS   Increases flexibility in the back

As a child, I always found something fascinating about the world-record-breaking domino contests, where the flick of one domino would affect many thousands more. The film Pay It Forward tells of a similar effect with powerful results, when one person does a huge favour to help each of three other people, and then those three "pay it forward" to three more. We can take the butterfly effect into our own hands and raise the whole world on such wings.

"When a woman gives birth to a male" appears to speak to only one half of the population until we analyse the Hebrew word tazria, which means "giving birth" but has the roots of zarua, meaning "planting", and zera, meaning "seed". Rabbi Elimelech of Lizensk explained that when we plant sparks of inspiration in others, stimulating them to bring more light into the world through their actions, we "give birth". He connects it to the Psalm, "A light is planted [*zarua*] for the righteous person, and gladness for the upright of heart" (Psalm 97:11). And so we lift others.

The space of the yoga mat is a private one, symbolising our own internal world, but the core of yogic philosophy is that there is no action without reaction. The *Yoga Sutras* are based around the principle of our actions impacting the world, such as *satya* (truthfulness), *asteya* (non-stealing), or *aparigraha* (non-jealousy). When we meet teachers who truly embody these traits (which are a lot easier to talk about than they are to practice), we are inspired to embody these values within ourselves. There is nothing more powerful than teachers who live what they teach, and few things more disappointing than the mentors who fall short.

The Hebrew month of Nissan represents a time of freedom. We can be free to recreate ourselves, remodel our behaviours, and get closer to our ideal self. Can you give birth to the true you inside, fulfilling the potential of whom you know you can be? Freed from the past, perhaps now is the time to start.

AHAREI MOT-KEDOSHIM
OFF THE MAT, INTO THE WORLD

KOSHER SUTRA   "You shall be sanctified" (Leviticus 19:2)
SOUL SOLUTION   Intensifying a spiritual connection
BIBLIYOGA POSE   Standing Leg Raise / *Utthita Hasta Padangustasana*, (p.70)
BODY BENEFITS   Builds balance and stability, tones the abdomen, firms
the legs

It can be tricky to find the balance between spiritual living and just getting on with life. These days, we have endless opportunities for "spiritual kicks", whether meditation classes, yoga retreats, shamanistic healing tents, and much more. This Kosher Sutra is about getting the balance to achieve that state of perfect holiness, to uplift our daily life into the spiritual realm.

The context seems obscure. The command to "be sanctified" or "be holy" comes in the wake of the death of the young priests Nadav and Avihu. Ironically, they died because they were addicted to spirituality and tried to get too close to God[1]. They went for too much of a good thing and paid dearly.

Yoga is about elevating our physical body into something greater, through the breath, movement, and moral principles[2]. The ideal is to find points of spiritual connection whilst practising on a yoga mat (which is why it's called "practising") and then maintaining that sense of connection throughout the "rest of the day. The

---

[1]   The Chassidic Explanation in Maamar Acharei Mot 5649, as quoted in Torah Studies, R
      Menachem Mendel Shneerson, adapted by Chief Rabbi J Sacks.
[2]   At least, according to the *Yoga Sutras*; although some scholars would argue that the moral
      principles are a later addition and that before the writings of Patanjali, yoga was more
      focused on asana (posture), vinyasa (breath-based movements), and pranayama (energy-
      breathing techniques).

nonprofit organisation, *Off the Mat and Into the World*, tries to do exactly this, using yoga "to ignite grass roots social change".

The Hebrew word for holiness, *kedushah,* actually translates as "separation"[3]. We achieve a state of sanctification and spiritual uplift by separating ourselves, whether through separating out time for meditation (e.g., a Bibliyoga class!) or putting aside a special day for a holiday or festival. The actual law "be holy" is mentioned immediately after a list of sexual prohibitions (e.g., "don't sleep with family members, animals", etc.) because a "holy" sexual relationship is considered to be one where two people are exclusively betrothed to one another[4].

Sexual energy is a key way to achieve holiness or to let it loose. The tantric aspects of yoga focus sexual energy through the increase of self-control. As you practice this Kosher Sutra's posture, the Standing Leg Raise, focus on breathing your energy through the base of your perineum to the top of your spine. Separate some time for this yoga practice and enjoy the benefits of increasing self-control and increasing the intensity of your spiritual connection.

---

3   "'Kedoshim—Be Holy!' This means, be separated." Sifra, Kedoshim, 1. "Wherever we find separation from arayot [forbidden sexual relations], we find holiness." Rashi 19:2. Translations: R Matis Weinberg.
4   The Talmudic formula for marriage is: "You are hereby betrothed [mekudeshet, from kiddushin] to me." The Talmud then comments: "Those words imply that [the husband] prohibits this woman to everyone as if she were consecrated [mekudeshet] to God." Kiddushin 2b.

AHAREI MOT-KEDOSHIM/ PESACH

A FAMILY BUSINESS

KOSHER SUTRA   "Don't get too close to your relatives" (Leviticus 18:6)
SOUL SOLUTION   Peace with your family
BIBLIYOGA POSE   Tree Pose / *Vrksasana*, (p.72)
BODY BENEFIT   Strengthens legs, increases balance

During Passover, I begin to ask what it truly means to be freed. The journey of Abraham was a profound mission, as he was told to leave his father's house, birthplace, and country so that he could become his own man and fulfil his destiny, free from the psychological trappings of his hometown.

During the festival of Passover, many children of all ages complete the opposite journey, as a three-line whip[1] is called for them to spend the festivities with their parents. In *Portnoy's Complaint*, Phillip Roth wrote that a "Jewish man with parents alive is a fifteen-year-old boy and will remain a fifteen-year-old boy until they die!"[2]. For plenty of people, the so-called festival of freedom is celebrated by going back to the house of bondage. Go figure. Eckhart Tolle wrote, "If you think you're enlightened, then go and live with your parents for a week". He wasn't kidding.

---

[1]   A three-line whip is a term originating from the British Parliament, describing an occurrence of each political party telling its Members of Parliament (MPs) to vote on a particular bill. A one-line whip is less imperative. British MPs don't actually use whips, at least not on official business, but what they do in their spare time is entirely their business.

[2]   Portnoy's Complaint p.109 [emphasis added].

I once tried to teach my parents yoga. The class lasted approximately five minutes. I finally realised that I have a lot of yoga to learn from them. Why? They give me the opportunity to practice every principle I am trying to teach, such as moderation [*brahmacharya* in the *Yoga Sutras*], being content with the moment [*santosha*], or being non-reactive and non-angry [*ahimsa*]. Spending time with one's family provides all of these wonderful opportunities…and many, many more.

The hilarious film *When Do We Eat*(subtitled: Sex, Drugs and Matzoh Ball Soup) shows a Pesach seder meal where grown children return to join their family and promptly resume old fights, old opinions, and old behaviours. Every Passover, my family says, "We were slaves but now we are Freed" (yes, and we are still amused every time we say it), but how many of us are truly freed? Do we have the power to free ourselves of the old behaviours that hold us back, of the old fears that we have carried through the decades? Are we still grown children, or can we truly be adults, able to maintain adult behaviours in the face of the emotional triggers that always used to get us sparked off?

"Don't get too close to your relatives" is the Kosher Sutra. It is a slightly free translation. The end of the sentence is, "Don't get too close to your relatives to have sexual relations with them: I am the Lord" (Leviticus 18:6). Hopefully the latter commandment is obvious, although the text then elucidates an entire list of forbidden relations, possibly because in the ancient civilisations, brothers married sisters and various other combinations[3]. Let us do a more palatable, contemporary reading of this. We are being encouraged to respect our family relationships, to be close with our families but not too close, to live the fine balance of

3   Chief Rabbi emeritus Dr. JH Hertz, Chumash, p. 490.

experiencing our Abrahamic freedom ("*lech-lecha*", i.e., get your distance and grow up), whilst respecting parents and coming home on occasion. 'Tis a fine, fine balance.

There's an old saying, "You can choose your friends but not your family", but I am not entirely convinced. From a spiritual perspective, we absolutely choose our parents. The kabbalistic concept of *tikkun* (literally, "repair") contains the idea that our purpose on earth is to fix the missing links within our soul— the things that we failed to achieve in a previous incarnation (if you go for the reincarnation aspect). Or, we are given the opportunity to be God's partner in creation by healing the parts of our soul that need to be healed through our work on earth. There is always something powerful to learn from our parents, even (God forbid) when people have had extremely rough upbringings. Oprah Winfrey was abused as a child but gained freedom from her parental *weltangshung* to become a highly successful teacher who has brought self-empowerment to millions of people.

This Kosher Sutra comes from the reading that begins with the death of Aaron's two sons. There are few things worse than the ultimate tragedy of parents having to bury their children, as I myself have seen in recent years, with three families I personally know having lost their children (the children all between the ages of 28 and 35). The healing from such loss, if indeed it ever comes, is slow and painful.

Despite the tragedy, God continues speaking with Aaron and his other sons as one unit, via Aaron's brother Moses (Leviticus

17:1). The family ties are strong, the Divine presence is channelled into the world through the work of a united family, and despite problems and obstacles, they still find a balance. When the family business is later challenged by their unruly cousin Korach, necessary actions are taken.

Of course we are ultimately supposed to leave our family. A physical reading of Abraham's instruction to "go forth from [his] father's house" takes us directly into the body. The Hebrew word for house, *bayit,* also refers to the body, albeit usually to the female body. We literally leave our parents' bodies as we go out into the world. The most famous person to try a return visit was Oedipus, and his path was disastrous. "Oedipus, Schmoedipus, what does it matter so long as the boy loves his mother?" one might ask. Well, it matters.

Have a peaceful experience. Know what it means to be freed.

EMOR – LAG B'OMER
BACK TO THE FUTURE

KOSHER SUTRA   "You must count until the day after seven weeks; fifty days" (Leviticus 23:16)

SOUL SOLUTION   Master time and master your world

BIBLIYOGA POSE Hero Pose / *Virasana*, (p.44)

BODY BENEFITS   Improves digestion, strengthens knees and ankles

Time travel is endlessly fascinating. Plenty of films have been made about it. We cried over The Time Traveller's Wife, marvelled at Back to the Future, and got a bit confused with Twelve Monkeys. The fantasy of time travel is that we might go back and change things to improve the present or at least to eradicate regrets. Simon and Garfunkel sang about lost time with more than a hint of reluctant regret: "Time, time, time, see what's become of me, as I looked around for my possibilities; I was so hard to please"[1]. The good news is, we have the technology to slow down time, and you don't need to be an Einstein to do it.

This Kosher Sutra is read in the context of *moadim,* which are festivals or "holy convocations", although the word *moed* actually means a kind of "specially appointed time", akin to a date. There are seven weeks in the counting of the *Omer,* an agricultural period that is underpinned with kabbalistic meaning. Day 33 of the Omer, *Lag B'Omer,* commemorates the end of the plague that killed the 24,000 students of Rabbi Akiva. It is a breath of fresh air in the middle of the counting, and we then continue the count until the climax of *Shavuot* in a couple of weeks, on Day 50.

---

[1]   A Hazy Shade of Winter by Paul Simon & Art Garfunkel.

One of the things I love about yoga is that it gives us the ability to slow down time. My teacher Edward has often commented on this, as we count our breaths in a way that is deliberately controlled and measured, and as a result, we clear our mind and can think more quickly. Time is relative, as Einstein taught, and by slowing down our mind we can actually think more quickly and gain more focus.

The stress of keeping to time is a human limitation. God isn't bound by it. Animals are not bothered by having to meet deadlines and instead work according to natural rhythm. Many predators will sleep by day and hunt by night, giraffes will go to the watering hole when lions aren't around, and there are no jungle tigers feeling overwhelmed at having to clear a brimming email inbox. We are the ones who have watches, schedules, and time-management programmes to try to get on top of it all. The rabbis stressed that time is within our control, and by controlling time we can reduce stress. The *Omer* is a simple count, day by day by day.

The focus here will be on counting breaths within the given posture and experimenting with the *pranayama* techniques of retaining the breath after the exhalation. Begin by taking the posture and counting 50 breaths. For the final 10 breaths, allow yourself to pause after the exhale, waiting until the breath "wants" to come back into your body. This technique further slows the mind and brings more clarity.

By mastering time, we become masters of our world, and much power of the mind sits within the breath.

EMOR
DATE NIGHT

KOSHER SUTRA   "These are the appointed festivals for God; you shall call
               them holy" (Leviticus 23:37)
SOUL SOLUTION Improved clarity and improved relationships
BIBLIYOGA POSE Bridge Pose / *Setu Bandha Sarvangasana*, (p.79)
BODY BENEFIT   Strengthens arms and legs, opens the heart space

One of the greatest afflictions of our age is the lack of exclusivity. There are high rates of marital infidelity among both men and women, placing an ever-growing pressure on the institution of marriage. Our once close-knit social circles now extend to lists of virtual friends that number in the hundreds or thousands. Worst of all, our incessantly texting generation has developed the inability to focus on the person we are with, as highlighted in a *New York Times* article entitled, *Keep Your Thumbs Still While I'm Talking To You*[1].

How does it feel when you are with a friend and they are not paying you full attention? Or if you are betrayed by a lover's affair? We do not like it. It's not the way we are wired, to enjoy such things. Often, though, the problem lies deep within ourselves, and, according to the yogis, we are in an age of mental distraction, which they called *vikshipta chitta* (a distracted mind) or *mudha chitta* (an infatuated mind). Oy.

Our Kosher Sutra: "These are the appointed festival times for God; you shall call them holy" (Leviticus 23:37). The term for

---

[1]   David Carr. "Keep Your Thumbs Still While I'm Talking to You". New York Times, April 15, 2011.

"appointed festival times" is *moadim,* which means "an exclusive time". I recently heard it translated as a "date with God".

It's date night!

The word *kodesh,* meaning "holy", is elsewhere defined as "separating something out to make it special". The Chernobler Rebbe and Sfat Emet explained that we can make time itself holy by marking it out for a specific reason such as a festival or Sabbath. In this sense we also make the private relationship with our spouses or partners holy because it's separate, dedicated, and exclusive. The commentator Rashi said that this word for holiness is often mentioned in conjunction with our intimate life (on Leviticus 19:2), and this is possibly because it is through sexuality that we have the greatest opportunity to be exclusive. Dating many people at once might sound fun, but it doesn't lead to good results.

How would a woman feel if she received a piece of jewellery from her husband, only to discover that he also bought an identical item for his mistress (and indeed to discover that he has a mistress at all)? The festival sacrifices are described four times in the following sentence as *milvad,* i.e., specially designated, or apart (Leviticus 23:38). In order to make a marriage special, it has to be exclusive, or the person will end up *levado;* the same word also means "alone".

The focus for our generation's yoga practice is *ekagratachitta,* meaning a one-pointed or singularly focused mind. As I have mentioned before in this book, a common objection I hear from would-be newcomers is, "I can't do yoga because my mind is all over the place". The appropriate response, which I actually rarely say, is, "You need to do yoga because your mind is all over the place". We learn to be at one with our thoughts, singularly focused in the moment. "If not now, when?" asked the sage Hillel.

In relationships, we can thrive spiritually, emotionally, and physically. When we learn to be focused in our thoughts and focused on the person we are with, we all benefit.

BRIDGE POSE /SETU BANDHASANA

"These are the appointed festivals for God;
you shall call them holy"

LEVITICUS 23:37

BEHAR-BEHUKOTTAI
THE LAW OF 7: REST & RECUPERATE

KOSHER SUTRA "The seventh year shall be a sabbath of rest for the land"
(Leviticus 25:4)
SOUL SOLUTION Create a powerful and sustainable future
BIBLIYOGA POSE Shabbat Pose / *Savasana*, (p.89)
BODY BENEFITS Aligns and grounds

Cause leads to effect. Physicist and Professor Stephen Hawking pushed out the scientific boat and boldly claimed that we are theoretically capable of traveling through time. Just as soon as we build a spaceship that can go close to the speed of light, it will be possible to move forwards but not backwards. The reason we cannot go back in time, according to the prof, is because it would be impossible for a scientist to travel into his/her own past and shoot themselves. In other words, although we can affect the future through our actions, we cannot remove the cause for a later event, because the law of cause and effect is immutable (again, presumably this theory will be provable once we have built said machine.)

This Kosher Sutra touches on a powerful law of nature that revolutionised the way that we see the world and act within it. The law of shemittah is the commandment to allow our agricultural lands to lie fallow once every seven years, thereby enabling the earth to rejuvenate and restore itself. It is described as a Sabbath for the land and makes sense in these days of sustainable and ethical living. Rashi later explained that shemittah is more than just a seven-year cycle to benefit the growth of our crops and, importantly, something that we ignore at our own peril[1]. If a farmer did not keep to the rule, he wrote, it could lead to the ruin of their business and eventual loss of faith, home, and livelihood.

Elsewhere we are taught to give everyone a break on the seventh day, including our employees and working animals. On a practical level, there is a danger otherwise of overworking everybody and long-term reduction of productivity. From a spiritual perspective, we are recognising that we are not the ultimate master but that there is a God above us, and we remember the process of creation through our working relationships, our business practice, and even the way we treat the land in its seven-year cycle.

The yogic posture *savasana* translates as "Corpse Posture"; I teach it as Shabbat Posture. More than just a resting posture, it is a space for rejuvenation and is as key to the overall practice of yoga as the more vigorous energy-burning movements. The *Hatha Yoga Pradipika* taught that "lying down on the ground, like a corpse, is called *savasana*. It removes fatigue and gives rest to the mind"[2]. Thus, we rest and rejuvenate—but without rest we are unable to rejuvenate. Today's culture encourages sleep deprivation through continual email and telephone contact, followed by ingestion of caffeine to stay awake, but medical studies continually prove that there is just no decent replacement for natural sleep. And what is the ultimate number of recommended hours' sleep? Between seven and eight. Of course.

My good friend Joshua Rudolph (the designer of this book!) taught me that, "we can't talk our way out of what we have

---

[1] Rashi commentary on 26:1.
[2] The Hatha Yoga Pradipika, 1:34, translated P. Singh, Sri Satguru Publications, Delhi, India, 1915, p. 37. As quoted by Gregor Maehle in Ashtanga Yoga: Practice and Philosophy, p.129.

behaved our way into". In other words, when we act a certain way, it is going to have consequences that we may not like, but we can save ourselves from those consequences by changing our actions in the first place. One way to do this is by applying the Kosher Sutra to today's posture and to begin to transform the way we live for the better. We have the opportunity to break free from the chains of unconscious living, to ensure that our actions bring sustaining growth to the world, and to improve the lives of those around us. Rest, recuperate, and then re-engage.

SHABBAT POSE / SAVASANA

"The seventh year shall be a sabbath of rest for the land"

LEVITICUS 25:4

BEHAR-BEHUKOTTAI
THE GOD OF SECOND CHANCES

KOSHER SUTRA   "If you walk...listen...do..I will give...give...give" (Lev 26:3-6)
SOUL SOLUTION Begin again!
BIBLIYOGA POSE Sun Salute A / *Surya Namaskar A*, (p.30)
BODY BENEFITS Gets energy flowing, gets you moving

We all have our personal restrictions: unhelpful behaviours that we've been repeating for years, relationships stuck in a negative cycle, or simply situations that we just wish were different. The quietly known festival *Pesach Sheni* is a subtle Biblical event that allowed people a second chance to bring the Passover offering if they had missed it the first time. No questions were asked about why they missed it the first time around, a month earlier. The Hasidic masters teach that this comes to remind us that we always have a second chance in life, no matter how bleak things may seem.

Yoga allows us to change our body, retrain our mind, and reprogramme our destiny. Such an undertaking isn't easy. The *Yoga Sutras* teach that "for those who practice with ardent intensity, *samadhi* [eternal bliss] is near" (1:21). The commentator Vyasa added that whoever practices with true intensity will not only enjoy *samadhi* but also "its fruit, which is liberation"[1]. That is, it offers the promise of nothing less than absolute freedom. Just because we've always done something, it doesn't mean that we always will. The past does not equal the future.

---

[1]   Translated and quoed in Gregor Maehle's Ashtanga Yoga—Practice & Philosophy, p.161.

And so, our Kosher Sutra: "If you will walk in My laws, listen to My commandments, and do them, I will give your rains in their time, the land will yield its produce, and the tree of the field will give forth its fruit" (Leviticus 26:3-6). The structure of the second verse mirrors the first: "[I]f you walk…listen… do, I will give…give…give". Rabbi Elimelech of Lizensk taught an astonishing explanation of this. He explained that the words "walking in my laws" refers to righteous people who have the ability to become partners with God, annul negative decrees, and actually change the future[2].

A lazy new-age approach teaches us that it is all about a positive attitude, but this is only halfway correct. It is about action. Hamlet did not sit back and just think happy thoughts when he wanted to fix a problem in the family, but did something about it when he uttered, "The play's the thing wherein I'll catch the conscience of the king" *(Hamlet 2:ii)*. We need to do something, we need to engage, we need to get involved. Pick your prize, and go for it. Turn and face the change.

---

[2]   "Such a Tzaddik is a partner with God in creation: God decrees and the Tzaddik abolishes" (BT Mo'ed Katan 16b); "any judge who gives a true verdict becomes a partner with God in creation" (based on BT Shabbat 10a). The Zohar explains that the Torah Sheb'al Peah, usually translated as "Oral Torah," actually refers to someone who has become a true Baal Peh, i.e., "Master of their mouth"—so following the laws involve becoming a master over our own words and deeds (Zohar, Vayikra 113a). As quoted in Mipeninei Noam Elimelech, p. 204–205.

NUMBERS

SHOULDERSTAND/ SALAMBA SARVANGASANA

"The holy service was upon them, carrying it on their shoulders"

NUMBERS 7:9

NUMBERS
HEAD HELD HIGH

KOSHER SUTRA   "Count the heads of the assembly" (Numbers 1:2)
SOUL SOLUTION   Achieve greatness whilst remaining grounded
BIBLIYOGA POSE Warrior II / *Virabhadrasana II*, (p.101)
BODY BENEFITS   Strengthens the legs, ankles, shoulders, and arms

Humility is a challenging mountain to climb. We all know when we spot false humility, and it reeks like a week-old fish. It is so obviously inauthentic when someone is going out of their way to appear humble and we know that they do not really mean it. Equally, somebody who is actively pushing themselves into a pit to achieve humility can effectively make themselves ineffective.

Our Kosher Sutra appears when Moses is asked to count the heads of all the tribes, and Rashi (Numbers 1:2) explains that the reason for the regular census-takings is because "God loves counting" the people. He is reminding us that we all count and that we all matter, regardless of what we are doing or achieving on any one day. Even though someone may feel alone or uncared-for, they are still dear to their parents, and their presence on the earth makes a difference.

Ramban comments the phrase *su'u et Rosh*, or "count the heads", can be translated as "lift up the heads" or "raise up the heads" (Numbers 1:2). The Hebrew word *su* appears when Joseph utters his dream-reading prophecies to the baker and butler; the latter has his head lifted up in a noose whilst the former receives

321

a job promotion[1]. This Kosher Sutra's Bibliyoga posture is to hold your head high, to "walk tall", but the challenge is how to claim our rightful status whilst maintaining humility. How can we walk tall and not become hoisted on our own petard, so to speak?

The primary aim of yoga is to lift our mind from the mire and confusion of earthly living. "Yoga is the suspension of the fluctuations of the mind"[2], taught Patanjali, and a large part of suppressing these fluctuations is to move beyond our ego.

This can appear to be an apparent contradiction: to walk with our head erect and yet free from ego. But who was arguably the greatest teacher of all time? Moses. Who was the most humble person of all time? Moses. Less is more.

Rabbinic wisdom teaches that true humility is an ideal quality[3], but the Hebrew phrase is *shfal ruach,* which we can translate as a "humbled breath" or perhaps a "lowered breath".

If we continue to connect our breath with the base of our spine and fully exhale using the abdomen, we can use this focus to support our head that is being held high. This humbled breath actually helps us lift up with dignity and humility. By keeping our head raised and our breath grounded, we can achieve humility and nobility, pursuing and achieving our true potential.

---

[1]   .With thanks to my teacher Rabbi Dovid Ebner for sharing this idea.
[2]   Yoga Sutras 1:1.
[3]   Ethics of the Fathers, 4:1.

NASO

A JEALOUS GUY

KOSHER SUTRA   "If a spirit of jealousy comes over him" (Numbers 5:14)
SOUL SOLUTION Emotional security and inner strength
BIBLIYOGA POSE Side-Angle Pose / *Utthita Parsvakonasana*, (p.56)
BODY BENEFITS Improves digestion, tones arms and legs

Jealousy is one of the most difficult emotions ,as it can twist, obsess, and compress our thoughts. Our Kosher Sutra refers to the husband who suspects that his wife has had sexual intercourse with another man. Although she is innocent until proven guilty, the Biblical law establishes the *sotah* process to clarify her innocence (although it is fairly high stakes, because if she is lying then her stomach will explode…but we are not focusing on that today). The male-female relationship is often compared to the connection between God and the Jews, and the sages say that the Jewish people were compared to a wife who was unfaithful on her wedding night because of the way that they created the Golden Calf so soon after the "wedding ceremony" of Mount Sinai[1].

One of the key principles of the *Yoga Sutras* is *aparigraha*, which translates from the Sanskrit as "non-jealousy" or "non-coveting"[2]. But what can you do if you are actually feeling jealous or even overcome with this emotion? We can do a closer reading of the Hebrew; the phrase for a spirit of jealousy is *ruach kin'ah*, which

---

[1]   This rather challenging image is hinted at all over, in Hosea Ch. 2, Jeremiah, Shir HaShirim, and more.

[2]   Sanskrit: aparigrahasthairye janmakathamtasambodhah; translation: "one who is not greedy is secure. He has time to think deeply. His understanding of himself is complete." Yoga Sutras II.39

we might translate as a "breath of jealousy" or even a "breath of possessiveness".

As we apply our Kosher Sutra, we can notice how we are breathing. We are unlikely to have jealous thoughts running through our mind and simultaneously find that our breath is free and unencumbered. Just as jealousy comes from trying to hold on to something that is not meant to be ours, we can hold in a breath that needs to be freed. By resuming the complete pattern of the respiratory cycle, we can cleanse further toxins from our body through the exhalation.

The Torah teaches the importance of quickly processing the emotion of jealousy through the *sotah* ritual because jealousy is unhelpful for our minds, our bodies, our relationships, and our spiritual life. The *Yoga Sutras* go one stage further and extol the "one established in non-greed/non-jealousy against knowledge of past and future births". When are able to become truly at one with the moment, we experience true liberation.

P.S. Yes, yes, yes, of course there is a whole discussion to be had about the feminist implications of the *sotah* issue, which involves establishing whether a woman is innocent by making her drink a ritually-prepared mixture..but what about a woman who considers her husband to be unfaithful? That is a great question—but for another day.

NASO – SHAVUOT
LEVATOR SCAPULAE!

KOSHER SUTRA   "The holy service was upon them, carrying it on their shoulders" (Numbers 7:9)
SOUL SOLUTION   Ground emotionally, raise your spirits
BIBLIYOGA POSE   Mountain Pose / *Tadasana*, (p.51)
BODY BENEFIT   Strengthens legs and improves stability

I once came up with a fairly arcane joke. It will be amusing perhaps to 10 people in the world: those who know both *Harry Potter* and physical anatomy. Here goes: A wizard walks into a bar, raises his wand high in the air, and says, "Levator scapulae!"

Allow me to explain. The levator scapulae is the muscle that raises (levator) the shoulder blade (scapulae). Yeah, yeah, it's too late to laugh now. Our Kosher Sutra takes us into the desert, where the priests are saddled with the task of carrying the tabernacle *(mishkan)* on their shoulders. Rabbi Elimelech of Lizensk explained that it is through our shoulders that we connect with other people and bring divine blessing into the world.

The Kabbalah associates the right shoulder with lovingkindness *(hesed)*, because we will often give gifts to others or perform deeds by leading with the right hand. Rav Elimelech connects another Hebrew word for shoulder, *shechem*, with Abraham, who "arose in the morning" to do goodness[1].

---

[1]   Mipenenei Noam Elimelech on Naso.

A balanced physical yoga practice contains *asanas* (postures) that open our shoulder blades and get them into the correct alignment. In Mountain Pose, we focus on planting the shoulder blades into the back and lengthening the neck. If you've ever experienced any tightness in your neck, such as the inability to turn your head right or left as the nerve pinches, try drawing your shoulder wblades downwards, thereby freeing the neck to be mobile.

There is a midrash that when the Levite priests carried the tabernacle on their shoulders, it was so light that it actually lifted them. Rav Matis Weinberg teaches that when the Temple was built in Jerusalem, the Hebrew people no longer had to carry anything physical, but their job was to carry a tune. What is the most powerful thing about a tune? If you start singing a tune and you do not feel good at the beginning, the tune will eventually lift you[2].

On Shavuot, we remember climbing the mountain and receiving enlightenment. Dance, sing, learn, and be lifted high through all of your holy actions.

---

[2] Thanks to Raphael Zarum for this teaching.

BEH'ALOTECHA
KNOCKED UP

KOSHER SUTRA   "Carry them in your bosom" (Numbers 11:12)
SOUL SOLUTION   Soothe troubles, connect with a caring God
BIBLIYOGA POSE Extended Child's Pose / *Balasana*, (p.88)
BODY BENEFITS   Relaxes, calms, heals, and nourishes

One night I truly succeeded in tapping into my feminine side: I dreamt that I was pregnant. Initially I was quite happy at the realisation that I would be having a baby but then experienced some pain in my lower back. This was uncomfortable, as I was somewhere towards the end of the second trimester and I was feeling quite heavy. But my concern about any back pains soon disappeared as I suddenly realised there was a bigger problem on my hands: How on earth was I going to deliver my baby?

Yoga continually seeks to balance the masculine and feminine energies within us. A couple of texts refer to the way that yogic practice can "devour time"[1] and take us back to the start of creation when Male and Female were all One (according to the *Hatha Yoga Pradipika*). "It is the reintegration of the primordial androgyne, the conjunction in one's own being, of male and female—in a word, the re-conquest of the completeness that precedes all caution"[22], writes one commentator. We have both masculine and feminine aspects to our persona and yoga helps us balance the these two different energies. On a basic level, the receptive, opening yoga movements tap into a feminine energy whilst the driving, forward motions are more masculine. Humans

---

[1]   Hatha Yoga Pradipika IV, 16–17.
[2]   Mircea Eliade, Yoga: Immortality and Freedom, p. 271.

are made in the "image of God", says the Book of Genesis; "male and female He created them" (Genesis 1:27). This Kosher Sutra leads us towards reconnecting with our feminine aspects and in turn towards connecting with the feminine aspect of God (*Shechina*).

In our narrative, the Children of Israel are finding life difficult and complaining to Moses. He wearily turns to God; "Did I conceive of this people? Did I bear them, that you should say to me, 'Carry them in your bosom as a nurse carries an infant'?" There is something unnecessarily sarcastic about Moses' complaint. God's response is to create more prophets who will share the burden with Moses, although the initial plan of 70 new protégés turns out not to be brilliantly successful, and there are only two fresh prophets who really cut the mustard. Their names are Eldad and Medad. Once we dig a little deeper, we will see that their names actually hold a coded message for us. A few verses earlier, we read about the *mannah,* a food from above described as tasting "like dough kneaded with oil". The commentaries teach that the taste was excellent and differed from day to day, depending on who was eating it. Rashi (12th century) provides a raunchy reading of the word *"l'shad"* which, rather than "dough" can actually be read as "breasts" (on Leviticus 11:9). The midrash raises the stakes further saying that "just as a nipple is of one variety and changes to many varieties [that is, the infant tastes many flavours from it], so would the manna change into whatever Israel wished" (Sifrei 89).

The names of Eldad and Medad hold a clue as to one mode of connecting with God. They share a final syllable that comes from the Hebrew *dud,* meaning "nipple". They were bringing forth prophecy that is like the milk of God, meant to nurture us and support us. Elsewhere Moses and Aaron are also described as being "two breasts"[3]. This Kosher Sutra is about re-tuning to feel our feminine aspect, and the posture, Extended Child's Pose, is an opportunity to feel the support of the ground and to contemplate the supportive and nurturing aspect of God. We are reminded of the child inside all of us, and that nurturing that can be felt when we are embraced by the *Shechina,* the feminine aspect of God.

---

3   Shir HaShirim 4:2. Rashi brings the more detailed explanation on this.

EXTENDED CHILD'S POSE / BALASANA

"Carry them in your bosom"

NUMBERS 11:12

BEH'ALOTECHA/ SHAVUOT

MAJESTY

KOSHER SUTRA   "Seven candles shall cast light" (Numbers 8:2)
SOUL SOLUTION Unify body and soul, be majestic
BIBLIYOGA POSE Mountain Pose / *Tadasana*, (p.50)
BODY BENEFITS   Grounds, strengthens

There are few things that rival the peaceful end of a successful yoga class. By "successful", I mean the state when all of the students are feeling physically invigorated (or calmed, depending on the intention of the day), everyone's minds are fully alert and their bodies are feeling that deep sense of calm. In short, we all feel tremendous.

Our Kosher Sutra comes from the passage where God presents Moses with a vision of the menorah, the seven-branched candelabra. Kabbalists explain that each of the candles actually represents one of the sefirot, the Divine attributes that reside within our body. The Ben Ish Chai (1832–1909) explained that: "When we call the *sefirot* 'light,' that does not mean that they are like the light that we see with our eyes. Rather, since our intellectual grasp is limited by our physical body and we cannot truly grasp the nature of spiritual things, we call the *sefirot* by the term light, since light is among the more important and lofty sensations. It is also the more spiritual of sensations"[1].

---

[1]   As quoted in Mipenenel Noam Elimelech, translated Tal Moshe Zwecker, p. 221.

By unifying the seven lights into one candelabra, we can discover hints towards a deeper process. Rabbi Elimelech of Lizensk explains that "the menorah alludes to the final complete unit. The ideal is to bring everything to complete and total unity since this is the root and fundamental purpose of everything. Understand this"[2].

This is why I love Bibliyoga—because it gives us tools to elevate our body and soul. Rabbi Elimelech could have been quoting directly from the *Yoga Sutras*. The purpose of yoga is to bring an internal unity among our body, mind, breath, and soul. We aim to heal our body through *asana* (posture), *vinyasa* (movement), *yama*, and *niyama* (moral principles/actions), and eventually reach a state of *samadhi* (enlightenment) when we are fully at one with ourselves and the world around us. There are many different kinds of yoga to suit different kinds of people, including Karma Yoga (through actions), Bhakti Yoga (yoga of love), Raja Yoga (the Royal path of yoga through meditation), and Hatha Yoga (i.e., your "standard" yoga class). Nonetheless, all are concerned with unification.

The festival of Shavuot is the culmination of seven weeks' preparation, and according to the Kabbalah, every week corresponded to a certain emotion and a specific part of the body[3]. On the final day of *Malchut,* we find our inner leader, our deep sense of grounding, and prepare to share our light with the world.

---

[2] Ibid.
[3] The Tikkunei Zohar explains that the week of Malchut ("nobility", "dignity", "leadership") corresponds to the mouth, possibly because it is through our words that we lead others.

SHELACH
GRASSHOPPERS

KOSHER SUTRA   "In our eyes, we seemed like grasshoppers"(Numbers 13:33)
SOUL SOLUTION   Positive thinking, positive feeling
BIBLIYOGA POSE   Backbend / *Urdhva dhanurasana*, (p.82)
BODY BENEFITS   Strengthens the back, abdomen, and digestive system

The new age mantra used to be to "Think Positive" but many of us gave up on that a long time ago. It is too difficult, too hard, too much work, especially when we are continually bombarded with the slings and arrows of outrageous emails and 24/7 media coverage, usually of bad news.

Our Kosher Sutra is taken from the incident when Moses sent 12 spies to scout out the land of Israel, and the majority of them returned with negative reports. They decided that the mountain was too high to climb, the inhabitants of the land too big, and the challenges too great. "In our eyes, we seemed like grasshoppers, and so we were in our eyes", they said (Numbers 13:33).

Today's yoga practice will reconnect us with our higher purpose. By focusing on our breath and concentrating on a visual point in front of our eyes, we work towards what the yogis called ekagrata, or single-point meditation. In the Bibliyoga practice, this is becoming truly *echad*, or one with the moment. We will use our eyes to bring focus, our breath to bring stillness, and our mind to bring healing for any negative thoughts that have held us back thus far. Try the pose, and stay confident in your abilities to conquer the world ahead of you.

When the yogic sage Patanjali wrote the *Yoga Sutras*, he incorporated elements of Samkhaya philosophy with a semireligious focus. What had previously been primarily a secular philosophy that denied the existence of God was soon to be combined with another stream of thought: Patanjali introduced the notion of *Ishvara*. Although it has its roots in Hindu idealism, *Ishvara* is expounded in the *Yoga Sutras* to direct one to reach a personal idea of God through one's asana and vinyasa practice. This is part of yoga's huge appeal to people of all spiritual (and non-spiritual) persuasions: it has a very clear reach towards a Higher Power in a non-dogmatic approach. Just as the rabbis taught that there are many paths to God, Patanjali taught that there are numerous yoga postures that will take us there as well.

SHELACH
POTTER AND THE SECRET
KABBALISTIC VESSEL

KOSHER SUTRA   "Send out for yourself men who will scout"(Numbers 13:2)
SOUL SOLUTION   Find your feet, follow your mission
BIBLIYOGA POSE Triangle Pose /*Trikonasana*, (p.54)
BODY BENEFITS   Strengthens legs

The aim of the mystic is to find meaning in the mundane, to uncover deeper secrets behind the texts that are in front of our very eyes. Thus, when Moses sends scouts or spies from the desert to explore the Land of Israel, the famed Kabbalist Sfat Emet reads a far deeper meaning into it.

He explained that on a spiritual level, we are all *shlichim,* or scouts/spies, and that the underlying essence of our life is to fulfil a Divine mission. He quotes his grandfather who said, "Every person is created to do a tikkun, a task that improves the world, for which he is uniquely qualified and which only he can do"[1]. The challenge is that we have to figure out our higher purpose, and only then can we put in the effort to pursue the task for which we alone are called to achieve.

The Sfat Emet taught that another word for scouts/spies is *cheresh,* which means "secretly", but the same Hebrew letters spell cheres, which means "vessel". It appears that the scouts disguised themselves as potters when they went on their mission, so that they would not be suspected.

---

[1]   Quoting the Chiddushei HaRim, p. 205.

How do we get in tune with our higher mission?

One approach is through meditation, to fine-tune our body. The essence of a physical yoga practice is to purify the body through asana (posture) to be a worthy vessel of the soul. From a yogic perspective, we start with the heavy external aspects of the pose and proceed to work on an ever-more subtle level. The yogis described five energetic layers to our body called the *koshas*. (Yes, that really is the Sanskrit word!) We use other yogic techniques to control the flow of our energy, including *bandhas* (energy locks), and *mudras* (seals).

Furthermore, during a yoga practice, it is as if each of our limbs were a scout, heading into a different direction on behalf of our mind and soul. In this Kosher Sutra's posture, *Trikonasana/* Triangle, our hands and feet point in different directions, reaching outwards and literally expanding our potential.

There is a profound aspect to this. From both yogic and kabbalistic perspectives, we can view ourselves as simple earthenware vessels, like those made by a potter. Our vessel contains the riches of *prana* (Sanskrit for "energy") and *neshama/nefesh* (Hebrew for "breath/spirit"). By reducing our ego and creating space within, we become vessels of the Divine and are on our way towards great achievements.

KORACH
LORDING IT

KOSHER SUTRA   *"Why do you lord yourselves above us?"* (Numbers 16:3)
SOUL SOLUTION   Peaceful relationships
BIBLIYOGA POSE Warrior I/*Virabhadrasana I*, (p.60)
BODY BENEFITS   Strengthens legs, teaches stability and focus

Think back to your last argument—specifically, the last argument you won. How did you feel afterwards? The problem with arguments is that their dynamic always involves anger, whether explicit or passive-aggressive. Do we feel better after winning? Maybe we do for a few minutes, while the ego is yet riding high, but it never does much good for the relationship. Personally, I usually find myself apologising before the sand has dropped to the bottom of the hourglass.

A key principle of yoga is *ahimsa*—the avoidance of violence, or non-violence (*Yoga Sutras* 2:35). We will come on to that again in a moment.

Our Kosher Sutra is spoken by Korach, the first cousin of Moses, who is jealous that Aaron and his younger brother have become God's chosen spokespersons. Korach begins with seemingly innocuous questions about why there is not a more democratic process for appointing the leadership, but the midrash makes it clear that Korach's agenda is to place himself and his followers at the helm of the Hebrews[1]. Korach's and his proponents'

---

[1]   Midrash Tanchuma Chapter 2. Korach's questioning over mezuzot suggests that his interest is in proving his point and elevating his status rather than finding genuine answers and bringing peace or furthering the spiritual aims of the community.

argument is driven by ego and vanity—and destined for failure, as the ground eventually swallows them up.

The rabbis later commented on the case of Korach, saying that any argument that isn't for the sake of heaven will be doomed to failure[2]. In other words, an argument that is ultimately self-centred and driven by self-aggrandisement can never end in success. We might win the battle but will ultimately lose the war.

This does not mean that we cannot disagree or enter a space of conflict when there is a legitimate reason for dispute. The Kosher Sutra is teaching that it will be futile if it is an argument driven by ego. How can we tell if our argument is ego-driven? We cannot. We are human. So what is the solution? The answer is to avoid arguments, to avoid violence wherever possible. That doesn't mean we should blindly turn the other cheek if someone is pursuing us, but neither should we go actively slapping the cheeks of others.

The posture here is Warrior One. We all have elements of the warrior within us, and emotions of anger and discontent can arise at any time. Our egos are easily inflated and reactive by nature, and once we have overcome the habitual impulse to fight back, then we are on the way to purifying the husk of this difficult nut to crack. It isn't easy; I speak from personal experience. Please join me as we breathe through the posture together and bring more peace into our troubled world.

---

2   Ethics of the Fathers, 5:21.

CHUKAT
STRIKING THOUGHTS

KOSHER SUTRA   "Moses struck the rock twice with his staff"(Numbers 20:11)
SOUL SOLUTION   Achieve results with ease
BIBLIYOGA POSE Staff Pose/*Dandasana*, (p.36)
BODY BENEFITS   Strengthens the back and shoulders, tones the legs

Life is not a self-development seminar. We are not given an official induction, and there is no operations manual. One thing we do get, however, is feedback. Whenever we mess up, we find out about it sooner or later. If we listen really closely to the feedback, we can start to function more effectively.

Moses is given one instruction: speak to the rock, and it will give out water, which will presumably stop his crowd of people from complaining. The instruction is simple: "Take the staff and assemble the congregation, you and your brother Aaron, and speak to the rock in their presence so that it will give forth its water. You shall bring forth water for them from the rock and give the congregation and their livestock to drink" (Numbers 20:8). Speak to it. How hard can it be?

Yoga is about achieving maximum results with minimum effort. There is a principle of *asteya*, of refraining from stealing, that encourages us not to force our bodies into positions that are not truly "ours" but only to receive them when ready. This is easier said than done; we may quickly find ourselves in a competitive frame of mind, for instance, when practising yoga with a group of people as opposed to when we are on our own. Regardless, there is always a price to pay when we try to force a result.

The only reason to steal something is if we feel that that there is a lack of abundance, fearing that we will not have enough unless we take matters into our own hands. Moses did not heed the simple instruction and instead hit the rock twice. Perhaps he felt that water would not come from the rock purely by speaking to it, and perhaps he felt imbued with more confidence by beating it[1]. But nobody responds well to repeated beatings, whether metaphorical, verbal, emotional, or literal. The practice here is Staff Posture, to ground ourselves and consider how we can be more trusting in situations where we are fearful and feel there is not enough flow of abundance. When we can truly enter a place of trust in a Higher Power, we will find we have all the water we need[22].

---

[1] There is a completely different way of looking at this, in that Moses may well have known exactly what he was doing and used it as his excuse for a graceful retirement.

[2] Rashi explains that the Children of Israel would have left the desert and entered the land immediately if Moses had not hit the rock (Rashi on 20:12). Because of this one action, Moses had to forfeit the thing he had been working towards for the best part of his career.

BALAK

MIDSUMMER NIGHT'S DREAM

KOSHER SUTRA   "Those whom you bless are blessed and those whom you curse are cursed" (Numbers 22:6)

SOUL SOLUTION Release the flow of blessing

BIBLIYOGA POSE Horse Stance Breathing /*Ujayi Pranayama*, (p.34))

BODY BENEFITS Purifies air entering the body

How can we turn a negative into a positive? Balak, the King of Moab, hated Israel, and he sent the inspired prophet Bilaam to curse them. Bilaam rode his donkey on the mission, but the donkey saw an angel blocking his path and swerved off the road. Bilaam beat the animal three times, and eventually the donkey started talking, asking his master, "What have I done to you?" (Numbers 22:28). Bilaam too eventually got ready to curse the Jews but found that whenever he tried to say a curse, blessings instead poured from his mouth. These blessings were so powerful that they are still said today.

This story reads like a fantasy. In the play *A Midsummer Night's Dream*, the character of Bottom wakes up to find his head has suddenly changed into that of a donkey, much to the bemusement of his friends Snout and Quince:

Snout
O Bottom, thou art changed! What do I see on thee?

Bottom
What do you see? You see an asshead of your own, do you?

Quince
Bless thee, Bottom! Bless thee! Thou art translated!

Bottom
I see their knavery: this is to make an ass of me...[1]

Shakespeare, too, has blessings pouring from one of the characters. The Baal Shem Tov taught a powerful interpretation of the verse: "When you see the donkey of your enemy collapsing under its load and are inclined to desist from helping him, you shall surely help along with him" (Exodus 23:5). He explained that *chamor,* the Hebrew word for donkey, can also be translated as "material matter" *(chomer).* This verse can be read as referring to the way we treat our body, teaching us not to treat ourselves as the enemy, not to beat ourselves up, and not to afflict or punish ourselves.

The path of yoga begins with *ahimsa,* or non-violence, and it is essential that we avoid doing violence to ourselves at all stages (*Yoga Sutras* 2:30). Harmful thoughts can leave us depressed, whilst self-denial can leave us feeling ill or damaged. But there is more to be revealed on the path of the yogic donkey, namely, a way that we can actually raise ourselves to a higher level, turning pain into pleasure and curses into blessings.

There are two men who began their journeys on a donkey: Abraham and Bilaam. The sages considered how we can learn from both of them and taught that someone who is amongst the "disciples of Abraham" should have "a good eye, a meek spirit, and

---

[1] A Midsummer Night's Dream III:i

342

a humble soul", whilst the "the disciples of the wicked Bilaam" have an "evil eye, an arrogant spirit, and an inflated soul"[2]. There is more than one way to ride a donkey.

A Bibliyogic reading takes us deeper into the soul, and the Hebrew phrase for a meek spirit is *nefesh shfalah,* which can be translated as "a contained or low exhale"—in other words, controlling our breath. "Humble soul," *ruach nemuchah,* can also be translated as "a sweet breath" or "pleasant breath."

The practice of *pranayama* (breath control) is central to yoga and allows us to focus our mind and achieve inner stillness. When we are truly still and focused, it is usually possible to see the blessings all around us and even consider how apparent curses might contain hints of blessings. If we are able to apply this pranayamic breathing in the midst of madness, we can find stillness in the most turbulent times and use this for strength and sanity.

Bilaam set out to cause trouble and curse Israel but ended up becoming an ass and praised the people for their ability to "get up like a lioness and rise up like a lion" (Numbers 23:24)[3].

This strength of a lion is within the reach of all of us; it is far better than being a donkey. Be strong, be blessed and be a blessing to others.

---

[2] Ethics of the Fathers 5:19. Rashi makes the connection between Abraham and Bilaam in his commentary on the Torah, noting that both were prophets and both began their journey with a donkey, albeit with very different outcomes. Bilaam has a "haughty spirit" according to Rashi, which is presumably why the Mishnaic sages were inspired to write this comment in Ethics of the Fathers.

[3] elavi can be translated as "lioness," or sometimes, "lion." It is one of the six Biblical words for "lion."

.01 .02

HORSE STANCE BREATHING /UJAYI PRANAYAMA

"Those whom you bless are blessed and those whom you curse are cursed"

NUMBERS 22:6

PINCHAS
COMM-UNITY

KOSHER SUTRA   "God of the breath of all flesh" (Numbers 27:16)
SOUL SOLUTION Self-mastery
BIBLIYOGA POSE Revolved Side-Angle /*Parivrtta Parsvakonasana*, (p.58)
BODY BENEFITS   Improves digestion, helps with balance

Moses, recognising that he will not see his mission through to fulfillment and lead the Children of Israel into the promised land, realises he will have to appoint a successor. At this point, he calls God by a rarely used name: "God of the breath of all flesh, set a man [i.e., leader] over the congregation". Sometimes translated as the "spirit" of all flesh, the word Moses uses is *ruach,* which is the Godly breath that hovered over the waters of creation.

This is a curious name, "God of the breath of all flesh", and one way of reading it would be to see the context of phrase. There is another occasion when it is also mentioned, in recent memory from the Korach incident: "O God, *Source of the breath of all flesh!* When one man sins, will You be wrathful with the whole community" (Numbers 16: 22). "Let the Lord, *Source of the breath of all flesh,* appoint someone over the community" (Numbers 27:15). In both instances there is a connection between God-as-breath-of-flesh, and community, or congregation (in Hebrew, the word is *edah*).

Our Bibliyogic process of spiritual development is about self-mastery and increasing the control we have over our thoughts and our body. We can read the Kosher Sutra figuratively, as we aim to connect to a sense of God within and become a leader of our internal "congregation", in other words, gain mastery over the fragmented aspects of our personality. Through self-control and discipline we can achieve greater heights, pursue goals, realise ambitions, and transform our life for the better.

The Hebrew word for "community", (again, *edah*) can also be translated as "witnesses". In this case, our limbs and thoughts can also be understood as witnesses to our mind. According to holistic medicine, when we have a mental illness, this may well be reflected by physical symptoms, and the body can subsequently be healed through the mind and spirit. Elsewhere God is referred to as the "healer of all flesh".

When the sage Patanjali introduced the idea of God into yoga practice, he wrote that yoga is achieved through "surrender to, or worship of, the indwelling omnipresence" or "persevering devotion to God" (*Yoga Sutras 2:321*). This indwelling presence of God is the idea of "God of the breath of all flesh", and through our *asana* and *vinyasa* practice we aim to realise this sense of divinity within.

Moses recognises the person who is the ideal protégé; his name is Joshua ben Nun, and he is described as a man "in whom there is spirit/breath" (Numbers 17:18).

The physical practice of yoga revolves around the movement of *prana* (breath), and we're told that "mental equanimity may be gained by the even expulsion and retention of energy"[1]. Focused *pranayama* - directed energy - allows us to become master of our bodies and minds. This is certainly easier said than done, but continual practice allows us to strengthen our world from within.

---

[1] Yoga Sutras 3:15

.01

.02

.03

REVOLVED SIDE-ANGLE /PARIVRTTA PARSVAKONASANA

"God of the breath of all flesh"

NUMBERS 27:16

PINCHAS
DON'T LOOK BACK IN ANGER

KOSHER SUTRA   "Should the name of our father be obliterated because he had no sons?" (Numbers 27:4)

BIBLIYOGA POSE   Standing Forward Bend / *Uttanasana*, (p.68)

SOUL SOLUTION   Freedom to live your potential

BODY BENEFIT   Stretches hamstrings and improves posture

We are all born into the world with different challenges. Some have a hard inheritance from their families, be it years of exposure to limiting beliefs or just being born on the tough side of the tracks. Others face obstacles later on in life. We can choose to be held back by these seemingly insurmountable difficulties or to tackle and overcome them.

This is a tale of two families. The sons of Korach are born with a father who is a rebel and outsider, an ego-driven man who eventually dies in a pit of public shame. Meanwhile the daughters of Tzelophehad are orphaned and quickly find that without a brother to inherit their father's land, they face the challenge of homelessness, because Biblical law does not allow women to take control of property. What were they to do?

Yoga teaches us to push beyond our past stories, to live in the present moment. The *Yoga Sutras* encourage us to free ourselves from attachments to fixed ideas, however strong they may be, and to work hard at identifying what our real limits are. When we engage with "faith, energy, memory, and concentration"[1], we

---

[1]   Rashi on Numbers 33:1

move one step closer to achieving a state of blissful, unlimited living.

The sons of Korach go on to become successful priests and turn their father's negative legacy into a positive future, while the daughters of Tzelophehad achieve a victory for Biblical feminism and have the law changed so that they can rightly inherit the land.

How do you believe you are held back? How would you like to be free? Try taking a moment to release an unhelpful belief or behaviour and move one positive step towards realising your unlimited future.

MATTOT-MAASEI
42ND STREET

KOSHER SUTRA   "These are the journeys of the children of Israel"
                (Numbers 33:1)
SOUL SOLUTION Journey to your spiritual home of stillness
BIBLIYOGA POSE Pigeon Pose / *Eka Pada Rajakapotasana*, (p.48)
BODY BENEFITS Opens the hip flexors, lengthens the hamstring muscles

I invite you to reflect on this question: how far have you travelled in the last year? This could be in geographical distance or personal growth, literal or metaphorical.

The Children of Israel have 42 stops on their journey from Egypt to the Promised Land, and each of the 42 stops is listed meticulously, as if to remind them of God's mercy along the way in that they were not abandoned[1]. Throughout the 42 stops, they resisted against continuing but kept moving forwards nonetheless. The Baal Shem Tov says that we experience 42 internal journeys through our life as we move from slavery to freedom.

Continually travelling is not easy. It's not always about getting from A to B. It can be tiring and exhausting, both physically and emotionally.

There is a certain yogic journey that differs from the path of Hebrew wisdom. The *Bhagavad Gita* and other yogic texts tell of a phase in life where someone becomes a *sanyasin;* old men renounce earthly desires and leave their families to become travelling yogis, seeking enlightenment as they go from town to town, free from the shackles of daily life. This isn't the Jewish way; it is enough of a journey to find this inner peace at home. Or maybe that is why the *sanyasin* leave in the first place. Who knows?

The yogic journey that makes sense is the daily visit to the yoga mat and the practice of daily prayer (*tefilla* in Hebrew). Visiting a yoga class or place of worship once in a while is fine, but if you try practising yoga on your own for 42 days in a row, or even 10 days for that matter, you will notice real progress. I have experienced immense journeys without ever leaving home.

Life has a habit of taking us through unexpected stops along the way, and we can either face them with resistance, screaming that we are not getting what we want, or we can journey within and discover a place of trust, stillness, and oneness with God.

Rav Nachman of Bratslav recommended daily *Hitbodedut* meditation, where we walk in nature and talk with God in a free-form one-to-one prayer. As we journey within, we journey home and realise that we are closer to our destination than ever before.

MATTO T- MAASEI
HIGHER AND HIGHER

KOSHER SUTRA "If someone takes a vow...according to whatever comes from his mouth he shall do" (Numbers 30:3)
SOUL SOLUTION Connect with the higher realms
BIBLIYOGA POSE Sphinx Pose / *Bhujangasana,* (p.76)
BODY BENEFIT Opens the back and shoulders

The 17th century play *Tartuffe* ridiculed people who feign religious virtue. Although Moliere's comedy was brilliantly written and finely observed, it was almost immediately banned by King Louis XIV due to the influence of the Archbishop of Paris. The latter threatened excommunication for anyone who saw the play, performed in it, or even read it.

The Kosher Sutra comes from the words of Moses, who discusses the issue of an oath, a *shavua.* Sincerity with our words is such an important virtue that it is a key part of Biblical lore, and there are large consequences for breaking a vow. As a result we are encouraged to avoid making vows wherever possible. Another word for an oath is *neder,* and the opening service of Yom Kippur, namely, Kol Nidrei, is framed around releasing ourselves from all vows that we may have made. We are encouraged to be true to our word, and we can do this without making grand public statements; far stronger is the person who can be quiet and sincere.

There was a revered yogic teacher known as The Mother (1878–1972) who ran the Ashram for famed guru Sri Aurobindo in

India for over fifty years. The Mother taught that sincerity is the "fundamental virtue to be cultivated" on the spiritual path and placed it at the centre of her yogic practice. Sincerity means not just being honest with other people but with ourselves. This is often the hardest path of all. She explained that we should "never try to deceive oneself, never let any part of the being try to find out a way of convincing the others…never to let anything pass, telling oneself, 'That is not important, next time it will be better.' Oh! It is very difficult…Try—try, to see, try for half an hour, you will see how difficult it is!"[1]. The words of our mouth count.

How do we develop this inner part of our yogic practice? The rabbis had an interesting practice. It is a set of physical tools that can effect an inner transformation. The Talmud gives two examples of specific choreography for prayer that work from the outside in, starting with the physical body and ending with our heart. The sages taught that when somebody bows during the standing prayer (*Shemoneh Esrei*), they should bow low enough that their heart is directly opposite the ground[2]. In other words, when we get down, we really have to get down in full-body prayer. This is the foundation of the Bibliyoga approach.

If we do not fully involve our body, there is a price to pay: "One who does not bow during the thanksgiving prayer [modim, in Shemoneh Esrei], after a while his spinal column is transformed into a serpent"[3]. We can therefore learn that the involvement of the spine is central for developing humility and sincerity, but if

---

[1]   p. 31, The Sunlit Path
[2]   "When one bows at the word baruch (in Shemoneh Esrei), he must bow low enough to see an issar, a coin opposite his heart" (Berachos 28b), Mipeninei Noam Elimelech, translated by Tal Moshe Zwecker
[3]   Talmud Bava Kama 110a

we don't fully engage the spine, then our body and mind will become locked into a place of arrogance, which is a barrier to spiritual growth. *Kundalini* yoga is based around the idea of a "serpent energy" in the spine, and it is fascinating that the rabbis came to a very similar conclusion as the yogis.

Our relationship with God is ultimately a private path. Certain ways of dressing and behaving can certainly help stimulate the path, but inner growth is something we have to cultivate. A deep yoga or other spiritual practice rarely happens overnight but by using this tool of developing sincerity, we can continue to take ourselves higher and higher.

STAFF POSE/DANDASANA

"Moses struck the rock twice with his staff"

NUMBERS 20:11

DEUTERONOMY

MOUNTAIN POSE/TADASANA

"You have dwelt long enough at this mountain"

DEUTERONOMY 1:6

DEVARIM - TISHA B'AV
LOVE CHANGES EVERYTHING

KOSHER SUTRA   "You have dwelt long enough at this mountain" (Deut. 1:6)
SOUL SOLUTION   Get motivated and bring healing to the world
BIBLIYOGA POSE Camel Pose / *Ustrasana*, (p.80)
BODY BENEFITS   Strengthens backs, releases thighs

Meditation and prayer form a crucial part of life because they connect us to our higher selves and to the source of our creation and help keep us from getting lost in the mire of everyday life.

Moses gets ready to motivate the people by reminding them that God spoke to them on Mount Sinai and that God had said, "You have dwelt long enough at this mountain. Turn and journey…" (Deuteronomy 1: 6–7). Whilst it is important to spend some time on our metaphorical mountains and even to revisit them on a regular basis, we cannot heal the world if we stay on the hilltop.

Rashi's interpretation was that God was reminding the people that they had spent time on the mountain and that they should also reflect on the things they had achieved and how far they had grown. It was not enough to just sit and "be spiritual"; rather, the essence of spiritual growth is interacting with the world.

One of the core principles of the yogic philosophy developed in Patanjali's *Yoga Sutras* is that the individual yogi affects the world through their actions. Although *asana, vinyasa, and pranayama* are central to one's personal yogic and spiritual development, so too are *yama and niyama,* the interpersonal ethics. Patanjali's view of yoga was firmly focused on healing and improving the world as a result of what we discover on the yoga mat. Whilst it may be admirable to develop a strong yogic practice or meditation technique, those around us will benefit when we are able to put these principles into practice.

The lowest point of the Hebrew calendar is the 25-hour fast of *Tisha B'Av.* The day commemorates the destruction of the Temple in Jerusalem, which was possibly the most significant tragic and negative event in Jewish history. The rabbis teach that this came about as a result of *Tsinat Chinam,* or baseless hatred between people. The ultimate healing for *Tisha B'Av* comes about not through the traditional routes of prayer, repentance, and giving charity (*tefilah*, *teshuva*, and *tzedakah*, respectively), but rather, the rebalancing comes through *Ahavat Hinam,* which is baseless or boundless love.

All you need is love, but it has to be translated from emotion to action.

TISHA B'AV

TALES OF LOSS AND LOVE

KOSHER SUTRA   "Why was the Second Temple destroyed?...Because of hatred without rightful cause" (BT Talmud Yoma 9b)

SOUL SOLUTION   Rebalance the world through unlimited love

BIBLIYOGA POSE   Lotus or Seated Pose / *Padmasana*, (p.96)

BODY BENEFIT   Opens the hips

We have all experienced the loss of something precious to us. Whether of a treasured relative, pet, friend, or important keepsake, we know what it is to suddenly feel a sense of loss. What is more challenging is when we have lost something but don't even realise it is missing.

Tisha B'Av, the ninth day in the Hebrew month of *Av*, marks a 25-hour fast to commemorate the destruction of the Temple in Jerusalem. These hours offer a powerful opportunity to find something that we are all missing.

"The Temple" can be read as a code for "Universal Balance". The Temple was seen as a centre of spiritual light for the entire world, and there is the description of window spaces in the brickwork that were designed back to front compared to most windows of the era: Rather than being wide on the outside and thinner on the interior side, instead, in order to better capture light on its way in, the Temple window openings were built in the reverse. That is, the windows were wide on the inside and narrow on the outside, because the building was seen as a container of powerful spiritual light that emanated to the entire world.

How ironic that the (geographical) place which had the potential to be a light unto the nations is now in the heart of an age-old political conflict. But it is never too late. The rabbis teach that when the Temple is eventually rebuilt, the entire world will experience an unprecedented level of harmony and balance. This is Isaiah's vision of the wolf living with the lamb and swords being beaten into ploughshares; we will see peace in our days.

Goodness knows we need it. The 25 hours of *Tisha B'Av* fasting are a time to remind ourselves of what we are missing: Universal Balance. Of course, we distract ourselves from remembering. Every email, Tweet, Facebook update, and SMS message serves to numb us to the balance that our society is missing. But we are still missing it, whether we are numbed to the fact or not.

Yoga is all about balance. When the mind is in pain, a yoga practice will be thrown off-centre. When we are internally distracted, it is hard to focus within the postures. When our ego drives us to get into postures we are not ready for, the body usually responds with a sharp sense of pain. When we are lethargic and avoid engaging in a practice, our body usually sends us a clear message that we are not doing enough. There is nothing easy or laid-back about yoga: if we choose to listen closely to our practice, the four sides of our mat reveal our negative traits, our bad behaviours, and show us what we are avoiding. Our postures reveal what is missing in our lives—for example, we may need more discipline or we may need more relaxation, depending on the individual—and once we have identified what is missing, we can start rebuilding from there.

How do we achieve Universal Balance?

To find an answer, we shall look to the Talmudic statement that explains how we lost it: "Why was the Second Temple destroyed?…Because of hatred without rightful cause" (Talmud Yoma 9b).

The concept of *Tzinat Chinam*, of baseless hatred, is something you may well be familiar with. But how many of us have overcome it? If this is what threw the world out of balance, it is also what can bring everything back into line. Just as every posture has a counterposture, there is a counterpart to baseless hatred: *Ahavat Chinam* is unlimited love.

Easy to say, hard to do: to truly love members of our family who annoy us, to be genuinely friendly to members of our community who rub us the wrong way, to open our arms to people who don't express any warmth, to step down from attacking (even in thought or speech) nations whom we are taught to hate, and most difficult of all, to switch off that internal voice that says, "You're not enough", and to love ourselves. Easy to say, hard to do.

As I have mentioned throughout this book, the first stage of the yogic journey is ahimsa, or non-violence—to truly step down from the fight, whether it be internal or external.

The *asana* to be practised during the 25 hours of *Tisha B'Av* is to sit on the floor whilst focusing on what we are missing. How would your world be better if you had peaceful relations with all of your family, your community, your enemies? How would your world be better if you had continual peace within?

"We look forward to the time when the Power of Love will replace the Love of Power. Then will our world know the blessings of Peace" (William E. Gladstone, 1809-1898).

If you are reading this Yoga Sutra during Tisha B'Av, I wish you an easy and meaningful fast. And otherwise, wishing you ease in achieving Universal Balance.

VA'ETCHANAN – TU B'AV
HUNGRY EYES

KOSHER SUTRA   *"Ascend the hill and lift your eyes"* (Deuteronomy 3:27)
SOUL SOLUTION Increase happiness
BIBLIYOGA POSE Dancer's Pose / *Natarajasana,* (p.74)
BODY BENEFITS   Stretches the shoulders and chest, improves balance

Humans are motivated by visual stimuli. We have entered an era that is more led by sight than ever before through pictoral advertising, and it is estimated that we are exposed to over 200 commercial messages each day. The problem is that this relentless eye-candy can often lead to unhappiness rather than deep fulfilment. We see pretty things (the latest iPhone, hybrid cars, you-fill-in-the-gap), we cannot always have them, and this can leave us frustrated.

Our Kosher Sutra is all about the eyes. Moses is denied his request to see the inside of the land that he has led the people towards (Deuteronomy 3:26) but told to look, "lift [his] eyes west, north, south, east" (Deuteronomy 3:27) to view from afar, because his successor Joshua will take the people into the land which he sees (Deuteronomy 3:28). In case they forget the miracles that they have seen (Deuteronomy 4:9), the people are later warned against "lifting their eyes to heaven" to worship stars or objects (Deuteronomy 4:19), lest their hearts follow the things they see[1] and they be led astray. Although we can imagine that Moses would be heartbroken about not getting to experience the land that he sees, we don't hear of this supposed pain and can safely

---

[1]   Rashi, ad loc.

assume that he learned to be content with what he was given, rather than lusting for more.

Ancient yogis taught the notion of *drishti,* that is, the visual focus in any yoga posture. Every single *asana* has a *drishti* and this is the place where our eyes are supposed to be looking whilst practising an *asana*. It can be a fixed point ahead of you, the tip of your nose, or even an imaginary internal point (e.g., centre of forehead). The *drishti* is a clear meditative focus that completes every posture, and if our eyes are wandering during a yoga practice, then we are not completely "there".

There is a value to controlling what we look at. The Kabbalists stressed the importance of this: since our mind is the ground for creating images in advanced meditation, we have to be careful what images we put in there. On the other hand, neither are we expected to wander through life with our eyes shut, and there is a daily blessing for opening our eyes.

In his comic-heroic poem *The Rape of the Lock*, 18th century English poet Alexander Pope reflected on the way that men have been swept away by visual beauty, losing their senses and acting like fools. He wrote:

> *"Say why are beauties praised and honored most,*
> *The wise man's passion, and the vain man's toast?*
> *Why decked with all that land and sea afford,*
> *Why angels called, and angel-like adored?*
> *Why round our coaches crowd the white-gloved beaux,*
> *Why bows the side box from its inmost rows?*

How vain are all these glories, all our pains,
Unless good sense preserve what beauty gains..."[2]

Indeed, we can attempt to keep everything in the balance, enjoy what our eyes see but maintain the "good sense" that Pope advocates. The newly revived festival of Tu B'Av marks a time when unmarried women would dance in the fields wearing white dresses and wherein single men were encouraged to take a look and propose marriage to the one who took their fancy.

Lest the virile men think that looks were everything, the women gave this warning: "Young man, lift up your eyes and appreciate whom you are selecting [to marry]. Don't look at our beauty. Instead, look at the family [from which we descend]"[3].

In his poem *Ode on a Grecian Urn*, John Keats (1795-1821) wrote that "beauty is truth, truth beauty", the Talmud reminds us that beauty is more than skin deep and that we should see with more than just our eyes alone. For all the talk of seeing, this is also the reading of *shema,* when the Israelites are invited to connect through listening (Deuteronomy 4:6).

Although we cannot have everything we see, we can learn to lift our eyes, focus our *drishti* on what's important and develop the art of looking beyond the surface to what really matters.

---

2   The Rape of the Locke, by Alexander Pope, Canto V.
3   Mishna Ta'anit 4:8. The full text reads: "Young man, lift up your eyes and choose wisely. Don't look only at physical beauty - look rather at the family - 'For charm is false, and beauty is vanity. A God-fearing woman is the one to be praised...' ("Mishlei"/Proverbs 31:30)".

.01

.02

DANCER'S POSE / NATARAJASANA

"Ascend the hill and lift your eyes"

DEUTERONOMY 3:27

EIKEV
HEART TO HEART

KOSHER SUTRA   "Circumcise the foreskin of your heart[s]" (Deut. 10:16)
SOUL SOLUTION   Create space for peaceful relationships
BIBLIYOGA POSE   Bow Pose / *Dhanurasana*, (p.78)
BODY BENEFITS   Brings flexibility to spine and neck

We have the possibility to bring lasting peace to the world by acting with compassion. The key to liberation, according to Moses, is to "circumcise the foreskin of your hearts and stop being stiff-necked" (Deuteronomy 10:16). It takes practice to be truly flexible when it comes to stretching our neck and seeing things from another person's perspective, to truly open our heart when it might otherwise be closed.

The most frequent phrase I hear people saying before I teach new students is, "I'm not good at yoga". They are, of course, referring to the fact that they do not feel physically flexible or able to touch their toes. This isn't the essence of yoga; instead, we are using external poses as ways to deepen our meditation and to cleanse our body. The goal of the practice is to refine our character, to become one with God, and to be able to act with compassion in every moment[1].

The Biblical commentator Rashi explained that "circumcising the foreskin of the heart" means to remove the "blockages and coverings of your hearts". The Kosher Sutra mentions the plural "hearts" rather than "heart" because we are in this together. This

---

[1]   The yamas and niyamas, that is, the principles of interpersonal development, are listed before the physical postures (asana) in the yoga system described by the Yoga Sutras. .

369

is a group exercise. If you are open and I am closed, then we can't create a peaceful relationship. This is about working to release the unhealthy blockages that stand in the way of strong connections.

The Hebrew word for blockages is *otem*, which actually means "seal". Classical yoga has all kinds of seals for keeping pranic energy sealed within the body[2], to allow us to keep in the good energy and flush out the bad stuff. We can use this yogic meditation practice to reflect on our personality and become aware of our negative behaviours. One aspect of yoga that continually amazes me is how it perpetually brings a spotlight on those aspects of our personality that need to be refined. Regardless of whether you can touch your toes or not, the whole yoga process enables us to grow on many levels.

Our hearts can become closed, and our hearts can become covered. Salty diets, high cholesterol, and an abundance of red meat can add an additional "covering" to our heart to stand in the way of realising our potential. Stress, anger, and negative feelings will further compound this problem, and it has been scientifically proven that psychologically induced stress is the cause of many illnesses.

Be blessed with an open heart and the flexibility to turn your neck to see the potential around you. Let's flood this world with peace and compassion.

---

[2]   As in the New Year's greeting, Gmar Hatima Tova, wishing people that they should be sealed in the Book of Life on Rosh Hashanah. The Yogic "seals" include Mulah Bandah and Uddiyana Bandah, which are energy locks around the perineum and abdomen

EIKEV

EAT LOVE PRAY

KOSHER SUTRA   "Eat, be satisfied, and bless..." (Deuteronomy 8:10)
SOUL SOLUTION Lift up your heart
BIBLIYOGA POSE Cow-Face Pose/*Gormukhasana*, (p.41)
BODY BENEFITS   Opens the heartspace

To almost everyone's surprise, praying has come back into fashion. It is called different things, because "praying" is no longer a word in vogue, but whether you call it "manifesting the Universe", "setting an intention", or "submitting to a Higher Power", these are all pretty much the same thing.

A key element of yoga practice is gratitude, and that is the essence of our Kosher Sutra: to appreciate the food we have and to say "Thank you" for it. But that is not enough. The essential thing is that we actually enjoy it. *V'savata*, says Deuteronomy, "and you shall be satisfied". We actually have to be happy (what a drag...).

The yoga teacher Aadhil Palkhivala, one of Iyengar's senior teachers and the founder of Purna Yoga, focuses on the attitude of bliss in his book *Fire of Love*, where he highlights the "inner smile": "Illness is a function of the loss of the inner smile... hidden deep within the veiled recesses of the Heart Centre is a smile that emerges from a sense of connectedness with all things. This unifying feeling is true love, far removed from the physical...Bliss is the connection with the heart and is not to be confused with excitement. Most of us equate bliss with a

371

thrill, and that is part of the problem. Bliss is a calm inner state, the manifestation of inner connectedness, while excitement is merely a passing fever"[11].

When we find this satisfaction, we automatically lift ourselves to a higher place. A few lines on from our Kosher Sutra is a caution lest we miss out the vital element of saying "Thank you" ("Then your heart will be lifted up and you will forget God" [Deuteronomy 8:14])—and we find ourselves in a place of arrogance. There is a difference between opening our heart centre, our heart *chakra,* the place the Kabbalists called *tiferet*— and becoming arrogant. In most yoga *asanas,* we are aiming to open and lift our heart and to do so in a spirit of gratitude and humility.

There is a famous Talmudic teaching imploring us to enjoy the world around us, saying that if we get to heaven and we have not enjoyed our time on earth, we will be asked why. So what are you waiting for? Go and have a good day already. Just don't forget to say "Thank you".

---

[1]   Fire of Love, p. 201-202

RE'EH

EVERYTHING'S ALL RIGHT

KOSHER SUTRA "You will dwell securely" (Deuteronomy 12:10)
SOUL SOLUTION Peace of mind and body
BIBLIYOGA POSE Inclined Plane/*Purvottanasana*, (p.40)
BODY BENEFITS Strengthens arms, wrists, and shoulders

Everybody likes security. We all want to know where the next meal is coming from, that there is a roof above our head, and that we are going to be safe in our old age. This is why we buy insurance policies, pay mortgages, and invest in pension retirement plans. Nevertheless, there are some basic facts we often choose to ignore: that our time on earth is limited, that we are not actually in control of the bigger picture, and that we are eventually going to die.

Our Kosher Sutra is spoken by Moses to the Israelites. He says that when they come to the land, they will dwell in security and that there will be safety from their enemies. This must have been a huge relief after a 40-year journey. They were safe at last. But we can imagine they had their doubts. How often have we had the rug pulled out from under us? When did you last feel completely secure, only to find that the wind changed and you were thrown into a storm of uncertainty?

The *Yoga Sutras* suggest that a yoga pose should be *sthirasukham*, or "secure and pleasant"[1]. We get into a difficult physical posture and then have to find a way of making it secure and pleasant.

---

[1] Yoga Sutras 2:46

This takes practice but it becomes possible over time, in even the most difficult of postures.

The title of the earlier Kosher Sutra, *Vayishavtem Betach,* means "you will dwell securely" (Deuteronomy 12:10) but could also be understood as "you will be seated securely". The Hebrew *Vayishavtem* comes from *yoshev,* meaning "to sit". The Sanskrit word for a yoga pose, *asana,* also means "seated" Our challenge is to sit securely wherever we are in life, whether it be in a challenging job, having a difficult conversation, or attempting an uncomfortable backbend.

How can we find this emotional and physical security if we feel turmoil around us? We find it by sitting still, breathing deeply, and connecting with God. The commandment of "dwelling securely" is based on the belief that we are not alone and that we are guided by a Higher Power. If we can fully align our body to find this secure and pleasant way of sitting—sitting with whichever activity we are doing at the time— then we can move into a place of deep joy[2] by knowing that everything is going to be all right.

---

[2] This state of joy is described two verses later: "And you shall rejoice before the Lord, your God, you and your sons and your daughters and your menservants and your maidservants, and the Levite who is within your cities, for he has no portion or inheritance with you" (Deuteronomy 12:12).

RE'EH

C B YOND

KOSHER SUTRA   "I set before you today a blessing and a curse"
               (Deuteronomy 11:26)
SOUL SOLUTION Freedom from pain through non-attachment
BIBLIYOGA POSE Supported Shoulderstand/*Salamba Sarvangasana*, (p.86)
BODY BENEFIT   Calms the nervous system

It is almost impossible to know who wins the lottery. What I mean is, the person who has the correct numbers and receives the prize money is not always "the winner". Dr. Steven J. Danish, Professor of Psychology at Virginia Commonwealth University in Richmond, has spent over a decade counseling lottery winners who find themselves facing huge problems after receiving their sudden windfall.

Stories abound of how the sudden abundance of money can magnify existing problems, with families descending into jealousy, arguments, and self-destruction. We may think that we have lost by not winning, but we may well have won by "losing". There are ominous words that form our Kosher Sutra, as Moses relates the words of God: "I set before you today a blessing and a curse". A list of blessings and curses follows, but Chassidic tradition reveals an underlying switcheroo. Likutei Torah teaches that the inner side of every expression is a blessing[1].

The yogis were keen to stress the importance of non-attachment, or *vairagya*, because it allows us "mastery over the mind and

---

[1]   "When I break your supply of bread, ten women shall bake your bread in a single oven" (Leviticus 26:26) is presented as a serious curse for times of distress. The Kabbalists explain that the "ten women" refer to the ten sefirot qualities of the soul that will be revealed through the "oven" of the body. Maybe this is where the phrase "bun in the oven" comes from...

realisation of the true self"(*Yoga Sutras* 1:16). As we get into a yoga posture, we focus on the actions rather than the result. It matters not if we can get into a handstand or drop into a backbend. What is important is that we commit to the action. We do not have to complete the full pose but neither are we free from refraining to start it. Underlying everything is a sense of ultimate trust (in Hebrew, *emunah*), and this can be attained through non-attachment. Another way of thinking about this is the idea of process versus results. If we focus on the process, the results will take care of themselves. An actor cannot force an audience to feel something, but if he/she fully commits to playing the scene, then the effect on the audience will take care of itself.

Think of an occasion when you had a huge disappointment but later realised that it was an unbelievable source of blessing. I was disappointed when I got waitlisted and then rejected from both the universities of Cambridge and Harvard (now that's *yichus!*), but in retrospect I would not have had it any other way. I'm even grateful for the times I sustained a couple of injuries through a somewhat reckless yoga practice, because it led me to learn new forms of meditation and alignment-based *asanas* that totally transformed my understanding of yoga. We cannot always see the bigger picture, but then, our job isn't to run the world. We just have to commit our best to each passing moment, to enjoy each breath, and let the result take care of itself.

The yoga practice for this Kosher Sutra focuses on getting into the postures but not forcing the results. Practice non-attachment, *vairagya,* and notice emotions of pleasure or disappointment as they arrive. Practice being the observer, revel in the process, and enjoy freedom from the mind's limited perspective.

SHOFTIM
THRONE POSITION

KOSHER SUTRA   "You say, 'I will set a king over myself'" (Deut. 17:14)
SOUL SOLUTION Achieve real change
BIBLIYOGA POSE Headstand / *Salamba Sirsasana*, (p.84)
BODY BENEFITS Improves focus and brain functioning

These are days of achievement and accomplishment. The month leading towards the spiritual new year, Rosh Hashanah, is a time for active reflection and dynamic change. We ask the questions:

- How effective have I been in the last year?

- How well have I used my personal talents in the world?

- What is the mark I'm trying to leave on the world?

- What do I need to improve?

- How can I be the best version of myself?

Our Kosher Sutra, "You say, 'I will set a king over myself'", refers to when the Israelites arrived in the land and they requested that a king be appointed over them so that they could be like the nations around them. They had three in close succession—King Saul, King David, and King Solomon—but it was not always the smooth ride that the people imagined. King Saul went crazy and paranoid, attempting to kill the young David on various occasions. King David faced numerous attempts at a coup d'état, in-fighting, and external wars, while King Solomon put the country into huge debt in order to finance his building projects, leaving the country in a state of disorder and on the brink of civil war.

Ruling is difficult, and we find this when it comes to self-discipline. We all have the option to rule over our own body, and Kabbalah identifies the mouth as the place of *Malchut,* the divine energy *(sefirah)* of Kingship[1]. The mouth wields a great deal of power of the body, through the food we eat, the words we speak to others, and the stories we tell ourselves. We can create powerful relationships through speaking healing words, or we can use our lips to create a hell on earth. The Kabbalah also identifies the top of the head as the place of *keter,* the crown. The mystics saw the top of the head as a place of receiving Godly energy, which is possibly why men and married women cover their heads during prayer and many religions prescribe covering the head.

The yogis discuss the path of Raja Yoga, or royal yoga, which allows us to fulfil our spiritual potential through our body. Headstand, *Sirsansana,* is referred to as King of the Postures[2]. We literally place the crown of the head on the ground and demonstrate mastery over our balance, as we determine exactly how prepared we are to work with gravity, rather than letting it just get us down. Our reading corresponds to the Hebrew month of Elul, a time of spiritual sensitivity when we are told that God is more accessible to us, like a king who goes into the field to meet his people[2]. We can apply this Kosher Sutra as an opportunity to remind ourselves that we can indeed take control over our own body and create the life we desire. We can also choose to seek help from a greater source above, as a further reminder that we are never alone.

---

[1]   BKS Iyengar, Light on Yoga," p. 189–190.
[2]   Likkutei Torah, Re'eh 32b.

SHOFTIM
SCAREDY-CAT

KOSHER SUTRA   "Let him return to his house, that he should not cause his
                brother's heart to melt, as his heart" (Deuteronomy 20:8)
SOUL SOLUTION   Banish fear, breathe in the light
BIBLIYOGA POSE Mountain Pose / *Tadasana*, (p.50)
BODY BENEFITS   Strengthens legs, improves posture

As a child I used to sit with my father and watch M*A*S*H*, the original medical comedy-drama that was set in the Korean War. One of the funniest characters was Corporal Klinger, who was so desperate to get discharged from the army that he claimed insanity by dressing up in women's clothing. He was not actually a transvestite and his plan never worked, but he did wear a fine selection of dresses and hats.

If Klinger had been in the Biblical army of Israel, he would not have had to go such outrageous sartorial lengths and would have been sent straight home. Our Kosher Sutra comes at the end of a list of people who do not need to go to battle: those who have just built a house, planted a vineyard, recently betrothed a woman but not consummated the relationship—or are just plain scared.

Nachmanides explained that this was not just a suggestion or an easy get-out clause; it was a commandment! ("If you don't want to fight, we don't want you in the army"). He went deeper to explain that the reluctant soldier is a spiritual and physical liability because their fear represents a lack of ultimate faith in

379

God, and as a result, they could actually encourage the loss of a battle by weakening the spirits of other soldiers.

A little fear can go a long way. The yogis explained that fear is one of the key obstacles to attaining enlightenment. *Abhinivesha*, translated as "fear of death" or "clinging to life", is one of the *kleshas* (obstacles) that ignore our spiritual side and cause us to over-identify with our body[1].

The traditional reading of *Shoftim* in August/September is a period of intense spiritual growth, punctuated by the psalm, "God is my light; who shall I fear?" (Psalm 27:1). We focus on revealing and seeing Divine Light and reducing fear.

If we allow just one fear to drive us, we can weaken our internal system. Everybody knows somebody who spends their life avoiding the pursuit of their dreams because they are held back by fear.

Just as the fearful soldier was banished from the army, we need to banish these fearful thoughts and be open to receiving the Light from beyond.

---

[1]   Yoga Sutras 2:3.

KI TEITZEI

WHEN TWO TRIBES GO TO WAR

KOSHER SUTRA "When you go to war against your enemies" (Deut. 21:10)
SOUL SOLUTION Banish negative thoughts
BIBLIYOGA POSE Warrior I/*Virabhadrasana*, (p.60)
BODY BENEFITS Strengthens arms and legs

The British band Culture Club sang it best back in the 1980s: "War, war is stupid. People are stupid. Love means nothing in some strange quarters". True though these lyrics may be, we all go to war on a regular basis.

While we may fight with family and friends, the most painful battle is the one that rages inside our heads. Our full Kosher Sutra reads as follows: "When you go to war against your enemies and the Lord your God delivers them into your power...." The Sfat Emet, a 20th century commentator, noted that we have negative thoughts that create fight-like conditions inside our heads. The *yetzer hara* is the slew of self-destructive thoughts that can stop us from living our life with joy and ease.

A key yogic text is the *Bhagavad Gita*, and it begins on the battlefield, although the commentaries make it clear that this war is representative of our internal war. The aim of all the warriors is to realise the sense of yoga—yoga means "oneness", and the objective is to see beyond the earthly turbulence and to realise that all is one. This takes practice, which is why all spiritual practices need to take place on a daily basis. Even if it is just 10 minutes of yoga, or 5 minutes of prayer or meditation, do what you can manage—but whatever you do succeed in accomplishing will reap great rewards.

There is a time to go to war, and that time is now: to beat our negative thoughts and stamp them out. But how? Negative thinking is often based around our limitations. ("How am I going to achieve X, Y, or Z?") We can win this battle by staying engaged and continuing to "fight" it. The idea of staying within a yoga pose when we are tired and feeling the fatigue is that we train ourselves to overcome the inner voice telling us to relax and drop out of it. We go to battle with our limiting thoughts and overcome them. The battle takes place inside, which, after all, is where all wars start, but this is a battle we can win when we commit our mind and body to the fight.

KI TAVO
TO INFINITY AND BEYOND

KOSHER SUTRA   "Blessed shall you be in your comings and blessed in your goings" (Deuteronomy 28:6)
SOUL SOLUTION See life from the infinite perspective
BIBLIYOGA POSE Mountain Pose / *Tadasana*, (p.50)
BODY BENEFIT   Improves balance, improves perspective

Can we ever know whether something is truly good for us? There are stories of lottery winners who thought their dreams had come true in winning before discovering that the sudden shower of wealth would come to tear their lives apart. Other people find that a seemingly awful occurrence, such as a sudden change of job, relationship, or physical comfort, results in a new lease of life that would become an ultimate gain. I have certainly cried real tears over painful situations that, in retrospect, changed my life for the better, and years later, realised I would have cried if I had been granted my original wish!

Our Kosher Sutra talks of extreme blessings, but it is preceded and followed by awful curses. There is an incredibly powerful Chassidic teaching that insists that at a future time of global enlightenment, we will see how all of the apparent "curses" in our lives were actually blessings. This is not easy to accept; but consider a time when something bad happened to you that you later became cognisant of as invaluably good.

The yogic technique of *dhyana* is an outwardly focused meditation that allows us to expand our consciousness and connect with the bigger picture. Our breath, movement, and posture are all focused on connecting the infinite part of ourselves with the infinite part of the Creator. We are limitless, we are bigger than our bodies, and we are bigger than our minds, but we need to stretch ourselves on a daily basis to keep our perspective as broad as possible.

Perhaps this is why the curses and blessings had to be given on a mountain. When we can step out of our daily life we can see the bigger view and consider for the moment that perhaps we do not actually know everything. However big we feel, we cannot always see the bigger picture.

NITZAVIM-VAYEILECH
WE ALL STAND TOGETHER

KOSHER SUTRA   "You are standing this day before God" (Deuteronomy 29:9)
SOUL SOLUTION Develop inner strength to take stand
BIBLIYOGA POSE Triangle Pose / *Trikonasana*, (p.54)
BODY BENEFITS   Relieves anxiety, aids digestion

Most of us take for granted the ability to stand. But what happens when we find it difficult to stand up? Our body might be in physical pain and our legs could be aching. Sometimes it is hard to stand up for ourselves if we are under attack. There can be challenges when standing up for what we believe in if we lack confidence, or it may be hard to stand up for others when we hear their pain but feel unable to do anything.

One focus of Bibliyoga is providing tools that will develop both inner and outer strength. This Kosher Sutra speaks of the Israelites' covenant with God, and they are all drawn together as one, whether they are rich or poor and regardless of whether they hold high or low status in society. In today's practice, we are going to consider how Bibliyoga can help us become stronger in our mind, body, and spirit, when it comes to taking a stand.

There are a group of standing yoga postures that have the benefit of creating physical strength and balance, but they also create emotional and psychological equanimity. Triangles, Standing Leg Raises, Forward Bends, and Mountain Poses all work our legs but make us focus on having a strong foundation that supports the rest of our physical activities. Everyone knows that a building has to have a firm foundation if it is going to stand and that a tree needs deep roots to survive, so why should it be any difference with humans?

This information does not necessarily help when we are having trouble standing—whether literally or metaphorically. There is a secret in our Kosher Sutra. The Hebrew says, *atem nitzavim*, or "You [pl.] are standing". The word choice is never accidental. It can be hard to stand alone, but we are stronger when we stand together.

This Bibliyogic approach provides a powerful tool for healing. Our pain is reduced when we stand together: practising yoga with a friend, meditating with a community, or dancing with a room full of people. In the words of King Solomon, "If two lie down together, they will keep warm. But how can one keep warm alone? Though one may be overpowered, two can defend themselves. A cord of three strands is not quickly broken" (Ecclesiastes 4:11-12). The ancient wisdom is as relevant as ever, but it only works when we stand together.

If our legs are hurting, we can see a physical therapist. If our heart is aching, we can talk to others. And if others are about to be knocked down, we can stand by them when they need a friend. There is never any reason to stand truly alone.

HAAZINU – 10 DAYS OF TESHUVA
TWIST AND SHOUT

KOSHER SUTRA   "You crooked and twisted generation" (Deuteronomy 32:5)
SOUL SOLUTION Return to your potential
BIBLIYOGA POSE Supported Backbend / *Urdhva Dhanurasana*, (p.82)
BODY BENEFITS Relieves tension in the back, calms the nervous system

When he was four years old, my nephew looked a little distracted during one of our weekly Skype calls. He had not quite adjusted to the fact that I had moved to live 3,000 miles away, and the computer technology was still a bit much for someone who had only been able to string together legible sentences for the previous 12 months (I mean him, not me). The key to his perplexed face was later discovered by his mother (my sister), when he asked her, "How are we going to get Uncle Marcus home?" It turns out that he thought that when we communicate by Skype, that I am trapped inside the computer, just like the characters in the film *Tron* (which of course my nephew is too young to have seen).

How often do you feel trapped? This sensation happens to all of us at some time or other. We can feel stuck in a routine, in a way of behaving, in a life that is not what we thought it would be.

Think back to when you were younger. What did you dream of becoming? What sort of person did you want to be?

Rosh Hashanah is the start of 10 days of *teshuva*. Often mistranslated as "repentance", *teshuva* literally means "returning", coming back to who you truly are. We think about our misdirected behaviours and try to get ourselves in tune with our potential selves.

Yoga practice is all about aligning our body and soul. The 20th century writer Merce Eliade explained that *asana* brings us back into shape. The postures help "put an end to the mobility and disposability of the body, by reducing the infinity of possible positions to a single archetypal, iconographic posture...the tendency toward 'unification' and 'totalisation' is a feature of all yogic techniques"[1].

One of the five names for Rosh Hashanah is *Yom Harat Olam*. It is the birthday of the world and remembers the creation of mankind. We press the reset button, and we begin again. There is a kabbalistic tradition to wear white on Rosh Hashanah to signify that we are brand new all over again.

There are two ways of changing ourselves. We can go from the inside, or we can go from the outside. I often drive from Los Angeles to San Diego, to teach, and soon after passing LAX airport on Freeway 5, there are huge billboards advertising cosmetic surgery and procedures: breast enhancements, liposuction, botox injections, and more. When we change from the outside, it can make us feel good for a short period of time, like when we get the latest digital gadget, but this doesn't bring about a true inner change. Once I was food shopping for Rosh Hashanah, and Michael Jackson's *Man in The Mirror* was playing

---

[1] Yoga: Immortality & Freedom p. 55.

in the supermarket. The lyrics had a message about how inner change affects outer change:

"I'm starting with the man in the mirror
I'm asking him to change his ways
And no message could have been any clearer
If you wanna make the world a better place

Take a look at yourself, and then make a change"

Perhaps the source of the wisdom is somewhat ironic considering our discussion about authenticity (and at least questioning the need for plastic surgery), but you get the idea.

The Kosher Sutra comes from Moses' final speech to the Children of Israel. He is calling people to think about their deeds, to consider how they can straighten up their ways. This has been the theme of many works of motivational literature, such as The Path of the Upright[1].

What have you done in the last year that you have regretted? How many times have you been rude to someone you love, upset your parents, or spoken too quickly, and regretted it later? When have you upset your husband, wife, girlfriend, boyfriend, lover? Or spoken in haste and regretted at leisure?

Rosh Hashanah brings days of cleansing, days of coming home. It is the time for returning to our potential. But we can summon

---

[1] Messilat Yesharim, by Rabbi Moshe Chaim Luzzato, 1707–1746.

the spirit of Rosh Hashanah any time, to return to the way we would like to behave in our relationships.

Another name for Rosh Hashanah is *Yom Hazikaron,* a Day of Remembrance. You can use it to remember who you can be, who you are meant to be—when you set your mind to it.

One of the prayers for the 10 days of Rosh Hashanah is the beautiful *Selichot* Meditation, when we consider how to re-tune ourselves so that we can make beautiful music with our body and soul. I love the phrase from the prayer, "Forgive us for being stiff-necked". How often have we been too fixed in the way we have approached our life? When have we been stubborn and close-minded and missed huge opportunities as a result?

Shake your body. Strike a pose. Breathe deep and long. Interlace your fingers behind your back and fold forwards to release the tension in your shoulders. Sit down, place your hands to the side of your legs, and twist to release the tension in your back. Rub your face to let the frowns disappear, and massage your jaw to free any residual tension.

Finally, smile. There is no longer any reason to be trapped. Use the Bibliyogic tools in this chapter and commit to the path of permanent change. The year ahead will be sweet and new, and that can start any day, including today. Be the best you can be.

V'ZOT HABRACHA
IT'S ALL GOOD

KOSHER SUTRA   "This is the blessing" (Deuteronomy 33:1)
SOUL SOLUTION   See and appreciate the blessings in our life
BIBLIYOGA POSE   Shabbat Pose / *Savasana*, (p.89)
BODY BENEFITS   Restores and heals

Life is all about cycles, and at various points we reach the conclusion of different journeys. Whether it is the end of a relationship, seminar, academic programme, or a calendar year, these are brief milestones that allow us the opportunity to take stock.

Our Kosher Sutra is spoken by Moses who is on the verge of his final breath and proclaims the words, "This is the blessing". Although he is saying it within a specific context, we can learn a huge amount from these words by firstly dropping into the present moment and questioning – where is your blessing right now? What are the blessings in and around your life? There's a rabbinic tradition to say 100 blessings every single day, and if we take the opportunity to count 100 good things in our life then we are bound to feel a sensation of joy.

The Sanskrit word for happiness or sweetness is *sukha*, and the *Yoga Sutras* proclaim that every posture should be happy or sweet—*sthira sukha asanam*[1]. One way of ensuring that they are sweet is to practice the posture until it is comfortable. A more immediate method is to mentally scan through the body, go

---
[1]   Yoga Sutras 2:46

through a checklist of all the body parts that are functioning well, and count these blessings until you are well into double figures.

When we can look at our life and see that it is good, we are on to a good thing. This is the first Kosher Sutra of our new cycle: "God saw that the light was good" (Genesis 1: 4), and there is a continual repetition of the Creator seeing the good throughout creation. We can do the same. It takes practice to keep on seeing the good, to appreciate the blessings, to taste the sweetness. May we all be blessed to continually see the good around us.

YOM KIPPUR
NO DAY BUT TODAY

KOSHER SUTRA   "I have found nothing better for the body than
silence" (Ethics of the Fathers 1:17)
SOUL SOLUTION Align with your true self
BIBLIYOGA POSE Fasting and silence
BODY BENEFIT   Cleanses the body

I write this Kosher Sutra just as the world has lost Steve Jobs, founder of Apple and a great artistic visionary. Most of us have been touched by his creations in some way or other. In a time of great recession and employment losses, he continued to create endless new jobs, and his impact on business and technology is substantial. From his example, the ancient questions become more relevant than ever: What is your ideal legacy to the world? How would you like to be remembered? If today were your last day on earth, how would you live?

Many of us would love the opportunity to start again, to press the reset buttons on our lives, to erase the hard disk of all the things we have done that we are embarrassed about, to think through those things that we wish hadn't said and make them go away. In a nutshell, that is Yom Kippur.

The yoga practice for Yom Kippur is a soul-focused deep meditation. We refrain from food, drink, physical relations, and the wearing of leather skins for which a creature had to die[1]. We realign with who we are and who we can be. That is, we engage

---
[1] ¹Mishna, Yoma, 8:1.

in what the yogis called "the continuous struggle to become firmly established in the stable state of the True Self" [2].

Yom Kippur is the day of atonement, or a day of at-ONE-ment—becoming one with our potential, one with whom we really want to be. Do you know what the Sanskrit word for re-tuning, reconnecting, becoming one with our ultimate self is? Yoga. And the Hebrew word? *Echad*. Hear, O yogis, all is One.

The Rabbis taught, "All my life I have been raised among the sages, and I have found nothing better for the body than silence" [3]. There is nothing better for the body than silence. I could add more, to explain this, but that would break the silence. The words speak for themselves. Enough talking, already. I have found nothing better for the body than silence.

Over the next 36 hours, try a little silence. I will not prescribe any yoga poses for this Kosher Sutra because your body already knows what to do, if you listen to it.

---

[2] *Yoga Sutras* 1:13.
[3] Ethics of the Fathers, 1:17.

THE YOGA OF SUCCOT
HAPPY ENDINGS

KOSHER SUTRA   "He showed His love to the peoples" (Deuteronomy 33:3)
SOUL SOLUTION   Feel loved and complete always, regardless of what is
                happening on the "outside"
BIBLIYOGA POSE Lotus of the Heart / *Anjali mudra*, (p.100)
BODY BENEFIT   Calms the body, increases inner peace

There is a poignancy to this Kosher Sutra; it represents a time for anticipating new beginnings. Nature runs its course, and we come to the end of various cycles. By Succot, the leaves are beginning to fall, the annual Torah reading is ending, another Kosher Sutra cycle has completed, and animals would begin to think about hibernating if we hadn't singed the ozone layer and messed up the timing of the seasons through global warming.

"He [God] showed his love to the peoples," explains Moses in his farewell speech (Deuteronomy 33.3). The rabbinic commentators (Onkelos and Rashi) go for an ethnocentric translation of this, explaining that the text is talking about the 12 tribes, but the Hebrew word amiym suggests a wider scope. Am usually refers to the Israelites, but the plural word refers to the other peoples on the earth, i.e., everyone, regardless of race or nationality. God loves you, baby. Hallelujah.

The final yogic teaching of the Kosher Sutra is simple: all is one. The teaching is also incredibly complicated: all is one. We can quote endless Sanksrit sources, or Hebrew sources for that matter, but such mind games will distract us from the work of our hearts, which is to understand that we are living in a space of Divine love and that we are all part of one huge spiritual organism. When we can live in this space of deep knowing, we remove our fears, pains, and sense of lack. This is an idea that our hearts understand but that our heads often complicate.

The yogic meditation of anjali mudra takes us into this place. It is performed by pushing both palms together into Prayer Position and lightly pressing your thumbs on the sternum, or heart centre.

During the festival of Succot, Jews gather in the temporary structure of the succah and invite guests in throughout the whole week. We sit in this physical-spiritual space and remind ourselves of the oneness of God and the Universe. We hold four species of plants together (the *Lulav, Etrog,* Willow, Myrtle) and remind ourselves that we are all one people. But can we feel it in our hearts?

Here is a simple meditation. Close your eyes and meditate on the word "love." Allow yourself to feel it in every cell of your body. If your heart is beating anxiously, breathe and allow yourself to come back to the meditation focus. If your mind wanders in another direction, bring your mind back to it.

My friend Peter Himmelman beautifully summed up Reb Aryeh Kaplan's approach to meditation: "Think of a thing. When you stop thinking of it, think of that thing again. Now do this for fifteen minutes."

Back in the days of the Temple in Jerusalem, Succot was a time of joint prayer for all peoples of the world, of all religions and nations. We all joined together as one. Succot really was a time for sharing the love. *V'zot HaBracha.* This is the blessing. This is the happy ending and the even happier beginning.

WARRIOR I/ VIRABHADRASANA I

"When you go to war against your enemies"

DEUTERONOMY 21:10

ABOUT THE AUTHOR

For more than 15 years, Marcus J Freed's passion and purpose has been helping people optimise their inner talents and live to their highest potential. Marcus has many entrepreneurial endeavours going on at all times, fuelling his enthusiasm for life. He believes that we are all born with different abilities and when used to good effect, can all contribute to improving the world we live in.

Marcus began his first serious yoga practice by accident. In the autumn of 2000 he was training to become a professional actor at the prestigious Webber Douglas Academy of Dramatic Art and was being taught yoga as a way to fine-tune the mind and ground the breath for acting work. Although he committed to a daily yoga routine for one purpose, it soon became clear that the yoga served as a gateway to more than he could have possibly imagined.

When he realised that yoga was providing a spiritual calm that he had not expected, Marcus began noticing the effect it had compared with attending synagogue on Sabbath mornings, and realised that there was a physical component missing from the traditional Jewish spiritual practice. He coined the term 'Bibliyoga' and the 'Kosher Sutras' in 2001 and began teaching experimental classes at the Limmud and Limmudfest conferences in England ('Limmud' is Hebrew for 'learning'). Soon afterwards he was being invited to teach throughout Europe and began sharing his ideas with students in France,

Italy, Germany, Austria, Switzerland, Greece, Macedonia, Israel and beyond.

There has always been a very strong spiritual aspect to Marcus' work. He became more religiously observant in the summer of 1994, deciding to fully embrace the customs of his Jewish heritage and aligning with the Modern orthodox movement. Marcus' approach to Sabbath observance has always been somewhat yogic, seeing the 25-hour period as a form of meditation that creates the space for a higher spiritual connection. Just as yoga is a practice designed to calm and focus our mind at every point during the day, he views the mitzvot (commandments) as a complementary system for staying grounded, focused and connected to a Higher Source of Being. The yoga journey continued more deeply as he sought to find connections to physical aspects of spiritual growth, and he wrote many hundreds of pages of Kosher Sutra-style essays that cover all physical aspects of prayer from the siddur (Hebrew prayer book), Jewish religious holidays and various Kabbalistic teachings. We hope that these teachings will be published over time.

As the community-themed yoga work developed, Marcus teamed up with Estelle Eugene, who had founded Yoga Mosaic, a network for Jewish yoga teachers. Together they rebranded and relaunched as the Jewish Yoga Network (www.jewishyoganetwork.org). Marcus served as its President for several years.

Marcus's academic training has included degrees in English Literature and Theatre Studies (B.A., University of Birmingham,

400

First Class Hons.), Twentieth Century Literature, Culture & Modernity (M.A., University of London), a full-time postgraduate year at Yeshivat HaMivtar (rabbinical seminary in Efrat, Israel, under the auspices of Rabbi Chaim Brovender and Rabbi Shlomo Riskin). He completed two 200-hour yoga teacher training courses, in London with Tripsichore Yoga (led by Edward Clark & Elizabeth Connolly) and San Diego with the College of Purna Yoga (taught by Rachel Krentzman).

While living in England, Marcus enjoyed regularly broadcasting for BBC Radio 2's 'Pause for Thought' segment, which was a short spiritual reflection piece broadcast at 6.15am for the early risers. His series of recordings were heard by millions of people and taught him how to present powerful spiritual ideas in a way that could be heard and understood by sleepy-eyed commuters.

GLOSSARY

HEBREW

Alef	First letter of the Hebrew alphabet. Kabbalistically, the letter *Alef* contains the secrets of Creation.
Amidah	The standing prayer that is said three times every weekday, and in different formats on the Sabbath and Festivals. Also known as the *Shemonei Esrei* ('Eighteen Blessings', it actually contains nineteen blessings).
Avodah Zarah	Idol Worship, a Biblical prohibition.
Bet	The second letter of the Hebrew alphabet.
Binah	Understanding. Also, of the upper *sefirot*, or energetic qualities of God that reside within the body.
Daat	Knowledge.
Ein Sof	'Without end', a Kabbalistic term and name for God that refers to His vastness and endlessness.
Gevurah	Strength or discipline. The *sefira* that is associated with the left arm.
Halacha	Jewish Religious law. The root, *holech*, means 'walking'.
Hanukkah	or *Chanukah*. The festival of lights, commemorating the rededication of the Holy Temple in Jerusalem at the time of the Maccabean revolt in the 2nd Century BCE.
Hesed	Lovingkindness, or giving. Also the *sefira* that is associated with the right shoulder and arm.
Hochma	Wisdom. One of the upper *sefirot*.

Hod	Humility or Glory. The *sefira* which is associated with the left leg.
Kabbalah	The Jewish mystical tradition. *Kabbalah* means 'receive'.
Keter	Crown: one of the upper sefirot, that resides on the top of the head.
Ketuvim	Writings. The third and final part of the Biblical canon that includes Psalms, Proverbs, Ecclesiastes and the Megillot (Esther, Ruth etc).
Ma'ariv	The evening prayer service.
Malchut	Kingship (from *Melech*, King). The sefira which is connected to the hands, feet, mouth and womanhood.
Midrash	Rabbinic commentaries, often told in the form of stories.
Minha	The afternoon prayer service.
Mishna	The oral law. Redacted by Rabbi Yehuda HaNassi c.220 CE. The mishna is written in short, memorable sentences, similar to sutras.
Netzach	Endurance. The sefira which is connected to the right leg.
Nevi'im	Prophets (singular: *Navi*). The section of the Bible which contains the major prophetic writings including the Books of Joshua, Kings, Isaiah, Jeremiah and the 12 'minor' prophets.
Or Ein Sof	A kabbalistic term to describe the endless light of the creator (*Or* – light, *Ein* – without, *Sof* – end).
Pesah	The festival of Passover, commemorating the exodus from Egypt.
Pirkei Avot	Ethics of the Fathers, a tractate of the Mishna that contains moral and ethical precepts.

Purim	The Festival of Lots that remembers the survival of the Jewish people through the earthly actions of Queen Esther, Mordechai.
Rabbi	Teacher or religious leader.
Rabbi Akiva	Rabbi Akiva ben Joseph (c.40–c.137 CE) was the leader of the generation. He is considered one of the major founders of rabbinical Judaism, and was eventually martyred by the Romans.
Rabbi Shimon Bar Yochai	The first century sage who is attributed with authoring *The Zohar*, the major work of Kabbalah. Also known by his acronym, Rashbi.
Rabbi Shimon Ben Gamliel	The leader of the generation (c.10 BCE – 70 CE) and head of the Sanhedrin (court), just prior to the destruction of the Second Temple. He was martyred by the Romans.
Rav	Alternative term for Rabbi.
Rosh Hashannah	The Jewish New Year festival that occurs at the 'head' of the year (*Rosh* - head) (*Hashannah* – the year).
Sefira	The mystical qualities of God that are manifested throughout creation, including within the body.
Sefirat HaOmer	The 49-day period between the festivals of *Pesach*/Passover and *Shavuot*/Pentecost. Originally an agricultural process, it was later revealed to contain Kabbalistic qualities that lead people from the state of impurity to liberation.
Shaharit	The morning prayer service.
Shavuot	The festival of Pentecost, during which the first fruits of the year's crops were brought to the Temple as offerings.
Shema	The most important Jewish prayer. *Shema* means 'Hear' or 'Actively Listen'.

SANSKRIT

Ahimsa — Non-harming or non-violence, one of the moral disciplines (*yamas*).

Asana — A physical yoga posture (lit. 'seat'). The third limb of Patanjali's eightfold path.

Ashtanga — The eightfold or eight-limbed (*ashto*, eight) (*anga*, limb) path of yoga described by Patanjali in the *Yoga Sutras*.

Ashtanga Vinyasa Yoga — The form of yoga developed by Sri K. Patthabi Jois which has become the basis of 'flow' and 'power yoga'.

Bikram Yoga — Bikram Choudry's yoga system consisting of a fixed sequence of 26 asanas, performed in a room that is heated to 95-100 degrees.

Niyama — The self-restraint aspects of Patanjali's eightfold path which includes purity/cleanliness (*saucha*), contentment (*santosha*), austerity/heat (*tapas*), study (*svadhyaya*) and surrender to God (*Isvara pranidhana*)

Dharana — Inward-focused meditation and concentration. The sixth limb of Patanjali's eightfold path in the *Yoga Sutras*.

Dhyana — Outward-focused meditation, the seventh limb of Patanjali's eightfold path.

Hatha Yoga — The most prominent branch of yoga practised in the West, that is centred around physical postures (*asana*), breath control (*pranayama*) and focused on physical transformation.

Iyengar Yoga — The system of yoga based on the teachings of B.K.S. Iyengar, which are primarily focused on strengthening and healing the body through improving alignment.

Kirtan	Call-and-response form of yogic chanting.
Kosha	The five 'envelopes' or 'energetic sheaths' that make up our physical, energetic, mental, psychic and spiritual bodies.
Kundalini	The spiritual energy or serpent power that must be awakened through the central column of the body.
Kundalini Yoga	A form of yoga that focuses on using the kundalini energy as a path to freedom.
Om	In yogic and Hindu teachings, Om or Aum is the sound which symbolises Absolute Reality.
Prana	Life force or breath that sustains our body.
Pranayama	The practice of breath control, and the fourth limb of Patanjali's eightfold path.
Satya	Truth or truthfulness. An aspect of moral discipline (*yama*).
Sivananda Yoga	A form of Hatha Yoga based on the teachings of Swami Sivananda.
Samadhi	The ecstatic, unified state of enlightenment and self-realisation. The culmination of Patanjali's eightfold path.
Sutra	A short phrase or aphorism in Sanskrit literature. Famous collections include the *Karma Sutra* and the *Yoga Sutras*. A Kosher Sutra is a Biblical phrase or verse that is used within the Bibliyoga context.
Vinyasa	A flow of yoga postures that are connected with steady breath, as with a Sun Salutation.

Yama   The moral aspects described in the *Yoga Sutras*, that form the first limb of Patanjali's eightfold path. They consist of non-violence (*ahimsa*), truthfulness (*satya*), non-stealing (*asteya*), abstinence or restraint of sexual energy (*brahmacharya*) and absence of greed or jealousy (*aparigraha*).

Yoga   Union or discipline. The path to achieve inner freedom, self-realisation and connection with God.

BIBLIOGRAPHY

Akers, Brian Dana (trans.) *Hatha Yoga Pradipika*. Yogavidya.com: Woodstock, USA, 2002.

Ashlag, Rav Yehuda and Berg, Michael (trans.) *The Zohar: by Rav Shimon bar Yochai: from the book of Avraham : with the Sulam commentary*. New York, NY : Kabbalah Centre International, 2003.

Bloomfield, Dianne, *Torah Yoga*. Jossey-Bass: San Francisco, 2004.

Boyarin, Daniel. *Unheroic conduct: The Rise of Heterosexuality and the Invention of the Jewish Man*. Berkeley: University of California, 1997.

Campbell, Joseph (1959), The Masks of God. New York: Viking Press, 1959.

Chapman, Gary D., *The Five Love Languages—How to Express Heartfelt Commitment to Your Mate*. Chicago: Northfield Pub.

Coakley, Sarah, *Religion and the body*. Cambridge University Press: Cambridge, 1997.

Coulter, H. David, *Anatomy of Hatha Yoga – A Manual for Students, Teachers, and Practitioners*. Motilal Banarsidass: Delhi, 2001.

Dekoven, Joel L., & Perlman, Dorothy. *The Rabbi Stands on His Head – A joyous venture into the worlds of YOGA, JUDAISM, SEX*. Tarnhelm Press: Georgia, 1974.

Eliade, Merce, *Yoga: Immortality and Freedom* (Mythos: the Princeton/Bollingen Series in World Mythology). Willard R. Trask (Translator), David Gordon White (Introduction). Princeton University Press (2009).

Feurstein, Georg, *The Deeper Dimensions of Yoga*. Shambala: Boston and London, 2003.

Frankiel, Tamar & Greenfeld, Judy, *Minding the temple of the soul : balancing body, mind and spirit through traditional Jewish prayer, movement and meditation.* Woodstock, Vt.: Jewish Lights Publications, 1997.

Gates, Rolf & Kenison, Katrina. *Meditations from the mat : daily reflections on the path of yoga.* New York: Anchor Books, 2002.

Ginsburg, Yitzhak, *Living in Divine Space – Kabbalah and Meditation.* Gal Einai: NY/Jerusalem, 2003.

Gold, Steven J., Om Shalom : Yoga and Judaism - explorations of a Jewish yogi. Georgia: Golden Glow Productions, 2009.

Green, Arthur, *Jewish spirituality. 1, From the Bible through the Middle Ages.* New York, N.Y: Crossroad, 1986.

Green, Arthur, *Jewish spirituality / 2, From the sixteenth-century revival to the present.* London : Routledge & Kegan Paul, 1987.

Heilbronn, Bill, *God is not an Uncle & Tikkun Olam, The Task of Healing – Essays on Jewish Spirituality, Yoga & Transpersonal Psychology.* Leamington Spa, 1997.

Heschel, Abraham Joshua, *God in Search of Man: A Philosophy of Judaism.* Noonday Press: New York, 1955.

Iyengar, BKS, Light on yoga : Yoga Dipika. New York : Schocken Books, 1997.

Iyengar, BKS, *Light on life: the yoga journey to wholeness, inner peace, and ultimate freedom.* Emmaus, Pa.: Rodale, 2005.

Jois, Sri K Pattahabi, *Yoga Mala.* North Point Press: NY, 2002.

Kaplan, Aryeh, *Meditation and Kabbalah.* Samuel Weiser: New York, 1982.

Kitov, Eliyahu, *The Book of Our Heritage,* by Eliyahu Kitov, translated from the Hebrew *Sefer HaToda'ah* Nathan Bulman and Ruth Royde. Feldheim: Jerusalem/NY, 1978.

Luzzato, Moshe Chayim and Shraga Silverstein (trans.), *Path of the Just/Mesillat Yesharim*, Feldheim: Jerusalem/New York, 1966.

Lyubomirsky, Sonja, *The How of Happiness: A new approach to getting the life you want*. New York: Penguin Press, 2008.

Mamet, David, Make-Believe Town—Essays and Remembrances. Boston : Little, Brown, 1996.

Mamet, David, *Three Use of the Knife—On the Nature and Purpose of Drama*. New York: Vintage Books, 2000.

Mezritch, R. Dov Ber, *Lekutei Yekarim & Maggid Devarav l'Yaakov*, #105, 106, Kolel Mevakesh Emunah: Jerusalem.

Michaelson, Jay, *God in your body : Kabbalah, mindfulness and embodied spiritual practice*. Woodstock, Vt. : Jewish Lights Pub, 2007.

Munk, Elie, *The World of Prayer*. Feldheim: NY/Jerusalem, 1961.

Myss, Caroline, *Anatomy of the Spirit: The Seven Stages of Power and Healing*. New York: Harmony Books, 1998.

Pitzele, Peter, *Our Father's Wells; Personal Encounters with the Myths of Genesis*. San Francisco, California: HarperSanFrancisco, 1995.

Pitzele, Peter A., *Scripture Windows: Toward a Practice of Bibliodrama*. Los Angeles: Alef Design Group, 1995.

Rapp, Stephen, *Alef Bet Yoga – Embodying the Hebrew Letters for Physical/Spiritual Wellbeing*. Woodstock, Vt: Jewish Lights Publishing, 2001.

Sacks, Jonathan, *To Heal a Fractured World*, Continuum: London, 2005.

Satchidandanda, Sri Swami, *Yoga Sutras – Commentary on the Raja Yoga Sutras*. Yogaville, Va.: Integral Yoga Publications, 1985.

Schiffman, Erich, *Yoga – The Spirit and Practice of Moving into Stillness*, New York : Pocket Books, 1996.

Scott, John, *Ashtanga yoga : the essential step-by-step guide to dynamic yoga*. Stroud: Gaia, 2000.

Shapira, Kalonymous Kalman, (author), Cohen-Kiener, Andrea (trans.) *Conscious Community – A Guide to Inner Work*. Rowman & Littlefield, Maryland, 2004.

Siddur KolYaakov, *The Complete Artscroll Siddur*. Mesorah, Brooklyn, NY: 1984.

Stiles, Mukunda (trans.), *Yoga Sutras of Patanjali*. Boston, MA : Weiser Books, 2002.

Swenson, David, *Ashtanga Yoga – The Practice Manual*. Houston, TX: Ashtanga Yoga Productions, 2000.

The Mother, *The Sunlit Path : passages from conversations and writings*, Pondicherry, India : Sri Aurobindo Ashram, 1984.

Tolle, Eckhart, *A New Earth*. New York: Plume, 1996.

Tolle, Eckhart, *The Power of Now*. Novato, California: New World Library, 1999.

Venkatesananda, Swami, *Enlightened Living (Yoga Sutra of Patanjali)*, online, and published through the Chiltern Yoga Trust: South Africa, 1975.

Webster, John, *The Duchess of Malfi*. New Mermaids, London, 1990.

Weinberg, Matis, *Patterns in Time, Vol 1: Rosh Hashannah*. Feldheim: Jerusalem, 1989.

Zalman, Schneur, *Tanya, Likutei Amarim*. Brooklyn: "Kehot" Publication Society, 1998.

Zion, Noam & Fields-Meyer, Shawn, *A day apart : Shabbat at home : a step-by-step guidebook with blessings and songs, rituals and reflections*. Jerusalem: Shalom Hartman Institute, 2004 .

DISCUSSION QUESTIONS

Thank you for purchasing *The Kosher Sutras*. Here is a way to deepen your experience, whether it is with a Book Club, friend (chevruta) or learning group.

PHILOSOPHY

1.   Which essay did you find to be the most personally meaningful, and why?

2.   The Kosher Sutras brings together two different traditions, interpreting Jewish wisdom through the light of yoga and meditation. How do you feel about the author's approach?

3.   "In his introduction to the *Sefer Yetzirah*, Rabbi Aryeh Kaplan explained that "Meditative Kabbalah...comprises a form of yoga" although some contemporary religious groups are critical of yoga practices because of their perceived connections to Eastern religions. What is your response?

4.   There is a Biblical precept not to bow down before idols (Leviticus 26:1). What is your approach to statues of Eastern religious deities (e.g. Ganesh, Shiva, Buddha) found in many yoga studios?

PRACTICE

1.   The Kosher Sutras for *Parsha Breisheet* are based around the themes of creation, and taking active steps to transform our own life. How might you apply these teachings to your own life, and which areas of your life would you like to transform?

2.   The Book of Exodus teaches us about freedom. On reading any of the essays from (p.59-187), how might you become more free and liberated in your own day-to-day existence?

3.   The Hebrew name for Leviticus is Vayikra – "and He called". Read and reflect on 'The Calling', (p.275)and share with

your group what your own calling is. If you aren't clear what your higher calling is, what could it be, or what would you like it to be? What are your unique gifts?

4. The first essays of Numbers/Bamidbar discuss humility and jealousy (p.321)-p.323) After reviewing these pages, how could you apply these teachings? What are the potential challenges you might face, and how can you use a yoga or meditation practice in your journey?

5. The final Kosher Sutra (p.395) advocates living in a state of happiness whenever possible. How might you apply it your own life?

6. What is the Kosher Sutra that would you like to write? What is the single biggest challenge you face in your life, and can you find a Biblical verse that provides an inspirational teaching? Finally, how would you apply that on the yoga mat or meditation cushion?

MORE RESOURCES

For more resources, visit **www.marcusjfreed.com**

INDEX

BOOK CLUB GUIDELINES

Thank you for purchasing *The Kabbalah Sutras*. Here are some thoughts on how to deepen your experience, using it as the basis of an event with your Book Club or whilst learning with a friend.

1. THEME - Pick a theme which interests you right now, such as Love, Strength, Balance, Endurance, Gratitude, Connection or Leadership. Then go to the corresponding section in the book, read one of the essays and discuss the questions.

2. LIFE QUESTIONS - What is a question that is most relevant in your life right now? Flip through the pages of the book, choose any essay and listen closely for how it may contain the guidance you are looking for. The answers may not necessarily be in the words themselves, but the thoughts they prompt while you are reading them.

3. KABBALISTIC DAY CYCLE - There is a Sefirah for every day of the week, so you might choose an essay that corresponds to the day you are reading. Based on the teachings of the Vilna Gaon, the cycle is as follows: Sunday - *Chesed*, Monday - *Gevurah*, Tuesday - *Tiferet*, Wednesday - *Netzach*, Thursday - *Hod*, Friday - *Yesod*, Saturday/Shabbat - *Malchut*. The "day" runs from sundown to sundown, so *Chesed* would be from sundown saturday night until sundown Sunday. *Gevurah* would begin at sundown Sunday, and so forth.

4. CREATIVE WRITING - You can use the Questions for Discussion as a basis for creative writing. Try answering some of the questions using "Free Writing" where your pen does not stop moving for a fixed period of time, e.g. ten minutes' continuous writing. This helps to switch off your inner censor and stay in the flow.

5. OTHER CREATIVE OUTLETS - You can also use these essays as the basis for other expressive media, such as visual arts, songwriting or plays. The key is to connect with the material in a way that feels truthful to your soul, and ideally maintains the integrity of the Kabbalistic teachings.

Good luck with your journeys!

For more resources and to join the mailing list, visit www.marcusjfreed.com.

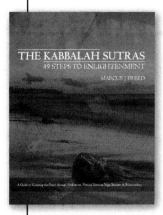

The Kabbalah Sutras: A Yogi's Guide to 'Counting the Omer'
by Marcus J Freed
Connect to Kabbalistic wisdom within your body: find deep peace, healing and fulfil your soul's mission. *The Kabbalah Sutras* shares a system to connect with Divine Light and apply it to your body, mind, soul, relationships, business and career. *"Marcus J Freed succeeds in a unique synthesis of traditional Kabbalistic thought, contemplative meditation and bodily expression. Bubbling with fascinating sources and insights, both traditional and modern, this book is a wonderful initiation into a compelling Jewish spirituality for the 21ˢᵗ Century".*
- Rabbi Dr Raphael Zarum,
   The London School of Jewish Studies.
6 x 9, 496 pages, Paperback,
ISBN 978-1797663043
$29.99/£19.99
Also: Kindle/E-book. $9.99/£14.99

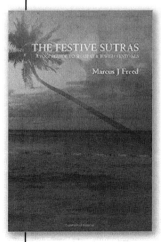

The Festive Sutras:
A Yogi's Guide to Shabbat & Jewish Festivals
by Marcus J Freed
How can we experience Jewish festivals & Shabbat through our body? *The Festive Sutras* contains a series of essays and practices to help get an experience of God within your body. Using the tools of torah wisdom and yoga postures, the reader is given very practical techniques to use physicality as a gateway to spirituality. *The Festive Sutras* is three-books-in one: The Festive Sutras, concerned with the Jewish festival cycle; The Shabbat Sutras - A Yogi's guide to the Jewish Sabbath; and Ethics of the Yogis - a Jewish commentary on the classic Yoga Sutras.
6 x 9, 272 pages, Paperback,
ISBN 978-0996350686.
$14.99/£9.99
Also: Kindle/E-book. $9.99/£9.99

THE KABBALAH SUTRAS

Made in the USA
San Bernardino, CA
22 August 2019